45.00

1990

Reversing
the Conquest

Reversing the Conquest

History and Myth in Nineteenth-Century British Literature

Clare A. Simmons

 Rutgers University Press
New Brunswick and London

Library of Congress Cataloging-in-Publication Data

Simmons, Clare A., 1958–
    Reversing the conquest : history and myth in nineteenth-century British
literature / Clare A. Simmons.
        p.   cm.
    Includes bibliographical references.
    ISBN 0-8135-1555-6
    1. English literature — 19th century — History and criticism.   2. Great Britain —
History — Anglo-Saxon period, 449–1066 — Historiography.   3. Great Britain —
History — Norman period, 1066–1154 — Historiography.   4. Historical fiction,
English — History and criticism.   5. Historical poetry, English — History and
criticism.   6. Anglo-Saxons in literature.   7. Medievalism in literature.
8. Middle Ages in literature.   9. Normans in literature.   10. History in literature.
11. Myth in literature.
I. Title.
PR468.H57S55   1990
820.9′358′09034 — dc20   89-48882
                                                                                              CIP

British Cataloging-in-Publication information available

To my parents,
Pam and Michael Simmons

Contents

Acknowledgments

Reversing the Conquest began as my doctoral dissertation at the University of Southern California, and I owe special thanks to the patient support of my dissertation director, Peter J. Manning, and my guidance committee, Joseph Dane, James Durbin, Jerome McGann, and Niall Slater. I would also particularly like to thank the staff of the Huntington Library, San Marino, California; Patricia Hodgell, for allowing me to read her unpublished dissertation on Scott and his sources; Raymond Wiley, for permission to quote his translations of Kemble and Grimm's correspondence; Alexander Ross, for picture research; and Leslie Mitchner of Rutgers University Press for her encouragement and guidance. Leo Braudy, Theresia de Vroom, Norman Fruman, Donna Landry, Eric Mackerness, Mark Schoenfield, and Frances Simmons are among many others who have offered material advice and moral support.

Reversing
the Conquest

Introduction

When in *Alice in Wonderland* the Mouse offers to tell Alice and other assorted creatures "the driest thing he knows," he begins, "William the Conqueror, whose cause was favored by the Pope, was soon submitted to by the English, who wanted leaders, and had been of late much accustomed to usurpation and conquest."[1] The Mouse proceeds to mention "Stigand, the patriotic archbishop of Canterbury," and the "insolence" of William's Norman soldiers. The recitation, which has been identified by Roger Lancelyn Green as from a schoolbook used by the historical Alice,[2] contains clear implications of what the Norman Conquest of England in 1066 should suggest to a right-thinking mid-Victorian child. William was a conqueror; he had the aid of the pope; the English — "English" itself being a far from neutral label — were in disarray; Stigand was a "patriot"; and the Normans were "insolent."

The Mouse's speech proves to be an ineffective method of drying the creatures, still wet from the pool of Alice's tears; but it appears to exemplify Hayden White's observation that histories "combine a certain amount of 'data,' theoretical concepts for 'explaining' these data, and a narrative structure for their presentation as an icon of sets of events presumed to have occurred in times past."[3] Outside of context, however, in the world of Wonderland, the Mouse's words are virtually without meaning. Even if it is accepted that Wonderland is contingent upon the historical Alice's world as a Victorian child, White's suggestion that history includes "theoretical concepts" and "presentation" may be of help to us, but not to Alice and the Mouse. In Clifford Geertz's anthropological image, adapted from Weber, Alice is suspended in the "webs of significance" her culture has created in order to define itself.[4] A Wonderland Mouse cannot be expected to know White; but neither is it possible for Alice to perceive White's concept of metahistory. Alice's education has surely never prompted her to question the certainty of historical fact. Even within the acknowledged narrative of Wonderland, Alice has what Hans Robert Jauss has called a "horizon of expectations," which assumes that history is correlative with objectivity.[5] To a Wonderland Mouse, the passage is simply dry. To Alice, a recitation recalling events of eight centuries ago only draws attention to its form when uttered by the Mouse. The strangeness is not in the content but in the re-creation in nonsense-context of an everyday world where references to Saxons, Normans, and the Conquest are loaded with specific cultural assumptions which do not include a consciousness of interpretation.

But if the Mouse reduces history to meaninglessness, Victorians of the 1860s did detect definite values in the events of 1066, and these present major difficulties for analysis. First, compared with the influence of certain other cultural models, notably those of classical Greece and Rome, upon Victorian self-definition, these values are less consciously articulated, since they are largely transmitted not through the writings of intellectuals, but rather through the attitudes of figures such as Alice. In White's definition, theoretical concepts may sometimes contribute to the forming of an orthodox position; yet the *doxa* of Alice's society is the ignoring of theoretical concepts of history.[6]

This contributes to the second difficulty. Since the characterization of the opposition between Normans and English is implicit in the culture rather than consciously articulated, one may reasonably surmise that the author of the Mouse's recitation would have refuted the suggestion that he had presented anything other than a purely factual outline of the story. Yet within a few lines can be detected fear of foreign domination, fear of Roman Catholicism, fear of anarchy — just sufficiently submerged to be presentable to a Victorian child such as Alice as nothing but fact.

And because the Conquest was perceived as fact, the possibility was overlooked that its significance might have changed, particularly since the eighteenth century. This point deserves emphasis because it is one that many Victorians, claiming a continuous tradition of the oppositions regarded as inherent in 1066, would have rejected. The following study is an attempt to analyze that change in the interpretation of a historical moment — the moment that came to be seen as the transition from "Saxon" to "Norman" — as an example of the interaction of the creative and the factual, and the effects of this interaction upon a culture.

The Problem of Established Fact

In 1777, Major John Cartwright argued that the English had a hereditary right to universal male suffrage.[7] In 1881, on a visit to the United States of America, Edward Augustus Freeman suggested that universal citizenship was an error and that only those of Germanic heritage should automatically be granted such privileges.[8]

Both Cartwright and Freeman based their claims on their understanding of British history in the Saxon and Norman period. Their views are not completely opposed to each other, each being based upon the assumption that the Saxon peoples (however these might be defined) have an innate regard for constitutionalism. Nevertheless, Cartwright uses this assumption to argue for inclusiveness; Freeman, for exclusiveness. The same historical example illustrates Cartwright's adherence to a theory that in 1777 was more than a century old, whereas Freeman's theoretical basis shows a new direction, a revised attitude towards the significance of the Saxons and Normans in England. Moreover, their claims to speak for their contemporaries are somewhat different. Cartwright, a campaigner for radical reform, was considered by many to be a political eccentric. Freeman's views, bigoted as they now seem, were acceptable to many respectable members of the mainstream Liberal party. In one hundred years, the conception of Saxons and Normans, while always retaining some oppositional elements, had undergone a series of changes and reinterpretations. While these retained some features of the old radical beliefs, at the same time they had become increasingly the means of affirming the status quo rather than criticizing it.

Such an example might suggest that historical interpretation, particularly of a confused and distant period, might be used to support any ideology. The idea is not new, even in the unphilosophical realm of British historiography. In *The Whig Interpretation of History,* his 1931 attack on earlier British concepts of history, Herbert Butterfield asserted, "History is all things to all men."[9] Most British historians of the nineteenth century, however, would emphatically have denied this. As the century passed, the belief grew that history was a science and that like a science it could be based upon empirical evidence. Michel de Certeau has pointed out the tension between fiction (identifying itself as "not fact") and western historiography (identifying itself with the fact of science).[10] But even if not fictional, history was principally a written form. The search for historical evidence was usually not archaeological, the testament of artifact being considered peripheral to, or inferior to, the written word. Consequently, in the search for established fact, the document was increasingly privileged as a fixed link with the past, the boundary of objectivity.[11]

Nevertheless, as Butterfield pointed out, even the document with an established text is open to interpretation. But does this prove that "History is all things to all men"? I wish to argue the contrary: that the nature of fact is not entirely open to interpretation, and that the recognition of the limits of subjectivity was a part of the nineteenth-century fascination with the Anglo-Norman past.

The question of Saxons and Normans imposes, if not material, then cultural limits on interpretation.[12] Acceptance of truth as absolute is not necessary in order to believe with historical certainty that in a Sussex field in 1066, the army of William, Duke of Normandy, defeated the army of Harold, King of England, and thus began the

Anglo-Norman dynasty.[13] Indeed, such is the certainty of this event in English tradition that in his influential series of lectures published as *What Is History?* Ernest Hallet Carr uses the Conquest as a principal example of established fact.[14] Yet in a society placing an increasing value upon "fact," the Conquest presented perhaps the greatest problem in all British history. The connotations inherent in the very word "conquest" clashed with the image that nineteenth-century Britons were creating of themselves. The task, then, was to interpret the Conquest as a historical corroboration of that self-image and not as a contradiction. Nineteenth-century considerations of the events of 1066 thus become questions of how a writer treats a historical fact that fails to conform with his or her personal ideal of history.

Given, however, that the historian might not have free choice in initial facts, cannot history still be interpreted to mean anything one chooses? I would suggest that "anything one chooses" is not a choice outside history itself but is determined by a historical moment within a culture and that the reconstruction of that historical moment may explain the choice. A product of the same historical moment as this new interest in history, after all, was Frankenstein. Like the creature, history is created by the historian from the remnants of the dead. Yet who is Frankenstein? Literature says the creator; tradition says the creature. Ideology states that the historian created history; yet culture created the self-conception that made the historian. The Saxon-and-Norman opposition reveals the extent to which self-definition is reflexive: having written themselves into history, nineteenth-century writers and readers could find themselves there.

As Geertz has remarked, the term "culture" is notoriously difficult to define.[15] Even within a culture sharing common concerns, great variety of thought is possible, and in pursuing "the spirit of an age" — a phrase that itself only entered British usage in the early nineteenth century — I do not wish to deny the power of human individuality. Yet certain trends predominate in British attitudes to history during the nineteenth century, and if Butterfield's polemical claim as to the nondeterministic nature of interpretation (which he almost certainly did not believe himself) raises questions, his identification of the predominant trends during this period as "Protestant, progressive, and whig" nevertheless deserves further consideration.[16]

With the advent of new scientific knowledge and wide acceptance of Darwinian theories of evolution, much contemporary thinking mused that history too might reveal constant progress and justify dominance of the the strongest. Lord Acton informed students at Cambridge in 1895 that history was an important science, "because in society, as in nature, the structure is continuous, and we can trace things back uninterruptedly, until we dimly perceive the Declaration of Independence in the forests of Germany." Acton concludes his speech by observing that:

> The historians of former ages, unapproachable for us in knowledge and in talent, cannot be our limit. We have the power to be more rigidly impersonal, disinterested, and just than they; and to learn from undisguised and genuine records to look with remorse upon the past, and to the future with hope of better things.[17]

He thus assumes two main derivations from science, both based upon a belief in fact: a theory of classification, and a theory of evolution.

First, the historian, as the arbiter of society, has a need to define and classify. As the very idea of Saxons and Normans (the two categories being mutually exclusive) suggests, the favored form of definition is binary. A thing or quality is defined by what it is not. Saxon is opposed to Norman, Teuton to Roman, freedom to tyranny, right to wrong, We to the Other.[18] The most heated historical debates of the nineteenth century were not over *whether* to classify, but over *how* to classify, as if by this means moral judgments might be scientifically beyond personal prejudice.

Classification of plants and animals, however, may not be the best model for the classification of abstractions. In the case of Saxons and Normans, a problem emerges when a belief in the need to define is combined with a belief in evolution — or in historical terms, in "progress." Central to nineteenth-century conceptions of historical periods was the belief that history, and particularly British history, progressed lineally, showing "constant ameliora-tion." This theory distinguishes nineteenth-century interpretations of the Conquest from those of earlier times. Christopher Hill's im-portant essay on the Norman Yoke perhaps gives the concept of progress insufficient emphasis, although his summary of the gen-eral doctrine which haunts all readings of the story hints at the problem:

> The theory of the Norman Yoke, as we find it from the seventeenth century onwards, took many forms; but in its main outlines it ran as follows: Before 1066 the An-glo-Saxon inhabitants of this country [England] lived as free and equal citizens, governing themselves through representative institutions. The Norman Conquest de-prived them of this liberty, and established the tyranny of an alien King and landlords. They fought continuously to recover them, with varying success.[19]

The similarity between this idea and the myth of a Golden Age is immediately apparent — as is Hill's sympathy for the Saxons. Yet particularly during Victoria's reign, the Golden Age began to be posited in the near future, or even in the present. In the introduc-tion to his triumphantly Protestant, Progressive, and Whig *History of England*, Thomas Babington Macaulay argued, "those who com-pare the age on which their lot has fallen with a golden age which exists only in their imagination may talk of degeneracy and decay; but no man who is correctly informed as to the past will be dis-posed to take a morose or desponding view of the present."[20] In his role as an Englishman fully in control of established fact, Macaulay expresses the Whig view that from the beginnings in the German forest (as in Acton's speech, cited as an unquestionable historical event) to the Victorian present, the course of British history has been one of progress.

Macaulay's linear view of history ignores the possibility that the theory of the Norman Yoke may owe even more to a cyclic conception of history.[21] When Arnold Toynbee returned to a cyclic conception of history in the present century, part of his objective was to demonstrate that the history of one country cannot be considered separately from the history of the world. This, however, was a deliberate rejection of the pre-1914 linear model which implied that British progess was essentially independent.[22] The rational-scientific stance of British history before Toynbee left it poorly equipped to approach the problem of whether it was necessary to go backwards in order to go forwards — whether, in effect, linear progress dictated a cyclic return to the Golden Age of the Saxons. Although Toynbee's focus on the development and disintegration of civilizations does not adopt the label of "cyclic," Toynbee himself continued the structural opposition by implying that the linear model must be rejected in favor of another. Yet the general assumption that the classifications of history were derived from science invites further scrutiny. Science may have made the stronger claim as the model of nineteenth-century historiography; but perhaps the claims of fiction should also be explored.

History and Fiction

Few nineteenth-century historiographers questioned the assumption that history and fiction are diametrically opposed. The very strength of this conviction gives rise to the question of why, simultaneously with the stress on established fact and the fixity of the historical document, the new genre of the historical novel should have emerged. If history by definition is not fiction, then a culture assuming such a definition might be expected to have no place for a bastard genre combining the two. As John Wilson Croker remarked in his review of *Waverley*, since a historical novel might confuse honest readers by mingling the surety of fact with "*mere* romance," the entire genre might even be dangerous in disguising truth.[23]

Croker's review shows conversance with the possibility of combined history and fiction, but his observations imply the superiority of fact and a belief that history is the surer way to literary immortality. The following years were to prove him wrong in his assessment of Scott, whose novels retained popularity for the entire century but whose *Life of Napoleon* was rapidly superseded. Croker's assumption, however, that history is the lasting genre is not unique in an age in which style was not perceived to alter the fixity of history, and in which history's relation to fact was regarded as permanent.

For practical purposes, though, Croker was justified in arguing from the basis that history does offer some fixed points. Even when employed by a writer prepared to change or ignore facts as expedient, history must place some constraint upon the imagination. In the case of Scott, who changes chronology where he chooses, this self-imposed constraint takes the form of authentic detail. Yet Scott also adheres to broad historical outlines. To return to Carr's example, no writer of this time would have dreamed of literally reversing the Conquest and of giving the victory of 1066 to Harold. I thus distinguish in this study between the historical novel and the Gothic or chivalric romance: whereas a historical novel may contain Gothic or romantic-chivalric elements, a historical setting does not provide an escape into the imagination but rather a constraint upon it. By adopting an editorial pose, a novelist such as Scott is playing with the self-imposed limitations of history. Interpretations of actions, and particularly of characters, may vary, but the ultimate outcome, however unappealing, is preestablished.

But while the preestablished outcome might seem a limitation, it may also be part of the historical novel's attraction, since individual indentity can also be seen as a product of history. Some proof of the egocentric nature of history even in the format of the early historical novel is suggested by *Quentin Durward*. Even though all Scott's novels were successful, *Quentin Durward*, set in France, was comparatively more popular in France than in Britain.[24] As the century progressed, the nationalist element in history became even stronger, but the historical novel contributed to the process by opening up the world of one's ancestors, the preoccupation with eating and sleeping arrangements found in Scott's earlier novels, for example, strengthening the sense of reality.[25]

Just as one's national ancestors ate and slept, so they also experienced hopes and fears similar to those of the present. Important also to the attraction of the historical novel is making the past as alive as the present, while simultaneously explaining the present in the light of the past. For this reason, Marxist critics have shown special interest in the nineteenth-century historical novel as a statement of important sociohistorical preoccupations. Georg Lukács, for example, sees Scott as the major British contributor to "the classical form of the historical novel." Lukács believes that Scott "endeavours to portray the struggles and antagonisms of history by means of characters who, in their psychology and destiny, always represent traditions and social forms."[26]

I would accept the impossibility of considering imaginative portrayals of English history without reference to the society that produced them, provided that this is not reduced to one-way process. Just as I have suggested that literature is both the product of a society and a means by which that society, like the historical Alice reading her own adventures, might perceive itself, I would further suggest that imaginative literature, and especially fiction, had a major effect on conceptions not merely of past and present but on conceptions of history as a discipline. The model for nineteenth-century history, claimed the historians themselves, was science. Yet as White has noted, history came to depend on narrative for form, and perhaps the literary genre of historical fiction provided a better model for history—and possibly even for the understanding of one's own society.[27] The historical novel (and to some extent the historical drama) gave a structure to fact. Events were not random, or even the product of specific natural and social conditions, but marked both progress and process: in short, they were part of a plot.

When this plot is reduced to form, the historical novel of the nineteenth century as exemplified by Lukács's reading of Scott involves a temporary disorder, earlier order reconfirmed, and marriage. Even, therefore, as a distillation of material historical truth— a truth that in the course of this study I have found ever elusive— the historical novel was comedic, not tragic. For this reason, the Conquest of 1066 presented a generic difficulty. The word "conquest" suggests an overthrow, not reconciliation. If history was to draw a narrative model from the novel while retaining a sense of England's linear progess, the tragic structure of overthrow instantly suggested by William the Norman's defeat of Harold and the Saxons had to be made to conform to a comedic pattern. Fiction imposed a narrative structure on history suggesting that the Conquest of 1066 was not a random event but an episode in a story. The challenge was to understand the whole story.

I hope to demonstrate that while a wish for a comedic rather than tragic conception of the historical event presented certain formalistic difficulties in the consideration of Saxons and Normans, the novel genre nevertheless provided a model for theory. That model was *Ivanhoe* — even though *Ivanhoe* itself was the product of certain social conditions and preoccupations. The conclusions to which use of this narrative model led, however, were not inherent in the novel itself. *Ivanhoe* provided a pattern for oppositions that the nineteenth century's need to classify — and to judge — took further than the earlier myth of the Norman Yoke implied.

In attempting to avoid categorizing works as literary or factual, I have assessed their importance not by aesthetics but by what Jauss has termed the "interaction" of the work and its influence on cultural self-conceptions.[28] Such an exploration of how the significance of the Conquest and of Saxons and Normans changed during the course of a century could scarcely be exhaustive. I have therefore adopted some of the more controversial oppositions discussed during this period in order to examine what was fixed in the conception of specific historical figures, what changed, and why the change occurred.

The first pair, King Richard and King John, can be seen as both a starting point and a finishing point. They lived at what came to be considered the end of the Anglo-Norman period, while their portrayal in *Ivanhoe* inspired the beginning of nineteenth-century popular interest in Saxons and Normans. Next follows the controversy concerning King Henry II and Archbishop Thomas Becket. The debate over their historical reputations became most heated in the late 1840s; why, at this particular time, was deciding which of the two was most Saxon and which the most Norman so important? Moving back to the first establishment of Anglo-Norman England and forward to the 1860s, I then consider how Harold, the last Saxon king of England, and William, the first Norman king, were interpreted by a society demonstrating an increasing belief in racial determination of character. The reverse chronological order concludes not with an opposition but with the comparisons drawn between Queen Victoria at the end of her reign and the Saxon king Alfred the Great.

Such pairings may suggest a lack of complexity, and indeed, I argue that by the end of the century the Saxon-against-Norman opposition was employed to provide simplistic solutions to difficult problems. Above all, however, I hope to demonstrate that even during a period when moral judgments and heroes and villains were seen to be a valid part of history, contrasts between individual characters and the sense of what constituted a Saxon or a Norman retained a flexibility dependent on both ideology and creativity. But first the question arises as to whether the nineteenth-century picture of Saxons and Normans was what it claimed to be — the continuation of a national tradition.

Chapter
1

Earlier Conceptions
of Saxons
and Normans

The very use of the idea of Saxons and Normans, the inhabitants of England from the sixth to the twelfth century, as a form of self-expression suggests a culture placing a value on history. Nineteenth-century British writers who used such references in their works were eager to claim the English attitude towards history and especially their own interpretations of this period as part of a continuous inheritance from Anglo-Saxon times. Examination of how the idea was used by earlier writers, however, reveals that it had undergone some significant changes since the English Reformation. Michel Foucault has remarked that the sense of history as a fact-controlling discipline was largely a product of the nineteenth century.[1] Hayden White has gone further in suggesting that from the mid-nineteenth century, the historical task had been seen as the discovery of "what happened." After having established a factual foundation, the historian is entitled to be "dissertative" and to offer an interpretation of those facts.[2] According to this model, the historian assumes the role of an empirical scientist, making a distinction between history and story that does not recognize narrative as having influence on the meaning of historical events.

Such an interpretation suggests that before this time, approaches to the past were less burdened by a need to distinguish between history and story. Perhaps for this very reason, interest in the Anglo-Norman past took a variety of forms during the eighteenth century: antiquarianism and language-study, the cult of Alfred the Great, and political radicalism. Even earlier, the use of the Saxon and Norman periods as exemplars is remarkably varied — from the sixteenth-century justification of the Reformed Church, to the seventeenth-century vindication of both change and conformity. And although the nineteenth-century claim to historical continuity may be rejected as applied to general definitions of what history signifies, certain specific historical interpretations are indeed part of an English tradition dating back at least to the Reformation.

Reformation and Revolution

A brief survey of opinions of Saxons and Normans before the eighteenth century cannot possibly do justice to the complexity of presentation and the variations in argument, of which Christopher Hill's work remains the best-known summary.[3] Certain assumptions do, however, recur — the most important being that the Saxon age and the Norman Conquest are a material reality that can be evinced as proof either of the way England used to be, or more polemically, of the way England should be.

The English Reformation itself, although sanctioned by the established power of the monarch, in many respects might suggest a rejection of history. Traditional conceptions of the role of a good English Christian were changed — perhaps not always drastically changed, but with the understanding that tradition alone was insufficient justification for continuing certain practices. That as far as anyone could remember there had always been monastic communities, for example, was not in itself enough reason for preserving them. The English Reformation, then, might potentially have been a reformation in the sense of creating something new, departing from historical precedent. In fact, the English Reformers assumed the role of *re*-formers, asserting that they were not abandoning the historical ways of England, but rather were returning to them. The attitude towards the past was ambivalent, and ways had to be found to respond to this ambivalence.

In seeking the mandate of history for the English Reformation, the Reformers were obliged to look back to the time before the Roman Catholic dominance (as they perceived it) of the High Middle Ages — the four-hundred-year period described by John Foxe (1516–1587) as the age of "the loosing of Satan"[4] — back to the time of a more primitive English church. The Reformer's patriotic task was the re-creation of this church. Foxe is usually remembered as a martyrologist, but as William Haller's examination of Foxe's historical techniques suggests, he should surely be credited as the constructor of a coherent English Protestant vision of history, in which the forces of the true British church were constantly at struggle with the ever more corrupt Church of Rome. In Haller's words, Foxe created "a comprehensive history of England based upon a conception of human nature and of the meaning and course of history which few of its readers were in any state of mind to do anything but accept as universally true."[5] With the support of Matthew Parker, archbishop of Canterbury from 1559 to 1575, Foxe looked for documentary evidence of the primitive virtue of the early English church as formed by both the Ancient Britons and the subsequent Saxon invaders. In the introduction to one of the most widely read English books of all time, his *Book of Martyrs* — or more properly, *Actes and Monuments* — Foxe presents himself as a true revisionist historian, writing from a less prejudiced stance than the hirelings of Rome:

> For, first, to see the simple flock of Christ, especially the unlearned sort, so miserably abused, and all for ignorance of history, not knowing the course of times and true descent of the church, it pitied me that this part of diligence had so long been unsupplied in this my-country church of England. Again, considering the multitude of chronicles and story-writers, both in England and out of England, of whom most part have been either monks, or clients of the see of Rome, it grieved me to see how partially they handled their stories.[6]

Foxe, Parker, and their associates hence claimed a role as creators of a truer history, one revealing that before the period of the Conquest, the age of the arch-necromancer Hildebrand (Pope Gregory VII), England's church had been very like the one they were now creating. To prove the early English church's position, Parker published some Anglo-Saxon works, including a sermon by Ælfric that was seen as a good English rejection of transubstantiation; and the Anglo-Saxon Gospels, which supported the claim that the pre-Norman church had valued the scripture in the vernacular.

Already in the sixteenth century, then, some contrast was being created between the time before the Norman Conquest, which Foxe, with an apocalyptic sense of period, saw as the time of the decline of the primitive church established by Christ, and the period after it, the four hundred years of the rule of Satan. Foxe and Parker, however, were working as official representatives of the established government. In the following century, the question emerged of how history should be used to create or assert authority when authority was in dispute.

Hill's important analysis of the Norman Yoke examines the first presentation of the Norman Conquest as a division of period that affected not merely religious practices but also politics. Hill describes how the Conquest was seen by subscribers to the theory as a major transformation that changed the independent (and moderate) English church, the long-established concept of equal laws and justice, and the system of government by an elected Parliament.[7] Two important points must be stressed from his study. First, even for those who believed that before the Conquest, the Saxon civilization was in decline, the Saxon way was an ancient inheritance, and thus more uniquely English, than what followed. Richard Verstegen, for example, whose *Restitution of Decayed Intelligence in Antiquities* was reprinted several times after its original publication in 1605, argued that the English were "descended of German race, and were heretofore generally called Saxons."[8] The Saxon period could thus be presented as a model of the way in which the English church and state should function. Second, the appeal to Saxon values was not, as it had been for Parker and Foxe, a state-sanctioned apology, but through its oppositional nature clearly opposed to the status quo.

Hill's examples, which include the arguments of the Digger Gerrard Winstanley and other seventeenth-century radicals who drew on Anglo-Saxon law to justify their claims for drastic voting and property reform,[9] emphasize this second point perhaps to the extent that the variation in use of the conception of an "ideal Saxon England" is less fully analyzed. An appeal to history, after all, implies discontent with the present, and the Norman Yoke argument is best known through its use by some of the more radical factions of the English Revolutionary period. Hill recognizes that two different interpretations are made of Anglo-Saxon law: either that the laws have been overturned, or alternatively, that their continuity has been maintained.[10] And indeed, most writers include instances from law. Even when specific mention of an ideal Saxon past is not made, the appeal for justice, whether to the king or later to Parliament and the various experiments in government that followed, is generally not to a concept of "natural rights" but to "traditional rights," rights that history demonstrates as having been granted to the English in the (implicitly Saxon) past. Many documents of the 1640s make appeal to such a past, even in a time of revolution insisting not on new ways but a return to the old. For example, the Parliamentarian general Thomas Fairfax, addressing Parliament on behalf of the army in 1647, assured them that "wee doe, and shall much rather wish, that the Authoritie of this Kingdome in Parliaments (rightly constituted, that is, freely, equally, and successively chosen, according to its originall intention) may ever stand, and have its course."[11]

Particularly influential in this appeal to law were the massive *Institutes*, or legal commentaries of Edward Coke (1552–1634). The second part of the *Institutes*, in which Coke examines English citizens' legal rights as established in the Magna Carta and other statutes and argues that these were the reconfirmation of previously existing rights, was too controversial for Charles I's government and consequently not published until 1642. In the new constitutionalist atmosphere, it immediately became one of the weapons of argumentation, a source of appeal to the hereditary rights of Englishmen.

At the same time, however, the written documents of law, those recognized as authentic history, were also augmented by tradition, notably in the form of the person of Alfred the Great as representative of ideal kingship. This idea became far more prominent in the following century, when it provided the inspiration not only for political argument but also for literature. Nevertheless, claims were made for Charles I as representative of the type of kingship of pre-Norman times, particularly as personified by Alfred the Great. One of the best books ever on Alfred and his times was written not by a Parliamentarian but by a Royalist, Sir John Spelman (1584–1643). Similarly, the first attempt at an Anglo-Saxon dictionary, William Somner's *Dictionarium Saxonico-Latino-Anglicum* (1659) was the work of an Oxford loyalist who during the Commonwealth saw a return to interest in antiquities as an important move against what Somner and his friends saw as the Protectorate's destruction of tradition.[12] From the Reformation onwards, then, the struggle for the possession of the Saxon-and-Norman past involved both aspiring reformers and solid conservatives, both antiquarians hoarding the documents of England's past and dramatists drawing on the power of the name of Alfred the Great.

Beyond the law, however, what was known about this happy past? A few scholars set themselves the task of learning more about the language and literature of the Anglo-Saxons, and while their discoveries were largely unrecognized by their contemporaries, they established the foundation for a broader interest in early England.

George Hickes and Anglo-Saxon Language

Interest in the documentary evidence concerning the Anglo-Norman past of the Reformation and Revolutionary periods had focused on religion and law. In each case, the pre-

Norman world was directly cited as evidence of the way England once was (and by implication how England should be). History was a very immediate tool for argument.

In contrast, interest in history for its own sake, or as a stimulus for creative literature, was slower to materialize. Advocates of equal rights such as the Leveller John Lilburne (1614–1657) might figuratively brandish Anglo-Saxon legal documents in the face of current practices, but very few could read the documents in the vernacular (now often known as Old English but until the mid-nineteenth century generally called Anglo-Saxon). Evidently, there were antiquarians whose interest extended beyond the question of legal precedent even in Elizabeth's reign: the work of William Camden (1551–1623), who claimed a knowledge of Anglo-Saxon, was widely known and extremely influential. Even then, Camden was clearly working to use the past to validate the authority of Queen Elizabeth. The relationships between theories of origin and authority from the sixteenth to eighteenth century have been explored by Samuel Kliger *(The Goths in England)* and Hugh A. Mac-Dougall *(Racial Myth in English History)*. Neither, however, gives much attention to the place of language. For the later development of creative use of the idea of Saxon and Norman, language became increasingly important because, antiquarians argued, its conclusions were not myth but supported by incontrovertible evidence. Mastery over the Anglo-Saxon language gave mastery over the written remains of an actual people. In the closing years of the seventeenth century, a small circle of antiquarians began to make a more systematic study of the Anglo-Saxon language.

The theory of a family of Indo-European languages was not to emerge until the late eighteenth century, when orientalists such as Sir William Jones (1746–1794) noted Sanskrit's affinities with the classical European languages.[13] Nevertheless, similarities between Anglo-Saxon and other European languages had been observed as early as the time of William L'Isle (1569?–1637), who set about learning it by studying "High and Low Dutch."[14] In the work of George Hickes (1642–1715) the Anglo-Saxon language began to be situated historically. In the 1680s, Hickes, a clergyman of the Church of England, published various sermons and tracts, mainly on the relative authority of church and state. After the revolution of 1688, Hickes became a nonjuror: he refused to take the oath of allegiance to William and Mary and was consequently deprived of his benefice. Seemingly, Hickes did not wish to embroil himself further in politics and instead devoted more of his time to his antiquarian interests. Questions of legal and historical precedent were less important to him than theories of language-transmission. With the help of his friends Hickes produced the first Anglo-Saxon grammar. His *Linguarum Vettarum Septentrionalium Thesaurus Grammatico-Criticus et Archaeologicus,* besides having one of the most daunting titles of all time, contains much otherwise unavailable information on the value and study of what he labeled "Northern Antiquities": Gothic, Norse, and Anglo-Saxon remains. If his essay "On the Usefulness of Northern Literature" is an accurate representation of his philosophy, Hickes does not seem to have wished to analyze his motives for his fascination with the topic beyond the fact that he found it interesting.[15] Although he was sufficiently reconciled to the succession to dedicate his huge work to the future Queen Anne's husband Prince George as the heir of the Danes, Norse, and Vandals, Hickes himself chose not to equate linguistic origins with politics. Still, his work provided the foundation without which the sense of a wider Anglo-Saxon culture could hardly have developed.

Hickes further contributed to the concreteness of the Anglo-Saxon past by initiating Humfrey Wanley's travels around England to catalogue Anglo-Saxon manuscripts: the list appears in Hickes's *Thesaurus.* As librarian to Queen Anne's chief minister the bibliophile Robert Harley, Humfrey Wanley (1672–1726) can claim an important part in Anglo-Saxon studies on his own behalf.[16] Hickes and his friends were not merely interested in the possession of Anglo-Saxon manuscripts, but also in their contents, and Wanley was the first to describe several of the major Anglo-Saxon literary records, including the *Beowulf-Judith* manuscript.

Other followers of Hickes included William and Elizabeth Elstob, both of whom apparently hoped to increase their study's popularity. William Elstob translated Wulfstan's Homily to the English into Latin, thereby giving it a potentially wider readership. His sister Elizabeth made an even more interesting contribution. Hickes's *Thesaurus* was written in Latin, but Elstob claimed that a "young lady" of her acquaintance was eager to study Anglo-Saxon, and this was her motivation for writing the first grammar in English. Essentially, her grammar was a translation of her guardian Hickes's work, but in a more modest, and far less confusing, format: the acquisition of the rudiments of Anglo-Saxon from her presentation would have been a far less formidable task than wading through Hickes's polyglot version. She moreover prefixed a reply to Jonathan Swift's letter to Robert Harley, his "Proposal for Correcting, Improving, and Ascertaining the English Tongue" (1712). In effect, Swift's essay was an appeal on behalf of the "ancients" who continued to see a superiority in classical literature. In her "Apology for the Study of Northern Antiquities," Elstob demonstrated that on some philological points, notably in his criticism of "monosyllabic" words, Swift's arguments were not invulnerable.[17]

Elstob's hope that young ladies would begin to study early English literature remained unfulfilled. Still, Hickes's *Thesaurus* had attracted contemporary interest. A cheaper and more straightforward summary of the large, expensive volumes was published by William Wotton in 1708. Even this did not satisfy the demand, since Maurice Shelton published an English translation of Wotton's abridgment in 1735, with additional notes.[18] But even in the early years of the eighteenth century when such studies were comparatively popular, the question remains of how widely disseminated these ideas were. Of the earlier group of Anglo-Saxon scholars, for example, Sir Henry Spelman the legal expert, John Spelman the biographer of Alfred, and William L'Isle, who edited Ælfric, were related.[19] Of the post-1688 group, Humfrey Wanley worked for Harley; he knew Hickes, who in turn was either in fact or in effect the guardian of the Elstobs.[20]

Perhaps this limited circle was inevitable. The problem of the unavailability of texts had yet to be overcome, the easiest method being to remain on good terms with someone with access to manuscripts, such as Wanley. Publishing also presented a problem. The leading scholars were not rich and most of the large printing costs were met by collecting lists of advance subscribers. The very enthusiasm of the scholars compounded the difficulties. Not content with only Anglo-Saxon type — the writing of the early scribes was believed to be a different alphabet, and hence a special font was believed to be necessary — many editors also chose to quote from Greek and Middle English sources, the latter usually being reproduced in Gothic type. Hickes even quoted "Moeso-Gothic" — the language from which he believed that the other "Northern" tongues were derived — and runes. Most printers would have been unable to supply the type, and so many antiquarian books, including Hickes's *Thesaurus* and several elegantly produced works by the respected antiquarian editor Thomas Hearne, were printed at the Sheldonian Theatre, Oxford. (William L'Isle, publishing a half-century earlier, was not so fortunate: the font in his edition of Ælfric is poorly made.) The London printers Bowyers had used Saxon type for William Elstob's edition of the Anglo-Saxon version of Gregory the Great's Homily in 1709, but the font was destroyed in a fire. Before her grammar could be printed, Elizabeth Elstob was thus obliged to produce her own designs for cutting new letters. Without funding from a sympathetic patron, this would probably not have been possible; and in her later years Elstob appears to have been too impoverished to continue publishing her researches.[21]

Of necessity, limitations in the knowledge of these early scholars, who perhaps called themselves Saxonists,[22] also presented problems. Many of the Anglo-Saxon works that later editors have designated as major, especially the poetry, were completely unknown. Junius had done some work on identifying manuscripts, and Wanley's catalogue was a major step forward. Yet while the *Beowulf-Judith* manuscript is listed, doubt remained even as to the language in which *Beowulf* was written. The main entry states of the poem: "In this book, which is a splendid example of Anglo-Saxon poetry, seem to be described the wars which a Dane called Beowulf, of the stock of the Kingdom of the Scyldings, fought against the Chiefs of the Sueciae."[23] But in the index the poem is described as "Dano-Saxonicus": indeed, the poem's first editor, the

Dane Grimur Jonsson Thorkelin, initially suggested that it was written in a form of Danish.[24] The Exeter Book, which contains the most varied collection of Anglo-Saxon poems, was mentioned by L'Isle in 1638.[25] Of its poetry, however, Humfrey Wanley merely noted that nearly all was riddles,[26] implying that poems such as the *The Wanderer* and *The Seafarer,* later considered important examples of early English poetry, were word-puzzles scarcely worthy of serious attention. Since the Vercelli Book was also unknown, a very incomplete range of Anglo-Saxon literature was available to the early enthusiasts, Hickes and his friends hence confining their linguistic researches to works of a theological nature.

Since there was no real corpus of "literature," the argument that in Anglo-Saxon writings could be found the origin of English literature and patterns of thought was as not as yet current, and generally, the early Saxonists avoided it. Despite his long Latin epistle to Bartholomew Shower, *De Utilitate Litteraturae Septentrionalis,* the best reasons Hickes could evince here and elsewhere in the *Thesaurus* for the usefulness of "Northern Literature" was a return to the old argument that English Common Law derived from the Anglo-Saxon tradition (Shower himself was an important jurist); and additionally, that study of Anglo-Saxon helped in learning the derivation of names and other words.[27]

Both what Hickes does and does not claim for his studies proves illuminating. First, Hickes notes that the study of Anglo-Saxon remains may disclose some origins of the contemporary world — although one might suspect that his own study was partly a retreat from that world. Particularly in his treatment of the law, Hickes supports the main contention of the Saxon constitutionalists: that Common Law derives from the practices of the ancient Gothic tribes. (Hickes, however, basing his conclusions consistently, if somewhat pedantically, on documentary evidence, was reluctant to rely on patriotic tradition: for example, he theorized that some of the Gothic practices had been introduced by the Normans, not the Saxons [*De Utilitate,* 41].) In contrast, he does not suggest directly that the appeal of the Anglo-Saxon is the characteristics held in common with their descendants, the dominant mood of his studies being presented as antiquarian curiosity rather than self-realization. Indeed, Hickes may have limited the potential popularity of his ideas by casting scholarly doubts on cherished traditions. He maintained, for instance, that Coke was "propemodum ignarus" (just about ignorant) of Saxon antiquities (*De Utilitate*, 152). He also — quite justifiably — questioned Verstegen's philology and disputed the authority of Andrew Horne, whose late thirteenth-century *Mirror of Magistrates*, presenting Alfred as exemplar of justice, was valued by many constitutionalists (*De Utilitate*, 148).

In addition, while Hickes is clearly taking a defensive stand against "ancients" such as Swift, his arguments still leave him vulnerable to attack. Skeptics might have replied that first, Anglo-Saxon law was already available — and well-known — in Latin; and second, that knowing the origin of names is hardly an instance of utility. Probably, however, the classicists simply ignored Hickes's work. Certainly, in the second half of the eighteenth century, the "ancients" appeared to have won the Battle of the Books.

This victory, however, was largely confined to intellectuals. And here again, just as the arguments of the Saxonists of both the Reformation and the Civil War had been aimed less at scholars and rulers than at an emerging, largely urban middle class eager to claim a share in the government of their country, so Saxonism in the eighteenth century assumed not an intellectual but a populist mood. Kliger has argued that even the fashion for the Gothic, the less specific appeal to past tradition, was partly intended to shock the supposedly civilized elite through its associations with barbarism.[28] But this populist mood may itself be subdivided into the celebratory and the socially critical. Unlike Hickes's and the Saxon philologists' attempts to escape from the world around them into a Northern Golden Age, each category assumes a close relation between past and present: either that the triumphs of the past are being repeated in the present, or that the failure of the present contrasts with the success of a past that should be reclaimed.[29] Both also assume that document and tradition are each a part of history. Of the two, however, the more optimistic (and in many cases, more consciously literary) strain concentrates on the traditional, and particularly on the cult of King Alfred the Great.

The Cult of Alfred the Great

The cult of Alfred the Great had some form as early as the late sixteenth century, when John Foxe used him as an example of the ideal English king. Alfred possessed such a rare combination of "heroical properties," Foxe remarks, that the martyrologist

> thought the same the more to be noted and exemplified in this good king, thereby either to move other rulers and princes in these our days in his imitation, or else, to show them what hath been in times past in their ancestors, which ought to be, and yet is not found in them.[30]

For Protestants, Alfred had the attraction of being a ruler of the English Golden Age, before the entry of Romish corruption. During Elizabeth's reign, indeed, as MacDougall has argued, Alfred effectively ousted the former holder of this position, King Arthur.[31]

The status of King Arthur as the greatest early king of Britain had been asserted by Geoffrey of Monmouth in the mid-twelfth century. Literature had come to the support of history in romances culminating in Sir Thomas Malory's massive Arthurian cycle, published by William Caxton in 1485. Arthur was a British, not merely an English, king, and from the accession of Henry VII in the same year, the Welsh Tudors attempted to assert their rights as new Arthurs, Henry VII shrewdly naming his heir Arthur. Arthur appears in Edmund Spenser's great confirmation of the Elizabethan worldview, *The Faerie Queene*, both as the fairy prince of book 1 and also as Britomart's husband Arthegall.

Already, though, Arthur is not merely a British prince defeating the Saxons, since he cooperates with the Redcrosse Knight Saint George — described as sprung "from ancient race/ Of Saxon kings."[32] Even Merlin's descriptions of the battles of Arthur's dynasty against the Saxons in the third canto of book 3 point to a reconciliation between Britons and Saxons. For with Foxe's new emphasis on the truth of history, the figure of Arthur presented certain problems. Caxton may have prefaced Malory's text with a claim for Arthur's historicity, but Arthur's existence was based on the flimsiest of documentary evidence. What was needed was an exemplary ruler whose existence was indisputable: a true English hero.

Alfred (Ælfred or Alured) was virtually the only pre-Norman concerning whom substantial documentary materials could be readily found. By the early eighteenth century, lovers of English history could read a variety of editions of what remains the main source of knowledge about Alfred's life, the *Ælfredi Regis Res Gestae* written by the king's friend, Bishop John Asser. An edition of the Latin text had been published by Matthew Parker in 1574; and William Camden's 1603 text, reprinted more than once in the seventeenth century, seems to have been made from this, following Parker's emendations and adding some more.[33] Other editions, such as that of Francis Wise in 1722, were not prepared directly from the manuscript (which in any case was destroyed in the Cottonian Library fire of 1731) but from these printed sources or misleading transcriptions. Readers consequently only had access to the manuscript as prettified by Parker's well-intentioned interpolations from other sources telling how the great king was scolded by a neatherd's wife for allowing her cakes to burn, and how he disguised himself as a minstrel to penetrate the Danish camp; and through Camden's perhaps less well intentioned addition of how Alfred founded Oxford University. Parker's treatment of the text is especially interesting: he had chosen it to provide unadorned fact and historical precedent for Tudor policies, yet he apparently believed that true history also contained good stories. Unfettered by a theoretical distinction between history and fiction, Parker seems to have had little doubt that his duty as a historian was to restore the narrative.

The materials contained in Parker's edition of Asser, supplemented by other early historians including Florence of Worcester and William of Malmesbury, were used by Sir John Spelman in his *Life of Ælfred the Great*. Spelman wrote the book during the Civil War: it first appeared in a Latin translation in 1678.[34] The decision to publish the history in Latin suggests that Spelman's study was seen as a serious work worthy of the University of Oxford, and even when Thomas Hearne published the English text in 1709 he included scholarly notes.

Several subsequent histories were greatly indebted to Spelman, including that of the French Protestant Paul de Rapin-Thoyras, which was translated into English by Nicholas Tindal in 1732. Here British readers could learn how Alfred succeeded unexpectedly to the throne in 862, was defeated by the Danes at Chippenham, and was driven into exile. Undaunted, Alfred soon had his revenge on the Danes at the Battle of Eddington and established a peaceful nation. Until his death at the end of the century he devoted his life to the encouragement of learning and the establishment of a centralized system of government.

A wealth of documentary material was therefore available to those who wished to develop the cult of Alfred. John Milton had noted that the life of Alfred would be a fit subject for an epic poem.[35] Several other writers, including aspiring epic poets and dramatists, apparently formed similar conclusions. The celebration of the great Anglo-Saxon king presented an ideal opportunity for patriotic expression.

The most notorious eighteenth-century venture into Alfredolatry is Sir Richard Blackmore's *Alfred, an Epick Poem*. Blackmore (c.1654–1729) had a long career as court physician and during the reign of William III presented the Protestant champion as a new Arthur. After the succession of George I, Blackmore apparently associated Alfred the Saxon (Saxons had been the villains of his earlier pieces) with the new German-speaking king and chose Alfred as the hero of his 1723 poem. Critics have yet to discover a redeeming feature in the twelve tedious cantos of rhyming couplets. Blackmore does not show much interest in the historical Alfred, nor does he make use of the more romantic exploits, such as Alfred's minstrel disguise or cake burning. Apparently, however, he knew a little about Alfred's life, since he includes an occasional fact, such as that Æthelbald, Alfred's brother, made an incestuous marriage with his stepmother.[36] Blackmore is far more interested in theories of the education of princes than in the literary possibilities of Alfred's history.

One minor point may be made in Blackmore's defense. While lacking in incident, his epic is at least more syntactically competent than another epic attempt, Henry James Pye's *Alfred; an Epic Poem in Six Books* (1801). Pye was poet laureate, but several passages in the poem show a complete inability to master even straightforward rhyming couplets. A stray Druid, for example, prophesies Britain's future freedoms and recounts the story of King John and the *Magna Carta:*

> Behold where Thames, through Runny's fertile meads,
> Placid and full, his waves pellucid leads,
> To England's swains, and England's chiefs, his brow
> Prone on the earth, the baffled tyrant bow,
> Imperial Freedom, waving in her hand
> Her charter, fixing rights by Alfred plann'd.
> Careful to foster, with protective wing
> The sacred pandects of a patriot king.[37]

The poem contains more action than Blackmore's effort and draws more on scenes from Alfred's life; but Pye is not striving for historical authenticity, for his Saxons and Danes fight on horseback in full suits of armor. Pye's poem is hence one of the last works where anachronistic details of some five hundred years are a matter of no importance to writer or audience. Still, Pye and Blackmore help reveal the extent of admiration for Alfred by implying that the comparison of their dedicatees to Alfred is an indisputable compliment. Blackmore's poem is dedicated to Prince Frederick of Hanover, who is informed by the poet that Alfred is "a Prince sprung from the ancient *Saxon* Race of your own native Land."[38] The clear assumption is that an association with King Alfred must of necessity enhance the image of the Hanoverian rulers of England.

The cult of Alfred seems particularly to have encouraged this favorable comparison with royalty in drama. Later commentators were to claim a place for Alfred in English folk-memory, but the question remains of what, if anything, Alfred would have suggested even to an educated nonantiquarian during this period. Dramatic realizations of Alfred hence provide an important means of assessing nonspecialist understandings of his significance. While comparatively few of the Alfred plays became standard favorites, they are of interest in presenting a conventionally acceptable view of the hero-king — and, I would argue, in revealing that deviations from the portrayal of Alfred as an ideal were unacceptable. As late as 1831, James Sheridan Knowles dedicated an only slightly historical but generally celebratory play, *Alfred the Great; or, the Patriot King,* to William IV.[39] But numerous published dramas on the subject of King Alfred had preceded it, in addition to pageants and burlesques.

Of all these dramas, probably the best remembered is one of the earliest, the Masque of Alfred. The first form of this work by James Thomson and David Mallet was *Alfred, a Masque,* which was performed in 1740 for the Prince and Princess of Wales, showing once again the association of Saxon themes with the current royal dynasty. Some general plot elements found here recur in other eighteenth-century dramatic versions of the Alfred story.

Most of the dramas span the period between the Battle of Chippenham, a major defeat for Alfred, and the Battle of Eddington, the important victory that forced a truce between Saxons and Danes. In this comparatively early version, Alfred and his followers are hiding from the "haughty, cruel, unbelieving Dane."[40] The plot follows a standard convention of romance when Alfred's son falls in love with a shepherd girl who fortunately proves to be of noble descent and hence marriageable. In the 1740 text the cross-historical references in the masque are elaborated when Alfred beholds a vision of English monarchs who will emulate his own authority and military prowess: specially highlighted are the apparitions of Edward III, Elizabeth, and William III. (Given these heroes, one suspects that the real enemies are conceived of not as Danish, but as French.) Finally, with the help of the earl of Devon, the Danes are defeated and Britannia is left to rule undisputed.

Most of the other surviving Alfred plays follow this general pattern. Names of characters in earlier versions such as the anonymous 1753 play *Alfred the Great, Deliverer of his Country* suggest that if any historical source was used, it was Tindal's translation of Rapin-Thoyras; after 1760 names were more often drawn from

David Hume's *History of England.* [41] In most cases, little more was taken from history than names, and the plot follows the general framework established by the 1740 masque. Within this framework, playwrights allowed themselves considerable license in the presentation of romantic disguises and barbarous Danes, but the central figure of Alfred, almost invariably played as an older, more fatherly figure than the historical Alfred would have been at the time of his greatest victory, remained sacrosanct. For example, critical response to John Home's *Alfred, a Tragedy* (1778) reveals that defamation of Alfred's character would not be tolerated. In the introduction to the published version, Home was forced to reply to charges that he had degraded his hero by presenting him as deceitful. Home had depicted Alfred (as a young man — actually closer to historical fact than in most other plays) entering the Danish camp in disguise, not principally out of a patriotic desire to learn the invaders' plans but to rescue his beloved. Alfred moreover tells a deliberate lie to preserve his disguise. Home defended his interpretation by pointing out that Sophocles had allowed morally virtuous characters to practice similar deceptions;[42] yet despite the legend that Saint Neot reproached the young Alfred for his early misconduct, Home had contravened the usual custom of portraying the king without a flaw of any kind. This surely suggests that even among nonantiquarians, the name of Alfred had resonances that a dramatist might explore, but not contradict: however shadowy a figure, there was an eighteenth-century mythic Alfred.

The celebratory nature of the Alfred plays contains an underlying assumption of the association of the past with the present. In portraying the greatness of the English king, the dramas, from *Alfred, a Masque* to Knowles's version, suggest that the current king of England may have some of the characteristics of his ancestor. Here the traditional concept of Alfred, so strong that Home found he could not contradict it, was more important than the documentary fact that was to obsess the nineteenth-century historians. The status of the great hero was simultaneously historic and mythical — a concept that in drama partly survived the new stress on fact. Nevertheless, much as Sheridan Knowles's play of 1831 seemed to be following this old tradition, it was affected by the change in attitudes to history, at least to the extent that Alfred's mythic kingly qualities are implicitly augmented by what was now accepted as a historical fact — that Alfred had founded the British navy. The parallel with William IV, whose interest in naval affairs was always emphasized, is thus more historically based. During the eighteenth century, however, the positive kingly comparison is usually less specific. Alfred had overcome his enemies; particularly during the struggle for the retention of the American colonies, emphasis on Britain's triumphs in adversity could not but be well received.

Critical Use of King Alfred

On the other hand, positive kingly comparisons were not the only ones possible. Not by everyone was Alfred merely seen as the mythic patron of Britain's successes. The great reverence for Alfred was shared by many Britons who followed the tradition of the seventeenth-century constitutionalists in believing that Anglo-Saxon social and political institutions had been the best in national history. More directly critical of the status quo, these Britons did not accept that their rulers displayed the pre-Conquest spirit of Alfred the Great. Instead, they repeated the Norman Yoke position by arguing that the Norman invasion had subverted the Saxon constitution so that the distinctive characteristics of the English people as exemplified by Alfred were submerged by oppression.

This view of the significance of Alfred and the Anglo-Saxon Golden Age required a more solid theoretical and historical basis. Obviously, the legal codes existed, but these were not necessarily specific on the most contested points. Since reformist groups were claiming a factual basis for their interpretation of the English constitution, and Alfred's symbolic value lay in his historical reality, the establishment of the Alfred story as history, as opposed to tradition, seemed especially important.

The difficulty was that comparatively little was known about

the early Saxons. As Kliger has noted, the seventeenth- and eighteenth-century Gothicists — those who believed the Goths to have
been the ancestral Germanic group — accepted that since the
Saxons were a Germanic people, their earliest recorded histories
were Caesar's *Commentaries* and Tacitus's *Germania*.[43] Reginald Horsman has drawn attention to a similar interest in Tacitus in America,
although the view of the American colonists of this period was
slightly different, tending to stress the Saxons as "yeoman farmers"
and property-owners, while British writers stressed their political
freedoms.[44] The *Germania* in particular ascribes to the ancient Teutonic tribes an unusual degree of personal liberty and a commitment to freedom. This at least appears to be documentary evidence
of early date. Modern readings have suggested that Tacitus's emphasis on the austerity and virtue of the Germanic peoples was
intended to create a stronger contrast with the standards of the
Romans of his own age.[45] If this is the case, English readers of the
eighteenth and nineteenth centuries did not favor such an interpretation. For them, the *Germania* seemed virtually the only trust-
worthy document concerning their ancestors, with the possible
addition of some hints from Caesar.

References by Sir Edward Coke, and later by Sir William
Blackstone (1723–1780), to some vague "time immemorial" when
the traditions of English Common Law were established were associated by many with these relics of ancient Germania, the "Gothic"
or Saxon heritage. The use made by jurists and historians of early
legal codes such as the Laws of Alfred and the slightly more dubious "Laws of Edward the Confessor" (several times reissued, but
always in expensive polyglot folios) spread their contents to a wider
readership — albeit in a necessarily interpretative form.

Eighteenth-century readers, then, could learn that English law
and constitutions had at least a thousand-year history. The problem
was that on the point seemingly most relevant, information was
comparatively scant. They could learn the rate of compensation for
the loss of a woman's hair under the Anglo-Saxon kings, but actual
constitutional arrangements, such as the law of succession and the
allocation of power between king, nobles, and people, could only be
reconstructed from hints. The same was true of perhaps the most

cherished English right, trial by jury. Yet the laws of King Alfred remained an established fact, and by a strange twist, the cult of Alfred, which seemed so clearly a confirmation of the existing form of government, became merged with a belief that he had been the father of English constitutional freedoms.

Yet only some of the earliest biographers of Alfred see him in this light. Just as the dramas and poems had supported a parallel between Alfred and the contemporary monarchy, Robert Powell, who wrote in defense of Charles I in the years preceding the Revolutionary War, used this comparison in his *Life of Alfred or Alured* (1634). Powell claims Alfred not as the father of English liberty, but rather as "the first institutor of subordinate government in this kingdom."[46] Powell had gleaned from his studies of Anglo-Saxon law "that the bodie of the common weale consisteth by an ancient monarchicall government, and that the KING is Vicarius Dei and Caput rei publicae, GODS Vicegerent and head of the Commonwealth."[47] The work concludes with: "CaroLVs aLVreDo, Charo aLVreDVs In CaroLo reVI VIscIt"—simultaneously presenting 1634 in Roman numerals and stating plainly that Alfred lives again in King Charles. Not surprisingly, Powell was expressing himself more cautiously by 1642, when he published another work based on Anglo-Saxon law. His *Treatise on Leets* is dedicated to the Speaker of the Commons, and the church is now implied to be subordinate not to the king but to Parliament—a good example of the flexibility of interpretation possible using the same documents.

Sir John Spelman, although also a supporter of Charles I, shows less evidence of having openly manipulated his materials in this way, but instead makes a conscientious effort to base his biography of Alfred on authentic history. Nevertheless, his Royalist sympathies are still in evidence. The Parliamentary party had argued that according to the strict laws of primogeniture, Alfred, whose elder brothers were survived by young sons, would not have become king at all, and that he was technically elected. In contrast, Spelman presents Alfred not as the archetypal constitutional monarch appointed by the will of the people, but as the first monarch to assume a position of "absoluteness." Spelman surmises that Alfred may in fact have been the most absolute monarch before the Norman Conquest, and that although he had an assembly, it should not be confused with the modern Parliament, since the king retained final control over it. He stresses that as the king and nobles controlled all land, "so what was then ordained by the King, his Earls, and Thanes, was a binding Law to the whole Kingdom; for it was the Act of those that had the Absolute Interest."[48] But even though Spelman thus places the institution of feudalism before 1066, he nevertheless regards the Norman invasion as "the fatal Visitation and Judgment of God upon the English nation."[49]

On this last point, political writers of the latter half of the eighteenth century may have been more inclined to agree with him. The American Revolution provided a major stimulus towards definitions of Englishness and of what rights English people should have. Interest in the Saxon heritage thus became a means of social criticism and a strain in opposition to the celebratory remembrance of King Alfred, under whose leadership the Anglo-Saxon culture had reached its pinnacle. From this high point, the kingdom was seen as having declined under successive invasions by the Danes and internal struggles, until William of Normandy took the entire legislature upon himself.

Thomas Paine was among the radicals who used the argument that a free Saxon constitution had been replaced by a Norman tyranny, and in some of his writings he draws deliberate parallels between George III and William the Conqueror as menaces to the traditional rights of Englishmen. Hence in *Common Sense* he remarks:

> When William the Conqueror subdued England, he gave them law at the point of the sword; and until we consent, that the seat of government, in America, be legally and authoritatively occupied, we shall be in danger of having it filled by some fortunate ruffian, who may treat us in the same manner, and then, where will be freedom? where our property?[50]

Paine is not, however, entirely consistent in his use of history, sometimes claiming that a return to former ways is necessary, but more often advocating the establishment of a new method of government. In his famous appeal to Edmund Burke to "produce the English Constitution," he insists:

> If he cannot we may fairly conclude that tho' it has been much talked about, no such thing as a constitution exists, or ever did exist, and consequently that the people have got a constitution to form. . . . Though it has been much modified from the opportunity of circumstances since the time of William the Conqueror, the country has never yet regenerated itself, and is therefore without a constitution.[51]

Paine touches on a recurrent problem in radical readings of history when he simultaneously claims that England "never did have" a constitution, and that William the Conqueror destroyed it. Another republican, Catherine Macaulay, displays the same contradiction in her writings. In her defense of the French Revolution she argues that since all previous governments were clearly imperfect, the creation of a new form of government needs no appeal to "historical precedent."[52] Nevertheless, Macaulay named her home Alfredhouse and placed a bust of King Alfred above the door.[53] Her own writings suggest conscious use of historical parallel at the same time she is arguing that England has not exploited its chances to establish something new. Early radicals were thus already encountering the historical difficulty that later liberals were also unable to solve: whether English history should be regarded as lineally progressive, or whether a return to a Saxon Golden Age was necessary.

Certain writers and politicians were absolutely committed to the cyclic concept of history inherent in the vision of an Anglo-Saxon Golden Age. Alexander Bicknell published *The Life of Alfred the Great King of the Anglo-Saxons* in 1777: this did not add to the factual basis established by Spelman but seems to have been written with the earnest intent of presenting the public with a portrait of the ideal king. Bicknell's biography contains guarded criticisms of the current political situation: he maintains that the constitution as established by Alfred leaves the English people "ever secure against the oppression of tyrants," a possible hint to the American Revolutionaries that a constitutional solution may exist for their grievances. But Bicknell also states that Alfred's laws are:

> so plain and simple, and yet so rational and efficacious, that we are apt to wonder that they were ever abolished, or being abolished, that they never were revived; how worthy are they of the attention of future Sovereigns? and how far from impracticable, even in the most luxurious and dissipated age, to a Prince who inherited a small share of the judgment, resolution, and patriotism of Alfred?[54]

Even in the mild contemporary criticism of Bicknell's history, Alfred becomes symbolic of an ideal that could be revived by his descendants.

But perhaps the most devoted and persistent admirer of King Alfred as constitutional monarch was Major John Cartwright (1740–1824). For half a century Cartwright remained firm in his conviction that England's best hope was to return as a nation to the ways of King Alfred. For Cartwright, the American war was "unnatural" in setting Alfred's descendants against each other. In *The Legislative Rights of the Commonalty Vindicated*, better known by its subtitle, *Take your Choice* (1776–1777), he quoted his favorite maxim from Alfred, the "godlike sentiment" that in all justice "the English should be as free as their thoughts."[55] Believing that "the title and authority of a king depends upon common consent," Cartwright claimed that in the time of Alfred annual assemblies had been called; that all citizens were part of an armed militia (an idea upon which he elaborated during the French wars); and that Alfred had invented trial by jury. From this he concluded that since these rights had been lost or eroded over the centuries, all Englishmen should defend them and reclaim their just inheritance.[56]

Cartwright's sentiments were openly nationalistic. In his extensive writings he almost deifies Alfred, repeatedly describing him as "godlike" and "divine."[57] Twenty years after *Take your Choice*, Cartwright was evidently still firmly committed to his ideal of Alfred and the Anglo-Saxon constitution. He was to continue to believe in Alfred until his death, although his last major work, *The English Constitution Produced and Illustrated* (1823), is more historically informed than his earlier works and attributes less of the Anglo-Saxon achievement to Alfred in person.

Not surprisingly, Cartwright has gained a reputation for being a quixotic bore. Nevertheless, his ideas gained some circulation among popular reformers. They especially achieved a wider audience through partial adoption by William Cobbett, who in turn was read by Carlyle and other influential thinkers. Thomas Jefferson, who demonstrated his interest in the Anglo-Saxon heritage in an essay on the language, also congratulated Cartwright, on having "deduced the Constitution of the English nation from its rightful root, the Anglo-Saxon."[58]

Cartwright was an important publicizer, then, of the Saxon myth: the question remains as to where he obtained his information concerning Alfred. J. W. Burrow has argued that "the more imprecise a historical myth the better it can perform its functions,"[59] which seems especially true of Cartwright's use of Alfred. His writings and speeches imply a belief that England actually had a Golden Age in the time of Alfred, but until his last works, this belief is based more on tradition than on historical sources. Cartwright was following this radical tradition when he claimed that the Saxon king had invented a general assembly and trial by jury. Yet historical evidence concerning how the Anglo-Saxon laws were carried out is extremely sparse. Even later historians were compelled to theorize on the basis of their knowledge of other Germanic peoples, or on scanty and dubious evidence from the Anglo-Saxon legal code.

The Laws of Edward the Confessor (actually a Norman document, a fact that Cartwright chose to ignore) contain some mention of the *folcmote*, or assembly, but the most substantial description of how it functioned is almost certainly a late interpolation.[60] Still more doubtful is Cartwright's assertion that Alfred himself invented trial

by jury. That this notion was part of popular tradition is indicated
by its inclusion in some of the Alfred dramas. In John O'Keeffe's
version, for example, Alfred condemns the hero Eustace to death as
as traitor, only to discover at the last moment that the young man
was in fact loyal to his country. The king consequently devises trial
by jury on the spur of the moment: "A man's life is too sacred to
depend on the capricious breath of an individual. Alfred decrees
that henceforth none shall be deemed guilty till convicted by twelve
of his peers."[61] A similar scene occurs in James Sheridan Knowles's
Alfred the Great; or, the Patriot King. The fact remains, however, that
no documentary evidence confirms the popular belief.

One possible source for the idea is Spelman's *Life of Ælfred the
Great.* Usually very careful in his use of evidence, Spelman may
perhaps have been misled by the researches of his father Sir Henry,
who did much to preserve the remaining records of early English
law, into confusing Alfred's law of frank-pledge, or binding men
into mutually responsible groups of twelve, with the institution of
the jury.[62] Although soon afterwards refuted by Hickes, who realized the cause of the error,[63] Spelman's version evidently gained
wider circulation than Hickes's contradiction, probably because his
book was a major source for Rapin-Thoyras's popular history of
England. Rapin-Thoyras hence observes that Alfred established a
system of equal justice, and to ensure that it was carried out without oppression towards the less powerful members of society,

> he ordered, that in all *Criminal Actions,* twelve Men, cho-
> sen for that purpose, should determine concerning the
> Fact, and the Judge give sentence according to their
> Verdict. This Privilege, enjoyed by the English to this
> Day, is doubtless the noblest and most valuable, that
> subjects can have.[64]

An alternative opinion was available after 1760, when Hume's
History of England pointedly does not attribute to the Saxons such
wisdom of legislation and even implies that they practiced super-
stitious trials by ordeal that depended on divine powers to reveal
guilt.[65] But certainly, Cartwright, who had read Rapin-Thoyras's

work, believes entirely in Alfred's creation of the system of trial by jury, assuming that under the Normans the practice was replaced by "Tryal by Battel," or single combat. Usually, Cartwright quotes Sir William Blackstone as a major source of his conceptions of law and constitution. Blackstone himself is more cautious in his estimation of the part played by Alfred, like Edward Coke tending to ascribe the jury system to a shared Germanic heritage. He observes that although "some authors have endeavoured to trace the original of juries up as high as the Britons themselves," they are found in most feudal nations and are ascribed to various ancient rulers, "just as we are apt to impute the invention of this, and some other pieces of juridical polity, to the superior genius of Alfred the Great; to whom, on account of his having done so much, it is usual to attribute every thing."[66]

Yet although Blackstone's opinion was available to Cartwright and other constitutionalists, in reference to Alfred the Great they were even inclined to doubt the great jurist. Consequently, the attribution of right to a trial by one's equals came also to be seen as part of the heritage from the Anglo-Saxons, particularly since it seemed to contrast with what was known of early Norman trial by battle. Alexander Bicknell had made his muted appeal to George III to follow the example of his illustrious predecessor as early as the beginning of the American War of Independence. Later, during the French wars of 1791–1815, certain civil rights (notably habeas corpus, that citizens could not be detained without charge) were withdrawn on the grounds of a national emergency. This provided a further stimulus to the idea that rights were part of a continuous tradition from Alfred's time (and also a reason for wishing to dissociate the democratic tradition from revolutionary France). George III was thus characterized not as the new Alfred but as the new William the Conqueror, once again destroying cherished Saxon institutions.

What the eighteenth-century Saxon constitutionalists had to bequeath to future generations, then, was a general reverence for an age about which they knew comparatively little. These early panegyrists of Saxon England focused their claims for tradition on limited areas, and principally in the political sphere. But although they had access to legal documents, knowledge of the rest of the Anglo-Saxon world — its religion, its culture — remained confined to those few who studied the language and, as yet, apart from the popular conception.

In the later years of the nineteenth century, this reverence for Saxon political institutions, and for their personification Alfred the Great, survived — with, however, some significant differences. Strangely, these later admirers of Alfred, even though they claimed to be following a thousand-year-old tradition, were not even fully aware of earlier attempts to portray their hero. In 1896, for example, Poet Laureate Alfred Austin wrote a dramatic poem about King Alfred called *"England's Darling."* Austin claimed that the "greatest of Englishmen has never been celebrated by an English poet"[67] — demonstrably untrue, since Henry Pye had exercised his laureateship in a similar manner one hundred years previously. Nor do nineteenth-century writers appear to know the earlier Alfred dramas, although Isaac Pocock's "musical drama" of 1827 seems to have connections with John O'Keeffe's 1796 version. Indeed, the tradition of Alfred as political example fades, even in works intended for the nonspecialist reader. Hence, in Charles Dickens's *Child's History of England* Alfred is transformed from political exemplar to moral exemplar. Here it is not so much Alfred's innovations as his character that is important. Like Cartwright, Dickens writes in a popular mode, but the Alfred of 1851 reminds English readers less of their commitment to the constitution than that "under the GREAT ALFRED, all the best points in the English character were first encouraged, and in him first shown."[68]

Historical works suffered less eclipse. Spelman's *Life of Ælfred*, recognized as a work of exceptional merit, remained the only widely known biography until well into the nineteenth century. But more than any definite facts there survived vague feelings: that Alfred had been in all senses a popular king; that at the Conquest something fundamentally English and exemplified by Alfred had been lost. As a character of stage and popular oratory, Alfred's role seems to suggest that the Saxon movement was largely the possession of the lower and middle classes, and particularly of those who had no political power. If all Englishmen had voted in the Saxon popular assembly, after all, Englishmen of later times should have the same right.

With the beginning of the nineteenth century, this reading of Alfred became complicated by interest in other possibilities of the tradition and particularly by its repossession by scholars. Still to be analyzed was whether a new stress on documentary evidence would confirm a healthy and well-governed state that had reached its highest glory under Alfred the Great but had been destroyed by the Normans; or whether a new view of the Anglo-Saxons would emerge — one that demanded their study not merely as creators of the constitution but as symbols of all that was inherent in English identity. If the true English were indeed the Saxons, then the status of the Normans as the ancestors of the English aristocracy was called into question. More historical fact was needed to support the myth of origins and to apply its message to the century's social, political, and religious situation.

Chapter
2

Nineteenth-Century Views of History

The role of the Saxon heritage in eighteenth-century writings might initially seem to support the nineteenth-century claim of a continuous English tradition. Later use of the theme, however, is distinct in two significant respects, both relating to a sense of the historical. First, a substantial increase in history-related publication indicates a more widespread acceptance of the importance of history. Second, more stringent standards were imposed in defining the very nature of history and of historical validity. Historical writers' increasing insistence on authenticating evidence on a more scholarly basis marks the nineteenth century as a new phase in historical methodology. Here, of course, "scholarship" does not imply professional study. Yet the relationship between popular culture and the scholarly search for the "fact" of history becomes far more complex.

History in the Marketplace

Until this time, the Saxon world had been inaccessible to most English people except through the imagination of poets, playwrights — and politicians. The early nineteenth-century believers in the fact of history, while encouraging new reverence for historical materials, failed to solve the problem of how accessible such materials could or should be. On the other hand, the believers prompted a new interest in Saxon and Norman history without which imaginative literature on these themes — literature from which the avowedly factual genre would in turn draw so much — could not have come into being. The formation of the nineteenth-century British view of Saxons and Normans, then, owes its origins to the stimulus to exploration of the past prompted by antiquarians through activities such as ballad collecting and historical-publishing societies, and to the contribution of historians who were prepared to search for new documentary evidence. By 1841, Thomas Arnold informed students of Oxford University not merely that he believed that the English national identity was unequivocally Saxon, but also that such an identity affected individual character. The confidence of his assertion was based on the newly developing sense that history was not myth, but concrete, and above all, relevant to patriotic Britons.

This is not to claim that in forty years all Britons had been convinced of the centrality of history. Nevertheless, in its different forms, an interest in history certainly reached a wider section of the population than before. In the early years of the eighteenth century, Hickes and his circle had pursued a path into a scholarly wilderness. Their emphasis on language appealed neither to students of the classics nor to antiquarian collectors. Hickes had believed that the "Northern" languages were derived from "Gothic" ones. If the word "Gothic" meant anything to his successors, it was in association with a more fashionable interest in antiquity, the acquisition of artifacts. The great leader of this fashion in England was Horace Walpole (1717–1797), who stocked his Gothic mansion Strawberry Hill with many curiosities of a historical nature. The urge of the most wealthy classes to own anything old and rare became sufficiently common to prompt the ridicule of satirists, particularly since, as Walpole himself realized, the connoisseur was vulnerable to the charms of items of questionable authenticity.[1] Sir Walter Scott's third novel, *The Antiquary* (1816) — his personal favorite —

features such an antiquary of the late eighteenth century. Scott's *Antiquary* is a likeable if pedantic old gentleman, but perhaps the comic actor and dramatist Samuel Foote expressed a more generally held attitude towards such enthusiasts in *The Nabob* (1772), in which Sir Matthew Mite, who has amassed a vast fortune in India, spends his money on very doubtful relics in an effort to be fashionably antiquarian.

Obviously, only the rich could indulge in this form of antiquarian collecting, but after Thomas Percy, later bishop of Dromore, published the influential *Reliques of Ancient English Poetry* in 1765, a new form of collecting became fashionable: that of old ballads. The popularity of Percy's work prompted others to collect and publish ballads and songs from England and Scotland.

Percy did not assert that these verses were Saxon, or even Norman, compositions; but in his introductory essay he laid claim to a continuous poetic tradition in Britain, dating back to ancient bards and scalds.[2] In editing these poems, he was asserting the value of heritage, and the interest in old literary remains prompted by the ballad "revival" (a term itself suggesting a concrete past) expanded to include other literary forms.

The sale of the duke of Roxburghe's antiquarian library in 1812 indicates how this interest in old ballads was associated with a more general wish to rediscover historical remains. At the sale, a collection of approximately three thousand ballads (some printed, some manuscript) fetched the enormous sum of 455 guineas.[3] But this same auction also prompted a group of aristocratic collectors to join together in the formation of the Roxburghe Club, the first of many historical publishing societies dedicated to expand interest in and knowledge of the documentary past.

The circumstances of the founding of the Roxburghe Club prompt the question of whether history was still only the possession of the very rich. Historical researches required a source of funding. Some of the ballad collections, such as Scott's *Minstrelsy of the Scottish Border* (1802) achieved a modest success. Yet some solution to the financial difficulties experienced by earlier antiquaries such as Elizabeth Elstob had to be found before major progress could be made in making early English works more accessible. With the possible exception of Joseph Ritson (1752–1803), who was widely regarded by his contemporaries as being insane,[4] most of the ballad editors of this period would unquestionably have considered themselves to be amateurs. Indeed, both in the time of Hickes and during much of the nineteenth century, medievalists of all kinds generally practiced one of the two main professions open to university graduates. Hence some (Sharon Turner, Walter Scott, and later Frederick J. Furnivall) had legal practices; many others were ordained in the Church of England. The main advantage of ordination was that with influence in the right circles, one or more church benefices could be obtained, which provided a secure income with flexible responsibilities. But while the professions produced most of the scholars, the scholars themselves were largely dependent on the interest of "gentlemen"—noblemen and other landowners—to finance their work. Few publishers would care to speculate on antiquarian ventures, and hence throughout the eighteenth century such books were generally published by collecting subscriptions from those who could afford to pay the not inconsiderable sum of a few guineas.

The conservative tendency of antiquarianism at this time may therefore partly be explained by the characteristics of those involved. Simply to be able to take a degree at Oxford or Cambridge it was necessary to subscribe at least in form to the doctrines of the established church, while the many antiquarian writers in orders actually depended for their livelihoods upon acceptance of those beliefs. Similarly, the wealthier men upon whose support most publishing ventures depended were unlikely to patronize works directly critical of the current balance of power.

How, though, could a broader interest in the past be fostered and made financially secure? There were countless unedited documents in the British Museum, private collections, and churches, but still so few people showed an interest in their contents that no publisher would invest in reprinting them. The solution to the problem found in the nineteenth century was through historical societies such as the Roxburghe Club: groups supported by subscription and principally composed of amateurs committed to rediscovering England as it used to be.

Although the first of these societies, the Roxburghe Club was not entirely a new invention. The Society of Antiquaries had been functioning since before 1750; other sources for obtaining antiquarian knowledge included publications such as the *Gentleman's Magazine*. Nevertheless, these groups were more oriented towards classical than "Gothic" antiquities and tended to stress archaeology and architecture rather than literary remains. (The records of the Society of Antiquaries, for example, show a remarkable fascination with Druids and with barrows long and round.) A few devotees of Norman architecture communicated their discoveries to their fellow antiquarians, but the Saxon period was still usually dismissed as the "Dark Ages," an area of conjecture scarcely worthy of scholarly study.

Philippa Levine has demonstrated that even in their period of greatest popularity most members of these societies had a comparatively narrow range of occupations, clergymen comprising the greatest number.[5] The Roxburghe Club was unusually aristocratic: of thirty-one founding members four, for example, were Spencers. Their group marked a new direction in history since it was dedicated to the pursuit not of ancient remains but of ancient literature. There were to be forty members, and each was to be responsible for the publication of an unedited manuscript, or the republication of some rare printed work.[6]

The founding of the Roxburghe Club is a key example of the muddled thinking that was to continue to dog the antiquarian societies. At first sight the intention would seem to be to make history more popular by increasing the availability of rare works. Yet according to the original regulations, only one hundred copies of each book would be printed, and these would be entirely at the disposal of the forty members. Nor did the club produce many of the "important works" promised, members tending to print family records and manuscripts and books readily accessible to them with little consideration of their general values. The subscription, at five guineas, was so high that in some cases the members could have bought the original works for little more. One significant early Roxburghe publication was Frederic Madden's edition of *Havelok the Dane,* but in this case, one of the few available professionals — Madden worked at the British Museum — was employed to carry out the work. Obviously, the exclusive nature of the Roxburghe Club limited not only its contribution to the rediscovery of ancient literature, but also opportunities for including in their number people who had made major contributions to history (the "Author of Waverley" was, however, permitted to join in 1823, and the constitutional historian Henry Hallam in 1836).

Still, the Roxburghe Club provided two important things for its imitators. First, it had a declared objective of rediscovering neglected texts. And second, the limitation of its membership to a very select few had undoubted snob appeal: antiquarianism was a fitting pursuit for gentlemen, and even for noblemen. Hence if the Roxburghe Club refused to open its membership to worthy citizens, then those worthy citizens would form their own historical societies.

The earliest of the many historical societies to follow were established in Scotland, Walter Scott having played a major part in making Scottish tradition fashionable. Scott, indeed, was founding president of the Bannatyne Club, established in Edinburgh in 1823 after the pattern of the Roxburghe Club. The Bannatyne Club, however, starting with the same number of thirty-one founding members, soon expanded its membership to one hundred, with the understanding that extra copies of its publications would be available for general sale.[7]

This slightly less exclusive membership became the pattern for the groups that followed. Among the first in England were the Surtees Society, begun in 1834 and named after the lately deceased Durham antiquarian Robert Surtees;[8] and the English Historical Society. The latter group announced the intention to publish "an accurate, uniform, and elegant edition of the most valuable English chronicles, from the earliest period to the accession of Henry the Eighth," of interest both to historians and to the nonspecialist reader[9] — a worthy goal, but one that proved impossible to achieve.

The historical society with probably the most influence,

though, was the Camden Society, founded in London in the 1830s. Whereas the Surtees Society's annual fee was two guineas (forty-two shillings), the Camden Society charged only one pound (twenty shillings), the intention being to attract twelve hundred members. Scarcely coincidentally, the first meeting was at the printing house of J. G. Nichols, who had realized the commercial potential of the scheme. In fact, in 1842, John Mitchell Kemble, then an officer of the society, described it as "the *most contemptible*" of all the historical societies and informed Jakob Grimm that it was "a *cheap* joint stock company, set on foot and kept for the benefit of Mr. Nichols the printer and publisher . . ."[10] Shortly before this time, however, the society had a waiting list of prospective members. Comparatively speaking, it seems to have been good value for one pound a year, and as Levine has shown, it did succeed in attracting a less exclusive range of members.[11]

In view of this success, many more regional clubs were formed. About the same time, other clubs focusing on specific interests, including the Philological Society and the British Archaeological Society (a splinter group from the Society of Antiquaries), provided alternatives. Clearly, historical interest was growing. Only some of this general feeling for national history, however, was directed towards Saxons and Normans.

Some societies did choose specifically to focus on the Anglo-Norman period. The Ælfric Society, named after the Saxon theologian and grammarian, and the first group dedicated specifically to Anglo-Saxon studies, was established in 1842 under the presidency of Sir Francis Egerton, later Earl of Ellesmere. All the English members of the council, which included Madden, Kemble, and Benjamin Thorpe, were fellows of the Society of Antiquaries. The Ælfric Society proposed "to give to the world of scholars every yet inedited remain of AngloSaxon."[12] Unfortunately, the society, which never achieved great popularity, also fell far short of the original plan — nor were these two societies alone in encountering difficulties with Anglo-Saxon works. The Society of Antiquaries commissioned Thorpe to edit Caedmon's metrical paraphrase in 1832 and the Codex Oxoniensis ten years later; Madden's long-awaited edition of Layamon's *Brut* finally appeared in 1847. But

Thorpe's books in particular were met with no enthusiasm: in her *History of the Society of Antiquaries* Joan Evans notes that "by 1844 the Anglo-Saxon texts had cost 1,135 pounds against sales of 712 pounds, and the series was suspended."[13] The English Historical Society found its promised "accurate, uniform, and elegant" series too costly and finally collapsed. One of its editors had been Joseph Stevenson. Stevenson began his career as a Presbyterian minister, became a curate of the Church of England, and died a Jesuit, but was to all intents and purposes a professional editor. In addition to his work for the English Historical Society, he was also employed by the Surtees Society to edit an Anglo-Saxon and Early English Psalter in 1843. This he carried through: but his edition of the Lindisfarne Gospels caused the society major financial problems for many years.[14] Whatever the enthusiasm for history, the issue of Anglo-Saxon texts repeatedly proved a stumbling-block for the societies.

Obviously, the comparative failure of societies specializing in the period reflects a continued lack of interest in access to Anglo-Saxon texts. Yet at least in part, the failure was also because of the enthusiastic amateurishness of many of the societies. Most were maladministered, the result of being only one part of the leading members' busy lives; and there were constant problems with collecting subscriptions. The majority of editors were not paid directly for their services, which meant that Madden might postpone completing *Brut* for a decade, and that gentlemen-amateurs could not be compelled to conform to any standard editorial principles. Often the publications were mere reprintings of a single manuscript or even of a transcript without collation with other available texts: notes and glossaries were left to individual whim.[15] The editors moreover employed transcribers, and this was an expensive process. Even when the societies used "professionals," additional complications ensued. Joseph Stevenson and Thomas Wright, for example, each edited a phenomenal number of books — Wright had a part in about one hundred such publications — and at the speed at which they worked inaccuracies were inevitable.

Had the societies continued to generate the initial level of enthusiasm, possibilities would still have remained. Yet not surprisingly, interest in historical societies soon reached a saturation point, the local clubs seeming to have attracted members away from the earlier groups. For example, although no mention is made of it in their official history, there appears to have been a secession from the Surtees Society in 1855; and the Camden Society, which at its peak was printing 1,250 copies, later reduced its print run to 600.[16]

Criticisms of the state of historical literature began even before most of the societies. The medieval expert Sir Harris Nicolas, clearly enraged by the Society of Antiquaries, published *Observations on the State of Historical Literature* in 1830, where he proposed that state records should be made more generally available and that the government might take an interest in historical publications.[17] About this time, the new government in France under Louis Philippe began to sponsor antiquarian research, including research into Norman-French materials. The French minister of state Guizot sent the antiquarian editor Francisque Michel to England to investigate Norman manuscripts in British collections. The result of this visit was Michel's most important publication relating to English history, the *Chroniques Anglo-Normandes* (1836–1840): this provided a major impetus to the Norman studies that had hitherto been even more unsystematic than Saxon researches. Michel subsequently edited Norman texts for several of the British historical societies.

France, then, had adopted the perspective that Norman remains were a significant part of French national heritage. The British government was slower to become involved, the Rolls Series of works in state collections only commencing publication in 1858. As late as 1848, Richard Garnett, whose principle interests were philological, was repeating Harris Nicolas's criticisms. Writing in the *Quarterly Review,* Garnett complained of the "niggardly spirit" both of owners of manuscripts and of societies such as the Bannatyne and Roxburghe clubs, whose goals appeared to be to keep access to antiquities to a select few. He further charged that the historical societies simply did not publish worthwhile texts: of the Camden Society's issues, for example, he judged much to be of "comparatively little interest." Moreover, fewer texts were in Anglo-Saxon or early English than had been promised, while some of the editing had been entrusted to "half-learned smatterers."[18]

But the very existence of so many historical societies — Levine has counted twenty-nine founded between 1834 and 1849[19] — indicates a widespread willingness to invest time and effort in history. One possible alternative for satisfying the historical desire was to publish antiquarian texts as regular ventures by commercial publishers. A very few publishers saw the possibility of profit, one of the most enterprising being William Pickering (1796–1854). Even at an early stage in his publishing career, old books fascinated Pickering, and his publishing house had a long-term association with Harris Nicolas. By the use of old-style letterpresses and woodcuts Pickering gave many of his books an antique appearance, but they were also available at comparatively moderate prices through his innovation of binding books in cloth boards.[20] Pickering's company, rather than the antiquarian societies, produced the first English edition of *Beowulf:* although only one hundred copies were printed, they were rapidly sold. The editor, Kemble, then produced a second edition with a modern English translation, evidently aimed at an even wider readership.

Henry G. Bohn, however, probably made most impact upon the accessibility of sources in early English history and literature. The son of the German Henry H. Bohn, also a publisher, Bohn commenced business on his own in 1831. He published an extensive collection of reprints, translations, and new works at moderate prices, his Antiquarian Library in particular helping make medieval works generally available in English translation. The first volume of the series, for example, was Thomas Percy's translation of Paul Mallet's *Northern Antiquities.* For five shillings, the interested reader could learn of Norse remains and the Prose Edda and also benefit from notes by the still-revered Walter Scott and several others. Many other books offered similar value for the money, the translation of Bede, for instance, containing in addition the Anglo-Saxon Chronicle. Many were edited by a diligent Anglo-Saxon scholar and admirer of King Alfred, the clergyman John Allen Giles: Wright also contributed some volumes. Thorpe's edition of Reinhold Pauli's influential *Life of Alfred*, with excerpts from the king's writings in Anglo-Saxon and a modern English translation, is another important example of how Bohn's Antiquarian Library made the Anglo-Saxon world more immediate to the nonspecialist reader.

The success of historical publications between 1820 and 1850 demonstrates a new emphasis on authentic, factual history, while the interest in local history further suggests that such history was interpreted personally, as a re-creation of the history-reader's own heritage. The cult of King Alfred had been fostered by radicals who through their social or economic positions had had little or no access to documentary materials about their hero. With the rise of publications that brought documentary evidence within the reach of the middle classes, knowledge of Saxons, and to some extent of Normans, was less dependent on a slender mythic tradition. To claim that the readers of England rushed to study the works that had for so many centuries lain moldering in private collections would be an exaggeration, as the bad experiences of the historical societies demonstrate. Yet the popular myth of the eighteenth century could now be complemented by the popularization of Anglo-Saxon writings themselves — or at least an interpretation of those writings.

Sharon Turner and Anglo-Saxon History

Increased interest in history was augmented by major new studies of both Saxons and Normans. The writers of these did not simply resummarize earlier chronicle accounts but instead drew on contemporary documents in an effort to create authentic pictures of these peoples. The lack of attention given by earlier writers and historians to the period between the Roman occupation and the Norman invasion in 1066 would suggest that until Sharon Turner began to publish his Anglo-Saxon researches in 1799–1800, it was simply dismissed as the "Dark Ages," with only the brief glimmerings of a culture as reflected in Bede's account of the early church and the reign of Alfred the Great. Admittedly, before 1800 some writers show a minor interest in Norse literature: Thomas Gray wrote some poems inspired by Norse mythology,[21] and Percy translated Mallet's *Northern Antiquities* into English Yet the Germanic languages were almost entirely unknown. Amos Cottle's publication of an English version of Saemund's *Edda*, for example, was probably not a translation from the Icelandic but from a Latin version. Cottle's brother Joseph subsequently produced an epic poem about King Alfred in no less than twenty-four books: Byron's sympathies were with the king whose life story had also suffered through Pye's poetic ineptitudes.[22]

Joseph Cottle's poetry is little better than that of most of the other Alfred bards, but his epic has a claim to interest in revealing both some knowledge of Danish antiquities and a crude sense of racial "character." Noting in his preface that "the turbulent and ferocious character of the ancient Dane has never yet been exhibited in poetry," he proceeds to make use of Norse mythology and tradition. The supposed Danish custom of "carving the eagle" on the backs of their enemies is hence described in repulsive detail:

> To the tree
> The wretched Ella now is bound! With joy,
> Wielding their monstrous knives, two Priests advanced,
> And from the neck, with an unshrinking hand,
> Downward the long gash draw; they pause awhile;
> Then, 'neath, the shoulder, either side, extend
> The murderous weapon, and, with straining hand,
> Rend the tough skin, till, o'er each elbow wide,
> The flaps are spread, and to the gazing eye
> The red nerve quivers![23]

Cottle seems also to have utilized a wider range of sources for his poem, combining stories drawn from Asser's biography of King Alfred with other anecdotes. The poet invents additional incidents of his own, but always in keeping with his conception of the historical characteristics of Danes and Saxons. As the upholder of English justice, for example, Alfred exiles one of his men since in the heat of battle he killed a Dane who asked for quarter. On one occasion at least Cottle terms the Danes "Normans" (JC, 1:146), and his treatment creates a clear opposition between the good defender of his people and the barbarous invaders.

Cottle's treatment of historical data and of racial characteristics was carried further by Sharon Turner (1768–1847) in the most important single impetus to Anglo-Saxon studies, his *History of the Anglo-Saxons*. Turner, a London lawyer, is said to have spent sixteen years studying Anglo-Saxon sources before publishing the first volume of his work in 1799.[24] This seems improbable, since Turner was even then only thirty-one years old; but he clearly familiarized himself not only with the Saxon sources in the British Museum, but also with the early Welsh chroniclers and bards. In subsequent volumes, Turner produced a wealth of new facts on Anglo-Saxon culture and literature.

Like many of his successors, Turner was an amateur forced to devise his own methods of study and research. He availed himself of Hickes's *Thesaurus*, but in many areas little guidance was available, particularly to a historian whose linguistic knowledge was uneven. Despite these difficulties, Turner seems at least to have looked through many of the Anglo-Saxon materials at the British Museum, and he produced a document-based history that provided his contemporaries with much new insight concerning their national history.

The very newness of the factual material concerning Anglo-Saxon life and civilization collected by Turner gives his book a major claim to consideration. Turner was always insistent, for example, that he was the first to realize the importance of *Beowulf*, which he brought to public attention in 1805. He cited *Beowulf* as evidence that, contrary to the prevailing belief, the Anglo-Saxons did have narrative poems — and even ones that might be described as "epic": "It is the most interesting relic of the Anglo-Saxon poetry which time has spared to us; and, as a picture of the manners, and as an exhibition of the feelings and notions of those days, it is as valuable as it is ancient."[25]

No complete edition of *Beowulf* was to appear for ten years, when Thorkelin, whose work on the manuscript actually predated

Turner's, published it with a Latin translation.[26] Before Thorkelin's work was known to him Turner was obliged to interpret the fire-damaged manuscript as best he could. Turner's renderings of select passages in his later editions, when he was able to make use of printed texts, are fairly precise; but his translations and explanations of extracts in his first edition are inaccurate both on points of syntax and of meaning — he identifies Hrothgar as Beowulf's enemy, and makes no mention of Grendel (ST 1799, 3:389–408).[27] His claims for *Beowulf* are comparatively modest: nowhere does he venture to suggest, as later philologists were to do, that this is the first great work in the English literary tradition. Still, the existence of a poem of such scope suggested that there was less cause than ever for the feeling that compared with other cultures British literature was inferior.

But *The History of the Anglo-Saxons* has further claims to consideration. First, it was a popular book, passing through at least six editions before Turner's death. The use of the writings of the Welsh bards as corroboration for historical theories particularly excited controversy. Still recovering from the blow to their critical acumen inflicted by Macpherson's *Ossian* poems and similar literary frauds, many scholars were inclined to doubt the very existence of Taliesin and the other Welsh poets cited by Turner, until in 1803 he was stung into producing an essay indicating his sources. Yet Walter Scott was particularly interested in the material on the bards and, as an ardent believer in the possibility of combining folk-tradition with other forms of historical evidence, found Turner's approach generally useful.[28]

Turner had even closer associations with other literary figures of his time. He met Samuel Taylor Coleridge at the publisher Longman's house, and considering Coleridge's avidity for books it would seem improbable that he never read *The History of the Anglo-Saxons*.[29] On a personal level, Coleridge's correspondence reveals that he knew Turner sufficiently well as to be annoyed by him: Wordsworth also met him.[30] Recommending Turner's work to a friend in 1802, Robert Southey described the first volume as the "very worst in style that ever can be written — but in research and novelty of information the best historical work beyond comparison that I have ever seen."[31] He also employed Turner for many years to conduct his legal affairs.

Turner's historical approach may therefore have influenced and also have been influenced by some of the leading Romantics. Not only was he personally acquainted with Southey and Wordsworth, but he echoed their political and religious orthodoxy. Whatever the "novelty of information" contained in the repeatedly revised three volumes, the editions of Turner's history known to the Victorians in no respect contradict the traditional view of the character and civilization of the early peoples of England. Thus in presenting the Anglo-Saxon system of government, he has no underlying objective of tacit criticism of the institutions of his own age but rather implies that the Englishmen of one thousand years ago conducted their political affairs with the same reason and moderation as their descendants. In direct opposition to democrats such as John Cartwright, who had conceived the Saxon king as something like a president, Turner even argues that in varying the succession from a strict system of primogeniture the Anglo-Saxons made a rare constitutional error, and that hereditary monarchy is by far preferable:

> Happy is the country in which the regal office is not elective, nor the right of succession permitted to be questionable! An hereditary monarchy, though, like all human institutions, it has its inconveniences, yet has not been the contrivance of childish thinkers or half-way politicians; it was the most benevolent institution of human wisdom, profiting from the most disastrous experience. (ST 1836, 1:409)

Turner also became an increasingly committed member of the Church of England, and as he produced successive editions of his history he revised the text to reveal a growing religious orthodoxy. By the sixth (1836) edition, for example, he does not question that a great flood occurred "about 2348 years before the Christian era," and that consequently Britain must have been populated much later than that time. He also pours scorn on contemporaries (Joseph Ritson, perhaps?) who believe the human race to be "deduced" from "fishes and monkeys" (ST 1836, 1:56). While Turner is not as extreme as some of his successors in claiming that the Anglo-Saxons never were true Roman Catholics, he still adopts a slightly apologetic tone when discussing the Anglo-Saxon church's relationships with the papacy. He accepts Gregory the Great, instigator of the first Christian mission from Rome to England, as a good man of his time, observing that although to his contemporaries the Roman Catholicism of that period might seem a debased form of Christianity, "it could not be better than that age or the preceding times were capable of receiving or framing" (ST 1836, 2:90). In Turner's opinion (one not shared by many other apologists for the Saxons) even this form of Christianity was better than heathendom: he could at least be proud of the moderate, English way in which the teachings were adopted. Recounting at length Bede's story of Augustine's reception by King Ethelbert of Kent and his Frankish Christian queen Bertha, and how the high priest pointed out that the pagan gods had never done anything for him and that Christianity could therefore hardly be worse, Turner fails to note the lack of religious ardor. Instead, he remarks with satisfaction: "In no part of the world has Christianity been introduced in a manner more suitable to its benevolent character" (ST 1836, 1:340–341).

These quotations, it must be noted, are from Turner's 1836 edition. The first edition of his history demonstrates a similar contempt for the "superstitions" of the Roman Catholic church, but is far less emphatic in its assertions that Christianity was of necessity preferable to paganism. Thus whereas the Pope Gregory of the sixth edition was sincere in his goal of saving Saxon souls, Turner in 1805 had presented a different view. When discussing the Anglo-Saxon translation of Gregory's Dialogues he had noted:

> That imbecility of thought which credulous fanaticism generates even in valuable minds, never left a more absurd monument of its perversion than the Dialogues of Gregory. . . . Piety, allied with nonsense or with falsehood, only degrades the tremendous being, whom it professes to extol. (ST 1799, 2:316, n.)

Evidently, he later revised his opinion, for by 1836 he was even willing to justify Alfred's attention to Gregory's works. He concedes that some may be surprised that Alfred was interested in such a Romish work as Gregory's *Pastoral Care* but explains that "as it contains many moral counsels and regulations, and was written by the Pope, who was called the apostle of the English, and no other book was then at hand which was equally popular or likely to be as effectual, it was an act of patriotism and philanthropy in the king to translate it" (ST 1836, 2:89).[32] Gregory's own superstition, so criticized in the first edition, is now seen as less important than his overall intentions.

Turner's increasing belief that writers should uphold religious orthodoxy and moral standards may have had some impact upon literature through his role as legal advisor to Byron's publisher John Murray.[33] Yet according to Butterfield's definition of "whig" historians, Turner may yet be considered "Protestant, progressive, and whig." His history's message is that an examination of the past may help in an understanding of the present, as the preface to Turner's sixth (1836) edition states with whig conviction:

> The increasing prosperity of the British nation, and the expansion of its empire by the new colonies which are issuing from it, and are forming, as they settle and enlarge, new branches of dominion to it in the distant regions of our globe, makes its first rudiments and humble beginnings more interesting to us. . . . The Anglo-Saxons were deficient in the surprising improvements which their present descendants have attained; but unless they had acquired and exercised the valuable qualities, both moral and intellectual, which they progressively advanced to before their dynasty ceased, England would not have become that distinguished nation which, after the Norman graft on its original Saxon stock, it has since gradually led to be.

Turner is one historian who found a way through the problems of linear and cyclic conceptions of history. For Turner, history is linear; nevertheless, the English people share with their ancestors aspects of character that at different periods have been more or less apparent. *The History of the Anglo-Saxons*, then, is the first study to raise in a systematic way the question that was to be repeated later in the century, namely, how much study of the Anglo-Saxons may reveal inherent national characteristics.

Doubtless, Turner's stress on continuity was one of the more appealing features of his history. He did not emphasize the strangeness of the Anglo-Saxons but rather the features held in common with their descendants. Above all, Turner helped make respectable the study of a people formerly dismissed as barbarous and uncultured. The young ladies of Charlotte Mary Yonge's novels, for example, demonstrate their immersion in medieval history, and although the main influence is Scott, they also think about Saxon themes. Proof of the strength and defects of one such maiden's character is that once "she had composed three quarters of a story of a Saxon hero, oppressed by a Norman baron, and going to the Crusades." In the same novel we find her advising her friend to read about Hereward the Saxon in "that delightful Norman Conquest." This blissful rural England of the 1840s, where radical extremists are seen almost as aliens from another world, is also where a vulgar village matron has been discovered "working in cross-stitch, a picture of St. Austin preaching to the Saxons, which she intended to present, as a cushion for one of the chairs of St. Austin's Church."

> "Oh, dreadful!" cried Anne.
> "Papa walked up and down the room for a full ten minutes after he heard of it," said Elizabeth, "but mamma came to our rescue. She, the mild spoken (Mildred, you know) set off with the Saxon Winifred, the peace-maker, to reject the Saint of the Saxons, more civilly than the British Bishops did."[34]

One wonders how deliberate was Yonge's naming of the unappreciated antiquarian needlewoman — Mrs. Turner.

Francis Palgrave and Norman History

While the Saxons had found a historian in Sharon Turner, the Normans found one in Sir Francis Palgrave (1788–1861). Like Turner, Palgrave greatly contributed to the sense of historic continuity rather than sudden change. Francis Cohen was the lawyer son of a Jewish stockbroker, but on his marriage he converted to Christianity and adopted his wife's family name. Perhaps because he had no vision of his own heritage as Anglo-Saxon, while his wife's was Welsh, Palgrave was even more sympathetic towards the displaced Ancient Britons than Turner was. Before his substantial work on the Normans, he wrote two books on the Saxons. The short *History of the Anglo-Saxons* (which appeared in 1831 and passed through several editions) and *The Rise and Progress of the English Commonwealth — Anglo-Saxon Period* (1832) are very different treatments of the same information, yet both reveal an earnest Anglicanism and conservatism.

The earlier book, as Palgrave explains in his preface, was originally conceived after the pattern of Scott's *Tales of a Grandfather,* and although it finally took the form of a continuous narrative, it remains directed at children. Notes are few, and much of the earlier part is an uncritical retelling of Bede. Palgrave's Anglo-Saxons are "faithful, chaste, and honest," even in their paganism retaining some vestiges of those truths lost at Babel.[35] Theirs was an ordered world, Palgrave argues, and their respect for institutions was an attitude from which their descendants in the troubled years prior to the First Reform Act might profit.

But Palgrave's first interest at this time was in the institution of law. Even in his history for children, which proved to be one of his most popular works, he notes the need for respect of the established law, albeit in imperfect form. He thus reworks the eighteenth-century conception of Alfred as lawmaker. Alfred's objective, he claims, was not to create the law but to preserve it.

Without doubt, Alfred must have seen that many portions of the laws of the Anglo-Saxons were defective; but he judged — and we have his own words before us, grounded upon such judgment — that it was better to permit the continuance of a defective law, than to destroy the foundation upon which all laws depend — respect for established authority — which sudden changes, even for the better, are apt to undermine.[36]

Like Turner, Palgrave dissociated himself from the radicalism that had so often been a part of earlier interest in his topic. Palgrave was a friend of the Whigs of Holland House who were largely responsible for the creation of the 1832 Reform Act. Yet he apparently disagreed with the Reformers' challenge, slight as it was, to "established authority," and from about this time his periodical contributions appear not in the pro-Reform *Edinburgh Review,* but the anti-Reform *Quarterly Review.* (William Gifford, editor of the *Quarterly,* was godfather to Palgrave's second son.) In sharp contrast to Cartwright's interpretation of the Saxon period, *The Rise and Progress of the English Commonwealth* is thus a direct response to the constitutional crisis of 1832. While the Holland House Whigs were not especially interested in Anglo-Saxon history, Palgrave's work might perhaps be seen as a rebuttal to the radicals who were still claiming an Anglo-Saxon precedent for an egalitarian system of political representation. Palgrave is not opposed to all legislative changes: as a supporter of Robert Peel, he shows himself to be in favor of penal reform.[37] But he argues that Anglo-Saxon political institutions were both hierarchical and dependent on respect for tradition.

Palgrave's *English Commonwealth* moreover advances an idea upon which he was to expand in his later works. In an emphatic rejection of the radical view, he insists that the English legal system is stronger than mere dynastic changes. In his more extensive work, the *The History of Normandy and of England* (1851–1864), he asserts even more clearly that the Norman invasion was not a historical reversal but in fact preserved the most vital institutions of the ancient English state. Palgrave claims that "Anglo-Saxon" is itself an incorrect name which falsely emphasizes the contrast of the England of before 1066 and the England of William the Conqueror.

We are accustomed to lament over Harold as the last of
the Anglo-Saxon kings and to consider the acquisition of
the crown by William as the destruction of independence
and nationality; and I must needs here pause, and substi-
tute henceforward the true and antient word English for
the unhistorical and conventional term Anglo-Saxon, an
expression conveying a most false idea in our civil history. It disguises the continuity of affairs, and substitutes
the appearance of a new formation in the place of a progressive evolution.[38]

Here as always, Palgrave's emphasis is upon continuity and legal
stability: he is even prepared to conjecture that since "the greater
portion of our antient writs consist of the principles of Anglo-Saxon
law, embodied in Anglo-Norman form," similar laws found in Normandy were possibly introduced from England.[39]

Palgrave died before completing his history, and the task of
assembling the final two volumes of the bulky work was left to his
son Francis Turner Palgrave, best known as the compiler of the
Golden Treasury. The result is a rambling, repetitive book, containing many moralizing digressions, but one that still formulates an
important thesis concerning the limits of the impact of the Norman
Conquest of England.

Unlike Turner's work, however, Palgrave's reading of the period gained comparatively few supporters. Even some of the conservative writers who referred to his study, such as Charlotte
Yonge, clearly have reservations about his presentation. Documentary evidence was less reassuring when it suggested that preconceptions about its subject matter might be wrong. Traditionally, the
Normans had been the ancestors of the aristocracy, and Palgrave's
history portrayed them as ruffianly adventurers. In the conservative
view, even if the Normans had originally been regarded as of inferior blood in comparison with the English nobility, time had
confirmed privilege. Since documentary records (notably the
Domesday survey) revealed that a major redistribution of land had
followed the Conquest through William's endeavors both to reward
his soldiers and to establish control over a large kingdom, Norman

ancestry was symbolically associated with landownership. Whether or not William had the right to bestow property upon his followers, eight centuries had ratified his action; and the sacrosanct nature of property had been repeatedly claimed as vital to national stability not only by opponents of the 1832 Reform Act but also by its most devout supporters.[40]

To claim Norman ancestry, then, was to declare oneself of noble blood, and here the aristocrats had their own favored documentary evidence. This was the list of Norman knights who had fought at the Battle of Hastings (or Senlac) in 1066, preserved for many centuries by the monks of Battle Abbey, which had been founded by William on the site of his victory. John Burke, whose researches began the listing of prominent British families known today as *Burke's Peerage,* noted in his new periodical of 1846, significantly titled *The Patrician:* "The Roll of Battle Abbey, the earliest record of the Normans, has at all times been regarded with deep interest by the principal families of the kingdom."[41] As Burke observes, so much did the inclusion of one's surname in this list support aristocratic descent, that the monks were later bribed to insert the names of those whose origins could support no such claim to Norman blood.

The "principal families," with their documented hereditary right to command, were hence predisposed to think favorably of the Normans, and to believe that, to quote Sharon Turner, their "graft on the Saxon stock" was both life-giving and ennobling. Palgrave had refused to exalt the Saxons in his earlier work; in his *History of Normandy and of England,* he simultaneously rejects the concept of the Saxons as egalitarian and the Normans as noble: whereas the Anglo-Saxons "seem to have had a strong aristocratic feeling," the majority of the Normans had been

> rude, and poor, and despicable in their own country; the rascalions of Northern Gaul; these, suddenly enriched, lost all compass and bearing of mind; and no one circumstance vexed the spirit of the English more, than to see the fair and noble English maidens and widows com-

pelled to accept these despicable adventurers as their husbands.[42]

Palgrave's history, then, is a work without heroes. His Normans do not forge a new political structure but rather contribute to a divided class identity. Doubtless he would argue that the center of his work is the English Common Law, a system developed over many centuries through the pragmatic considerations of both Saxons and Normans and the true fixed point in a definition of what it was to be English. But in making theory the heart of his organizational structure, Palgrave had neglected myth. His work is important because until the later 1860s, when Freeman published his massive *History of the Conquest of England by the Normans*, it was the most substantial work on the Norman world. Yet Palgrave's Normans, shadowy figures in a society dominated by the law, could not compete with the fictionalized realizations of the novelists — or even with the work of scholars who, although presenting their materials in nonnarrative forms, detected in early English history not universal human weakness but the triumph of the English spirit.

Subsequent Advances in Scholarship

Turner's and Palgrave's work demonstrated that the times of the Saxons and the Normans could not simply be dismissed as the "Dark Ages": subsequent scholars were to go much further in their claims that essentially the English people of one thousand years ago were the same as the English of the present day. This idea was not confined to self-proclaimed works of history in narrative form. A number of scholars took up the original intentions of the historical societies and published specimens of literature surviving from the period, once again asserting the reality of the past.

Besides the selections published in Turner's *History of the Anglo-Saxons*, the first nineteenth-century additions to knowledge of early English writings came from John Josias Conybeare, who became Oxford Professor of Anglo-Saxon under the eccentric conditions of the Rawlinson Bequest in 1808.[43] In a series of communications to the Society of Antiquaries' journal *Archaeologia*, Conybeare drew attention to hitherto-ignored Anglo-Saxon poetry, notably the Exeter Book.[44] Conybeare died without having published any extensive works, but his papers on Anglo-Saxon poetry, including a study of early poetic meter, were edited after his death by his brother Daniel.

The careers of three other leading figures in British Anglo-Saxon studies had a stronger influence on later interpretations. Unlike Turner, who demonstrates comparatively little interest in the Saxons outside England and who does not use German sources, Joseph Bosworth (1789–1876), Benjamin Thorpe (1782–1870), and John Mitchell Kemble (1807–1857) shared unusual educational backgrounds for Englishmen of their time since each spent some years studying abroad. If Anglo-Saxon studies were to become a part of what an educated Victorian could reasonably be expected to know, these men were the self-appointed missionaries. Their success — and perhaps more, the limited nature of their success — helped shape Victorian attitudes to Anglo-Saxon culture.

Of the three, Bosworth was probably the most successful in popularizing the study of Anglo-Saxon language and institutions. The authoritative *Oxford Anglo-Saxon Dictionary* still bears his name. A minister of the Church of England, Bosworth served as a chaplain in Holland between 1829 and 1840. Among his interests were Poor Law reform and grammar texts, which he produced in a variety of languages. Bosworth's first Anglo-Saxon grammar was published in 1823; he later revised it in the light of advances made by the Danish philologist Rasmus Rask. A dictionary followed in 1838, the more expensive edition including a "History of Germanic Tongues" and a comparative sample of Scandinavian literature. Although his first dictionary incurred much criticism, notably from Kemble, it was simply the only one available, and it sold well. At the time of his death Bosworth was still working on a "definitive" Anglo-Saxon dictionary and claimed that he had the assistance of "most of the eminent Teutonic scholars at home and abroad."[45]

Even then, upon its eventual publication under the supervision of A. Northcote Toller in 1893, the dictionary was found to be not quite as definitive as had been hoped. Nevertheless, Bosworth was rare among Anglo-Saxon scholars in making a substantial sum of money from his writings and for many years might have justly claimed to have played the most substantial role in raising levels of knowledge on the subject.

Benjamin Thorpe was not so successful. Indeed, his publication record reveals the difficulties encountered by the new enthusiasts for Anglo-Saxon. Thorpe himself remains a shadowy figure but is believed to have traveled to Copenhagen in about 1826 to study with Rasmus Rask. Rask had compiled an Anglo-Saxon grammar, and Thorpe, who — unusually for his time — knew both Danish and German, translated it into English; the book was favorably reviewed in the *Gentleman's Magazine* in 1831. About the same time Thorpe returned to England and worked on some texts for the Society of Antiquaries. He was also responsible for the first edition of the Vercelli Book (although it never circulated) and worked on the new edition of the Anglo-Saxon Charters, which appeared in 1840. With the exception of the last, in which his name appears only at the end of the introduction, Thorpe's books were remarkably poor sellers. Although pioneering, then, his work can hardly be said to have made a major impact on the English consciousness.

Both Thorpe's and Bosworth's lives reflect a Germanic or, as it was often called, a "Teutonic" interest. In the attitudes of John Mitchell Kemble, however, the commencement of the Teutonist spirit that was to influence Liberal thinking in the latter part of the century is most clearly revealed. Kemble, a member of the famous acting family and a personal friend of Thorpe, also studied abroad, and during his years in Germany he began to identify himself as a "disciple" of the great German philologist Jakob Grimm, with whom he corresponded for several years. Like Thorpe, Kemble may have been induced to adopt a non-British mentor simply because at this time early English studies were still neglected in his home country. But clearly Kemble developed a reverence for Grimm close to devotion, and Grimm's influence strengthened the young Englishman's commitment to Teutonic tradition. Linda

Dowling has pointed out the irony of Kemble's insistence on the superiority of German scholarship when the Germans themselves acknowledged the inspiration of British eighteenth-century language studies.[46] As the translator of *Beowulf*, Kemble further contributed towards the creation of the idea of a common Germanic heritage by presenting the poem as a relic of Germanic prehistory.[47] Taking the Germanic ideal even into his private life, he married the daughter of a German professor; in a further irony, the union proved a failure. The concept of *Volk* is strong in Kemble's writings: his book *The Saxons in England* (1849) suggests in its very title that he conceived of the Anglo-Saxons as part of a common Germanic heritage, as opposed to a separate race, and he repeatedly cites facts known of European Germanic tribes as evidence of how the ancestors of the English would have behaved.

Kemble shows an almost fanatical zeal for his studies. In 1838, he contributed an English introduction to an Anglo-Saxon bibliography compiled in French by Francisque Michel, in which he criticized virtually all Anglo-Saxon scholarship to date. Of Thorkelin's edition of *Beowulf* he had previously stated that "not five lines . . . can be found in succession, in which some gross fault either in the transcript or in the translation, does not betray the editor's utter ignorance of the Anglo-Saxon language."[48] Kemble's overview of British Anglo-Saxon studies adopted a similar tone. He noted that Conybeare committed "blunders"; Ritson was "profoundly ignorant of Saxon"; Turner's work, while "learned and laborious," was in aspects of literature "often deficient, often mistaken."[49] While he grudgingly conceded that Bosworth's grammar was "yet of some use to the student," in 1834 he had privately informed Jakob Grimm:

> We cannot get on in England for want of an Anglo-Saxon dictionary; and though one Mr Bosworth threatens us with one, I fear we cannot rejoice in the prospect of its filling up the void. He is a sad dull dog, as I need not tell you if you have met with his grammar.[50]

Kemble also despised Joseph Stevenson and Thomas Wright, repeatedly accusing the latter of misappropriating other scholars' transcriptions; while he described Frederic Madden as "utterly abominable." This contempt for his fellow editors may not merely be personal paranoia. As a "serious" scholar, Kemble saw reason to criticize editors such as Stevenson and Wright, who produced so many works for the historical societies. The sheer quantity of books published by Wright prompts the suspicion that very often he did little more than print transcriptions of one manuscript, even when others were available for collation, and that very often the transcriptions were not his own. Wright was principally interested in the later Middle Ages, but Kemble took credit for having taught him Anglo-Saxon, while noting that he was "superficial and unscrupulous."[51]

Perhaps Kemble had reason for distrusting Wright. In Madden's case, however, even if he was "utterly abominable" as a person, there was no particular justification for questioning his scholarship.[52] Madden was largely self-taught, and although as Keeper of Manuscripts at the British Museum he may indeed have been high-handed in his control over the greatest collection of Anglo-Saxon materials, possibly what Kemble objected to most in Madden and in some of the other editors (including Michel) was that they did not conform to his lofty Teutonic image of what Anglo-Saxon scholars should be like.

The success of Bosworth's work suggests that his stay in Holland did not cause him entirely to detach himself from an English point of view. Kemble and Thorpe, on the other hand, were perhaps premature in placing Anglo-Saxon studies within a broader Germanic framework that Carlyle was to term "Teutonic." Thorpe, for example, translated the German Reinhold Pauli's *History of Alfred the Great*. Although this is an ably written history and won critical praise, it was the work not of an aged master but a man young enough to be Thorpe's son. Considering the limited research sources available concerning King Alfred, Thorpe's choice to prepare an English edition of a German book rather than write one of his own suggests a definite sense of cultural inferiority.

The truth seems to be that Kemble, and probably also Thorpe, were inclined to disregard even the little work on Anglo-Saxon studies carried out by their compatriots. Kemble, indeed, in his essay for Michel, traces the origin of modern Anglo-Saxon studies back to Thorpe's teacher Rask and his own mentor, Jakob Grimm, with the observation: "a new and powerful impulse has been given to Saxon learning by two continental scholars." He further claims that these men had shown the laborious persistence that the historical societies had had no leisure to foster. Kemble concludes:

> From the activity which all at once appears to prevail among the Saxonists of England, there is hope that we may make some important advances, and escape the reproach, at present too well deserved, of suffering foreigners to outstrip us in acquaintance with our native tongue. Surely while we have all the MSS., it cannot be right that they should have all the knowledge.[53]

The reference to "Saxonists" suggests that at least some British scholars were beginning to see themselves in this light. Yet ten years later, Richard Garnett made a similar observation.

> So incurious are we of our riches, that till within a very recent period, the number of Anglo-Saxon works published averaged about three in a century, and of Middle-English ones in their genuine form scarcely so many. It is well something has been done of late to redeem us from this reproach; but still a great more remains to be done.[54]

The fact remained that the type of scholarly devotion advocated by Kemble was unlikely to penetrate the general reading consciousness. Multiple editions of Anglo-Saxon laws were less effective in reminding English readers of a Saxon heritage than the writings of Scott and Carlyle. Nevertheless, the force with which those few scholars claiming philological knowledge argued for a shared Germanic heritage had a major impact. Ultimately, the relationship between "scholarship" and "literature" had to be a reciprocal one: only when a Saxon consciousness had been created by more immediately captivating works would English readers turn to books such as Bohn's edition of Pauli's *Life of Alfred the Great*; and only in a society that had already accepted the characterization of its ancestors created by the "serious scholars" could novelists present polarized characterizations of Saxons and Normans. In an overview of Anglo-Saxon studies published in 1840, John Petheram expressed a hope that "the Anglo-Saxon tongue will, within a few years, form an essential part of a liberal education."[55] The goal hoped for by Hickes and his circle more than a century earlier was still not a reality, but the study of Anglo-Saxon culture was already no longer the esoteric province of a scant few.

Petheram, though, was surely right in arguing that education could make the English more conscious of the Anglo-Saxon past, and through the educational ideals of teachers such as Thomas Arnold, the myth of the Anglo-Saxon inheritance reached far more people than exacting scholarship was ever likely to do. Thomas Arnold, headmaster of Rugby School from 1828 until his early death in 1842, had little professional interest in Anglo-Saxon literature and indeed was responsible for imposing a regimen of almost exclusively classical literature upon his students.[56] Nevertheless, the idea of the Saxons, and of a Saxon identity, is strong in his writings. Arnold believed that philologically at least, Saxons and Normans still had a presence in the English class system. He described class distinctions as

> an evil arising from causes which run back to the earliest period in our history; and which have tended silently and unconsciously to separate the higher classes from the lower in almost every relation of life. For instance, it is an enormous evil, yet one for which no one is to blame, that the rich and poor in England have each what is almost a distinct language; the language of the rich, which is of course that of books also, being so full of French words derived from their Norman ancestors, while that of the poor still retains the pure Saxon character inherited from their Saxon forefathers.[57]

Although Arnold so valued the classics, the use of the word "pure" to describe Saxon speech, particularly when opposed to a language "full of French words," indicates that Arnold did not consider being a Saxon a reason for social inferiority. Schools such as Rugby helped shape the self-image of the middle and upper-middle classes, those who made no attempt at an aristocratic identification with the Normans but who claimed for their blood a different kind of nobility.

In 1841 Arnold became Regius Professor of Modern History at Oxford University. In his inaugural lecture, like all history professors before and after him, Arnold asserted the importance of his subject. But for Arnold history was not merely important in providing precedent and example; it was also a means of determining national character, of special significance when a nation "may have duties of vast importance to perform in its national capacity."[58] Arnold moreover asserted that despite repeated invasions, English history began "with the coming over of the Saxons."

> We, this great English nation, whose race and language are now overrunning the earth from one end of it to the other, — we were born when the white horse of the Saxons had established his dominion from the Tweed to the Tamar. . . . So far our national identity extends, so far history is modern, for it treats of a life which was then, and is not yet extinguished.[59]

In Arnold's unquestioning assumption that the English Saxons were born to rule can be seen the beginnings of an attitude that was to become more common as the Oxford students who formed his audience matured into national leaders. Cultural imperialism was no new phenomenon, but Arnold combined his sense of cultural superiority with a new sense that the actual bloodline of the English gave them a special place in the world.

Arnold hence saw his task at Rugby to be to form "a place of Christian education,"[60] an objective that had certainly been lacking in Rugby for many years previously. *Tom Brown's School Days*, set at Arnold's Rugby, is a romanticization of the formative years of a muscular Christian; whether or not school was the place where boys learned honorable conduct towards each other, Arnold's lead-

ership clearly contributed to the creation of the myth. Tom Brown
himself was not a boy to rush into the study of Anglo-Saxon remains. Arthur Penrhyn Stanley, however, thought to be the prototype of Hughes's fictional Arthur, went on to make a personal
contribution to Anglo-Norman scholarship. A high proportion of
Arnold's Sixth Form, the boys with whom Arnold had most direct
contact, were ordained in the Church of England; many of these
also became schoolmasters and were thus in a position to dissemi-
nate further the concept of "character."[61] Arnold also presented in a
new form the idea that the Anglo-Saxon church was the most truly
Christian of all, particularly when compared to popery. Planning a
work on "Christian Politics," Arnold noted of the conversion of Europe:

> One real conversion there seems to have been, that of the
> Anglo-Saxons; but that he [Satan] soon succeeded in
> corrupting: and at the Norman Conquest we had little I
> suppose to lose even from the more direct introduction of
> Popery and worldly religion which came in with the
> Conqueror.[62]

This belief in the Anglo-Saxons' "real" conversion does not square
with Bede's account but conforms to Arnold's conception of English character.[63] Even more than Sharon Turner, Arnold easily accepts that the modern English are Anglo-Saxons and thus the
Anglo-Saxons must have been good Church of England men of liberal views like himself, an assumption that was to remain an important part of Broad Church Saxonism.

Perhaps, then, Lytton Strachey was right in detecting "a
slightly puzzled look upon the face of Dr. Arnold."[64] Almost in spite
of himself, the editor of Thucydides and Roman historian had
helped create a slightly anti-intellectual environment in which a
sense of character, and above all of English character, was seen as
the way to social success and also as the standard by which to
assess the past. For English readers at least, Arnold's interpretation
of history reflected the happy ending of the romance combined with
the certainty of fact. Indeed, as I shall argue in Chapter 3, the
model for the interpretation was a romance.

Chapter
3

The Condition
of England:
Richard and John

Even works in apparently nonnarrative form such as Arnold's essays seem influenced by a belief that history can be seen as narrative and that, in the case of English history at least, narrative has a happy ending. The ways in which forms of history presented as fact were both constructed and perceived therefore have much in common with the historical novel. The historical novel's re-creation of specific historical moments proves not to be the deviation from "authentic" history that a distinction between fact and fiction might suggest, but a major source of inspiration for later essays and prose history. In particular, the presentation of characters emblematizing Saxons and Normans in self-consciously literary treatments of historical material cannot be detached from the development of a nineteenth-century model of "factual" history. Works by Scott, Carlyle, Bulwer-Lytton, and many others contain instances of oppositions not only between Saxons and Norman characters, but also between characteristics seen as Saxon and Norman. The portrayal of King Richard and King John provides one of the earliest and most influential examples.

Literary interpretations of King Richard I (Coeur de Lion) and King John, who have become known (but only from this time onwards) as the last two Norman kings of England, reveal how the concept of Saxons and Normans might be interpreted not racially but conceptually. As full brothers, the sons of Henry of Anjou and Eleanor of Aquitaine, whatever their ancestry (which was mainly French and Norman, but included through their great-grandparents some Saxon-English stock), each was genetically as "Saxon" and as "Norman" as the other. In imaginative interpretations, however, the tradition has developed of portraying John as an unsympathetic Norman, and Richard, if not as a Saxon, as having a stronger sense of identity with his English subjects. Yet this interpretation of the end of the Norman period dates only from the early years of the nineteenth century — and, indeed, can largely be traced to a single source, although that source is itself indebted to other evidence.

Scott's Ivanhoe

Sir Walter Scott's 1819 novel *Ivanhoe* is the one work to which all later depictions of Saxons and Normans, either directly or indirectly, owe a debt. As late as 1938, when the Warner Brothers studio decided to make a movie incorporating "as much of the traditional Robin Hood stuff as possible," the resulting portrayal of King Richard and Prince John was very like Scott's: *Ivanhoe* had actually become the tradition.[1]

The debt, however, was not always acknowledged. Scott's novels, with their seemingly casual anachronisms and delight in musty antiquarianism, were an easy target of attack for later students of the Anglo-Norman period, who nevertheless assumed that all their readers would know them. Particularly in the case of *Ivanhoe*, the contrast between Saxons and Normans may seem sufficiently well known as to require little further examination. The Saxon and Norman motifs in *Ivanhoe* nevertheless deserve reconsideration. First, Scott's use of racial characteristics has been read in the light of subsequent works, notably Thierry's *Norman Conquest*; in fact, it is simultaneously more complex and less theorized than later interpretations. Second, Scott's compression of chronology has been widely accepted, but seemingly without full consideration of its effects on early and later readers. The Saxon and Norman theme in *Ivanhoe* is all-encompassing; but here it will be considered principally in relation to the depiction of its most historically based figures, Richard and John.

In creating *Ivanhoe,* Scott shaped much of his source material to emphasize the opposition between Saxons and Normans. Even characters' names reflect the theme, a partial exception being Ivanhoe, which Scott apparently knew from an old rhyme, although one of his reviewers devised an Anglo-Saxon origin for it.[2] Most probably he found the Norman names, including Bracy and even Front-de-Boeuf, on the Roll of Battle Abbey among the purported list of Normans who had fought at Hastings in 1066. The name Malvoisin is found on a similar list in Brompton's Chronicle, and doubtless its meaning (bad neighbor) appealed to Scott as appropriate for Cedric's wicked Norman neighbor and his Templar brother. Rowena is the traditional name of Hengist's daughter, the first Saxon princess in England. Cedric is a modernized version — which Edward Freeman ridiculed him for using — of Cerdic, the founder of the Wessex royal line that concluded with Edward the Confessor. His thrall Gurth bears the name of King Harold II's brother: Gurth's father is said to have been one Beowulph, a name that Scott would have known from Sharon Turner. From Turner he would also have known the name Hereward, although whether Scott identifies Cedric's father with the legendary Hereward the Saxon is not quite clear.[3] Athelstane (noble stone) is a name found among the royal family of Wessex. Many of these names suggest a return to origins: Rowena and Cedric, last of the Saxons, bear the names of the first of the line; Athelstane's name recalls the foundations of English law; the Normans' names recall their first arrival in England.

Scott's use of sources also reflects his strong interest in early historical materials. From his friend George Ellis, who published *Specimens of Ancient Poetry* in 1805, he would have known of the *Romance of Richard Coeur de Lion,* a fourteenth-century English version of a French *geste* that tells of the fantastic adventures of Richard the Lion-Heart.[4] Very probably, the idea of King Richard's disguise as a Black Knight originated with the ballad, in which

Richard participates in a tournament disguised successively as a Black, a Red, and a White Knight. Scott quotes extensively from Ellis's notes on the episode of Richard's cannibalism in his 1831–1832 Preface to *The Talisman,* a subject of more interest at this time than his sexuality. If the possibility that Richard might be homosexual occurred to any writers of the period, none mentioned it.[5]

In using such materials, Scott's novels were in many respects innovative works, although he chose to ascribe the beginning of his interest in the historical novel to his editing of Joseph Strutt's *Queenhoo-Hall.*[6] *Ivanhoe* was the first of Scott's novels to make extensive use of the type of antiquarian detail found in *Queenhoo-Hall.* Previous novels in the Waverley series had had detailed period settings, but *Ivanhoe* was set in the more distant England of the Crusades. Where *Ivanhoe* rises above Strutt's *Queenhoo-Hall*—and above some of Scott's own novels—is in having a thematically unified plot. *Ivanhoe* is a depiction of a closing chapter in history, the end of the sense of division between Saxons and Normans; and the two kings Richard and John represent in unidealized form the possibilities of reconciliation and continued division.

As we have seen, the distinction between England under the Saxons and England under the Normans was not new. *Ivanhoe* nevertheless contains an important innovation. The eighteenth-century constitutionalists had seen the Conquest as being a disastrous historical moment for the English, but *Ivanhoe* presents the division between Saxons and Normans established in 1066 as outlasting William's reign by several generations. In this respect, Scott's reading provided a bridge between the old radicals and later, more optimistic reformers who assumed that British history since 1066 had been a fight back to the state of the nation in the Golden Age of the Anglo-Saxons.[7] Yet *Ivanhoe* suggests that the division is not exclusively one of constitutional beliefs identified with race, so that two brothers, Richard and John, might be the exemplars of Saxon and Norman characteristics.

How Scott originated the unprecedented idea of seeing the struggles of the late twelfth century in racial terms is a difficult question. In the introduction to the 1831–1832 collected edition of his novels, Scott explained that he chose the period

not only as abounding with characters whose very names
were sure to attract general attention, but as affording a
striking contrast between the Saxons, by whom the soil
was cultivated, and the Normans, who still reigned in it
as conquerors, reluctant to mix with the vanquished, or
acknowledge themselves of the same stock. (*Ivanhoe*, 537)

Scott attributes this idea to John Logan's play *Runnamede*. The
play depicted discontented Britons, both Saxon and Norman, in
opposition to King John and forcing the grant of the Magna Carta:
as Scott remarked, there was little attempt "to contrast the two
races in their habits and sentiments." Logan had probably merely
intended to be patriotic when he wrote: "Let every Briton, as his
mind, be free . . ." but the play was refused a performance license
in London.[8] Scott saw *Runnamede* as a boy in Edinburgh in 1783,
and when he came to write his first chivalric novel, perhaps he
recalled the formerly hostile Saxon and Norman leaders uniting to
preserve the freedom of Britain and pledging never more to divide.

But Scott very probably derived much of the characterization
of the period from his readings in other historical materials, including Strutt and Sharon Turner.[9] Scott's writings amply demonstrate
his attraction to the romance of history and particularly to the chivalric period,[10] and his use of Turner's generally unromantic *History
of England from the Norman Conquest* may at first seem surprising.
But Scott's attitude towards this historical moment neither entirely
coincides with radical idealization of Saxon freedom nor with conservative nostalgia for feudal order. In fact, *Ivanhoe* can be read as
novel whose ideal, as much as it has one, is less a return to an
idyllic past than to achieve Turner's vision of progress as epito-
mized by "the Norman graft on the Saxon stock." Unlike later interpreters of the Saxon-and-Norman dichotomy, Scott does not
entirely identify the Saxons as "We" and the Normans as "the
Other."

Superficially, Scott might seem to be repeating the roles of
Saxons and Normans as presented by the old radicals. The Normans in *Ivanhoe* are admittedly evil characters. They have no compassion for the subject Saxons, and their lust for power is

supported by the wiles of the Roman Catholic church as represented by the Hospitalers and Templars — orders supposedly created to defend Christianity but in Scott's portrayal a source of corrupt power. Even the Normans' claimed chivalry becomes a form of self-parody, particularly as represented by the Templar Brian de Bois-Guilbert's unrequited passion for Rebecca. Other Normans include the vengeful Waldemar Fitzurse, said to be the son of the Fitzurse who murdered Thomas Becket; and the Malvoisin brothers, Norman villains in the Gothic style.

But the arch-Norman is the king's brother, Prince John. John identifies only with the Normans; and whereas he knows the Saxon language perfectly well, he affects not to understand the barbarous tongue (*Ivanhoe*, 109; chap. 9). On no historical authority, Scott notes that John "hated and condemned the few Saxon families of consequence which subsisted in England." Scott's sketch of John as "light, profligate, and perfidious" may now seem to be the conventional view; it is completely in accord with most of the medieval sources, where John is always presented as the unworthy successor of Richard.

This was not, however, the only possible interpretation of King John, one of the subjects of the early English Protestants' historical revisionism. Whereas the monkish chroniclers had repeatedly stressed John's licentiousness and wickedness, the sixteenth-century Protestants wondered whether John had been the victim of a Roman Catholic conspiracy. John Bale and the anonymous author of *The Troublesome Raigne of King John*, following John Foxe, had suggested that John's character had been maligned by the Roman Catholic church.[11] He had desired to make the crown independent of the church, and was defeated only by treachery and murder.

Traces of this characterization survive in Shakespeare's *Life and Death of King John*, so Scott may reasonably be assumed to have been familiar at least with the presentation of King John as a man placed in an impossible situation. Yet Scott apparently prefers the historical method of Turner, his main source. Turner weighs up conflicting evidence, but his claim of compiling a document-based history seems to include the presupposition that where evidence is not self-contradictory it should be taken at literal value. Turner's King John, following the chronicle sources, wastes "his nights in debauch, his days in sleep,"[12] and Scott's characterization is not very different.

That the chronicles portray him as a bad man is not, however, the usual motivation for the general nineteenth-century dislike of John. Both politically and religiously, John becomes seen as an alien monster. John's reign may have produced the Magna Carta, but only because he attempted to keep all power to himself and ignored the traditional rights of the people. John is thus presented as the archetypal tyrant depriving the people of their Anglo-Saxon freedoms; and for this reason, plays concerning King John — particularly during the reign of George III and the suspension of habeas corpus — were politically sensitive.

In characterizing the woes caused by the Normans, *Ivanhoe* further highlights the problems of a regency. Richard I had left England in the control of an unworthy prince through personal choice. By the time of the publication of *Ivanhoe*, if not through the king's personal choice but by reason of his mental incapacity, Britain had been ruled by a regent of doubtful character, the future George IV, for nine years.[13] Scott, as a Tory, identified politically with the group who were to favor George IV in the coronation crisis of 1820; but his characterization of the weak-willed and extravagant John, surrounded by favorites and marrying his interests to the Roman Catholic church, bears a distinct similarity to Prince George, always in debt and in fashionable company, who had caused a constitutional embarrassment by his marriage (or quasi-marriage) with the Roman Catholic "Mrs. Fitzherbert." Whereas the progressivists might see John's reign as a necessary step in the consolidation of English freedoms, it remained to be seen whether the freedoms of the Magna Carta, eroded under the new prince regent, might be restored.

The Normanness of John's character was also seen in his relationship with the church. John lost his battle of wills with the pope, thereby humiliating himself — and hence England. Whereas the early Protestant writers had seen him as a victim, nineteenth-century Protestants were more inclined to see him as a failure who, as representative of the state church, should never have submitted to the authority of Rome.[14] That the association of John with George IV was a Tory prophecy of the dangers of Roman Catholic emancipation—which finally removed restrictions on Catholic political participation in 1828—is, however, less certain than the existence of a general Protestant suspicion of Roman Catholic involvement in affairs of state.

Thus far, Scott's portrayal of the Normans and their leader John conforms with the traditional pattern. Yet according to this pattern, the converse of Norman tyranny is the Saxon Golden Age. In *Ivanhoe,* the question remains whether the Saxons represent any form of ideal: whether, indeed, the novel supports Alice Chandler's contention that "Scott regrets the end of Saxon society."[15] The titular hero Ivanhoe is of the Saxon nobility and marries a Saxon lady. But other characters are portrayed as more consciously Saxon, and these figures often fall far short of the prototypical Teutonic stock imagined later in the century.

Sharon Turner had written in 1814 that at the time of the Norman Conquest the Anglo-Saxons' condition

> was rather degeneracy than civilization. Their sovereigns were men of feeble minds; their nobles, factious and effeminate; the clergy, corrupt and ignorant; the people, servile and depressed. All the venerated forms of the Saxon institutions existed, but their spirit had evaporated. . . . Amid all these means of prosperity, an intellectual torpidity had since the days of Athelstane pervaded the country. (*MA* 1:73)

Perhaps Scott had read this passage before he named the decadent Saxon prince Athelstane. Athelstane is the representative of the Saxon line whose passing Scott is said to regret. With an ironic appropriateness, Athelstane is described as the blood-successor of both Edward the Confessor (who was childless) and Harold son of Godwin (who was not a member of the Wessex royal house); he is, in fact, the child of a barren stock. His weaknesses—indecision, drunkenness, rich living, a want of intellectual stimulation—are precisely those ascribed by Turner to the later Anglo-Saxons. This is the Saxon alternative to Norman rule.

The other personification of the old Saxon nobility is Ivanhoe's father Cedric. Chandler states that Cedric "illustrates many of the medieval virtues that Scott found praiseworthy."[16] And certain aspects of Cedric's personality are attractive. Like a true lord of the mead hall from the poetic past, his hospitality is without restrictions, and unlike the Normans, he extends it even to the Jews. He is a kind master who has earned the loyalty of his servants — a factor that Scott clearly believes is greatly to a nobleman's credit. But nevertheless, Cedric is an intellectual dinosaur and, as is the Valkyrie-like Ulrica, a survivor of a lost past. He has disinherited his blameless son for aspiring to the chivalry of the Normans and tells Prince John that "in the days of King Alfred that would have been termed disobedience — ay, and a crime severely punishable" (*Ivanhoe*, 159; chap. 14). Prince John scarcely cares but might have remarked that the days of King Alfred are long past. Wilfred's further offense is that his liaison with Rowena interferes with his father's hopeless plans for a new Saxon royal line; and Cedric's judgment of individuals solely on the basis of race and particularly for their closeness in blood to Alfred the Great is implied to be a source of weakness. When Cedric and Athelstane are captured in the Castle of Torquilstone, the degenerate Saxon Athelstane thinks of his dinner, and Cedric of how many years before from this same castle "the valiant and unfortunate Harold" had shown the nobility of his Saxon nature in his response to the invasion of his brother Tosti and Harald Hardrada (*Ivanhoe*, 220–221; chap. 21). Neither of these is a particularly useful response to the predicament, and it is left to the ordinary Saxons Wamba and Gurth, with the assistance of the Saxon yeoman Locksley — significantly, Scott has converted Robin Hood from Norman nobleman to Saxon commoner[17] — to contrive a rescue for their masters. Any regret for the passing of the age of these Saxons cannot be tinged with hope for their restoration.

Nevertheless, Scott evidently likes these examples of the fading Saxon nobility. Cedric's impracticality is reminiscent of Scott's favorite creation, the Antiquary — a kindly man, but one scarcely fitted to survive the trials of a world of evil barons. Athelstane, like Shakespeare's Barnardine, seems created to die: his death seems both symbolic of the last of the Saxon line and a convenient means of making Rowena available to Ivanhoe. Yet having killed Athelstane, Scott contrives a miraculous escape for him, while allowing the "progressive" Saxon Ivanhoe to keep his bride. Perhaps after all, this is a more appropriate solution: the Saxon nobility of *Ivanhoe* are not tragic figures but the impotent representatives of the past. The Saxon commonalty, in contrast, displays a more enduring spirit; and the announcement of Athelstane's supposed death is followed closely by the emancipation of Gurth the thrall.

If, then, *Ivanhoe* does not present a cozy medieval alternative to the problems of industrial society, what form of happy ending remains possible? Having created a dichotomy between Saxons and Normans, *Ivanhoe* shows most hope in a limited level of assimilation. And here the contrast between Richard and John is of key significance.

Scott's portrayal of Richard the Lion-Heart in *Ivanhoe* steers a central path between the chivalric exemplar of Kenelm Digby and the shirker of duty primly criticized by Sharon Turner. Although Turner, earnest in his Christianity as always, believes that the Crusades were inspired by "disinterestedness," he suspects that Richard was not motivated by such generous religious feelings to undertake a crusade. He deplores Richard's cruelty, his belief in human progress causing him to remark: "Let us rejoice that our own time, and especially our own country, has learned to make its military humanity a portion of its national honour" (*MA* 1:345). But above all, Turner considers that Richard neglected his duty in leaving England under uncertain control.

Scott follows this condemnation in *Ivanhoe* when he observes that:

> The condition of the English nation was at this time sufficiently miserable. King Richard was absent a prisoner, and in the power of the perfidious and cruel Duke of Austria. Even the very place of his captivity was uncertain, and his fate but imperfectly known to the generality

of his subjects, who were, in the meantime, a prey to every species of subaltern oppression. (*Ivanhoe*, 74; chap. 7)

Richard has deserted his people, and his very role as a great warrior, or, as Scott phrases it, his assumption of the "brilliant, but useless, character of a knight of romance" (*Ivanhoe*, 471; chap. 41), is occasionally portrayed as slightly ridiculous. For example, Richard is eager to fight twenty of Malvoisin's men single-handed, and in the ensuing struggle ignores the more prudent strategy offered by the supposed fool, Wamba. As in Turner's history, it is also implied that Richard is at fault in immediately and unconditionally forgiving Prince John (*Ivanhoe*, 511; chap. 44); and although the end of a romance might be expected to anticipate a happy future, the restoration of order by Richard is stated in the concluding lines of the novel to be of as short duration as Richard's life. Having deserted England once, Richard is to desert England again through his untimely (and unnecessary) death.[18]

Yet Scott's Richard remains an attractive figure. In the end it is Richard's generosity of spirit and his compassion for the ordinary people that mark him as more Saxon than John in spirit. In developing the idea of an alliance between Richard and Robin Hood, Scott brings the Norman king into close contact with the English people. Whereas his brother refuses to communicate with the Saxons, Richard apparently has little difficulty, addressing them in a language that Scott imagines to be a mixture of Anglo-Saxon and Norman-French. Richard is accepted by the Saxons, including the reactionary Cedric, almost as one of their own race and throughout the novel is depicted in their company. Although the promise of reconciliation personified by Richard remains unfulfilled at the king's death, Wilfred of Ivanhoe, a true Saxon but with the energy and chivalric nature of a Norman — and with more Norman prudence than the misplaced generosity of Richard suggests is possessed by the born Norman — represents the possibility of progress.

Scott's use of racial identity more as a moral structure than as a support for a specific theory is further stressed by his presentation of the Jews. When first seen, Isaac the Jew seems little more than a stereotype, concerned only for his property and private affairs. Yet Scott emphasizes that if the Jews seem to have unattractive characteristics, they are probably only conforming to expectations: they are a race "alike detested by the credulous and prejudiced vulgar, and persecuted by the greedy and rapacious nobility, and who, perhaps owing to that very hatred and persecution, had adopted a national character in which there was much, to say the least, mean and unamiable" (*Ivanhoe*, 50; chap. 5). In the course of the story Isaac proves true to his friends and ready to sacrifice everything to save his daughter. Rebecca herself shows a generosity of spirit that made her the most popular character in the novel — and according to early reviewers, one of the greatest female characters of all time.[19]

Having created a division between Saxons, Normans, and Jews, Scott emphatically does not proceed to suggest that in his view of history race is deterministic. The effects of one's upbringing — Cedric's generous treatment of Gurth, Richard and John as the spoiled children of Henry II — and of one's strength of character are still important. Above all, while the opposition between Normans and Saxons is not entirely racial, it nevertheless provides a means of expression for tensions between classes, the "ordinary" Saxons in particular being portrayed as victims; and hence there is a release from the medieval context into Scott's own world. Although *Ivanhoe* implies a rejection of the religious solution (that Roman Catholic England was more compassionate), the constitutional solution (that a return to Saxon England would restore freedom), and to some extent, a romantic-chivalric solution to England's difficulties, the novel's direct relation to its readers' society is perhaps seen more in the moral structure of the Saxon-Norman contrast than in a conscious attempt to address the condition of Scott's England. The good and bad actions of the book have a universality so that some early readers — and even those who, like Francis Jeffrey, were more committed to a critical social perspective — saw the historical content as a dressing for a romantic plot.[20]

Scott is unquestionably doing more than Jeffrey chose to see: in his delineations of heroes and villains he is drawing upon the concepts of Saxon integrity and Norman ruthlessness, and even when presented by a nonradical writer, this must be influenced by the reality that in 1819, as in the 1190s, the "condition of England was sufficiently miserable" (*Ivanhoe*, 74; chap. 7). Yet while *Ivanhoe* may suggest that Scott's commitment to the preservation of existing social structures was not without recognition that those structures were far from perfect, Scott's conservatism seems to have placed limitations upon the extent to which he was prepared to draw conclusions from his social observation. The distinctions between Saxons and Normans in *Ivanhoe* are hence simultaneously more formalistic and less the embodiment of theory than they were to become in the hands of other writers; but the novel still has a crucial role as the inspiration for a racially based sense of origin. Hayden White has suggested that viewed "in a purely formal way, a historical narrative is not only a *reproduction* of the events reported in it, but also a *complex of symbols* which gives us directions for finding an *icon* of the structure of those events in our literary tradition."[21] White is not speaking primarily of the historical novel; but the symbols of *Ivanhoe* nevertheless helped later writers, and not only writers of novels, to find an "icon" for the reigns of Richard and John. Even though Scott himself stops short of analyzing English society through a theory of race, *Ivanhoe* provided the symbols through which such a construct became possible.

The Influence of Ivanhoe: *Thierry*

In his critique of *Ivanhoe* in the *Edinburgh Review*, Francis Jeffrey had chosen to read and enjoy the story as "just" a romance benefiting from the supposedly unknown author's best-constructed plots and many interesting characterizations. Ivanhoe may be an insipid hero, disappearing from sight for a third of the story, and Rowena an uninteresting heroine; but Scott's readers did care about Rebecca, who, as Thackeray pointed out, deserves better than what Scott grants her.[22] Yet the use made of *Ivanhoe* by later writers indicates that to many of its readers it was far more than a romance. By showing them, in White's phrase, "what to take for an icon,"[23] the novel actually transformed the way in which they conceived of the medieval period.

Scott's topographical and architectural errors and major mis-calculations of chronology in *Ivanhoe* may now seem an easy target for criticism. Freeman's savage mockery of the book's historicity, presented in the 1860s in an attempt to discredit Augustin Thierry's style of history, summarizes the major mistakes:

> When we believe that the keep of Coningsburgh castle is older than the Norman conquest — when we believe that Englishwomen, whether of the fifth, or of the twelfth century, bore the names of Rowena and Ulrica — when we believe that the Christian English folk of the twelfth century prayed to the Slavonic idol Czernibog, or swore by the soul of the heathen Hengest, when we believe that there was a time when Normans and English differed about the time of keeping Easter — when we believe that there were lineal descendants of Edward the Confes-sor — when we believe that the son of a man who had fought at Stamfordbridge was alive, and seemingly not very old, when Richard the First came back from Ger-many — then we may believe in the state of things set forth in the History [of Thierry], and of which Cedric (Cerdic?) is the popular embodiment.[24]

Some of these are comparatively minor slips, and Scott himself cor-rected an error of his first edition, in which he placed Stam-fordbridge not in Yorkshire but in Leicester (*Ivanhoe*, 554; note on chap. 21). Others are major miscalculations, such as the glowing description of the Saxon fortress of Coningsburgh (*Ivanhoe*, 476; chap. 41), when the construction is far later. Yet most of Scott's major errors of chronology are not random but form a pattern that helped create a new interpretation of the period.

The most obvious historical revisions in *Ivanhoe* are those relat-ing to the Norman Conquest. Cedric the Saxon and his Norman neighbor Front-de-Boeuf are only the second generation from the

Battle of Hastings in 1066 — which would make them centenarians in the 1190s. Cedric nevertheless insists that his father Hereward was "not the worst defender of the Saxon crown" and had feasted with King Harold at Torquilstone prior to the battle of Stamfordbridge, which also occurred in 1066 (*Ivanhoe*, 221; chap. 21).[25] In the same Castle of Torquilstone lives Urfried, later revealed as Ulrica. She is the daughter of Torquil Wolfganger, King Harold's host in 1066, and after the Conquest she was taken as a concubine by the father of Reginald Front-de-Boeuf, the current lord. Ulrica informs Cedric that "age, premature age, has stamped its ghastly features on my countenance" (*Ivanhoe*, 277; chap. 27); but since she must be nearly 150 years old, her wrinkled appearance is not entirely unexpected. Ulrica further offended Freeman by her pagan death-song "such as was of yore raised on the field of battle by the scalds of the yet heathen Saxons" (*Ivanhoe*, 344; chap. 31). Ulrica is the only pagan in the novel, but Cedric's thrall Gurth is still solidly Teutonic, retaining "the whole of the superstitions which his ancestors had brought with them from the wilds of Germany" (*Ivanhoe*, 121; chap. 10). Scott apparently expects his readers to accept that pagan memories have survived for half a millennium.

In Scott's playful antiquarian form, moreover, his "chronicle" is derived from the "Wardour MS." This supposed document bears the name of a friend of the Antiquary Jonathan Oldbuck and is said to be written in Saxon — highly improbable by this date, but perhaps giving some indication of where the supposed narrator's sympathies may lie (*Ivanhoe*, 91; chap. 8).[26]

In his opening pages Scott is at pains to stress that the distinction between Saxons and Normans did not end with the Conquest. He originally wrote that the events were parted from the Conquest by three generations, but he changed this in proof to four.[27] But whether three or four, these

> had not sufficed to blend the hostile blood of the Normans and Anglo-Saxons, or to unite, by common language and mutual interests, two hostile races. . . . Yet the great national distinctions betwixt [the Saxons] and their conquerors, the recollection of what they had formerly

been, and to what they were now reduced, continued, down to the reign of Edward the Third, to keep open the wounds which the Conquest had inflicted, and to maintain a line of separation betwixt the descendants of the victor Normans and the vanquished Saxons. (*Ivanhoe*, 8–10; chap. 1)

Scott's revisions scarcely alter the effect of his original conception, which brought the time of the Conquest closer to the time of the Age of Chivalry. This chronological compression is useful in terms of his plot: characters such as Cedric and Ulrica with first- or secondhand knowledge of the "time before" provide an effective form of contrast. The Saxon memory of, in Scott's phrase, "the unfortunate King Harold" — and even of Alfred the Great — remains fresh, and the wounds of defeat are still unhealed.

Scott's successful construction of a myth more powerful than the supposedly factual histories is indicated by the immense influence of *Ivanhoe* on two popular historical works. Macaulay published the first volumes of his *History of England* at the end of 1848. The main focus of this work was to be the period following the succession of James II in 1685, but before commencing his study in detail, Macaulay presented a brief review of English history prior to this time. Macaulay's sketchy realization of the Anglo-Norman period reveals him as an enthusiastic reader of the Waverley novels yet also as tinged by the conceptions of the old radicals. He observes that the Conquest "gave up the whole population of England to the tyranny of the Norman race" and has no doubt that "the Conqueror and his descendants to the fourth generation were not Englishmen: most were born in France." Only John's unhappy reign prevented the "calamities" of Englishmen becoming French; and on the signing of the Magna Carta: "Here," Macaulay notes, "commences the history of the English nation. . . . It is certain that, when John became king, the distinction between Saxons and Normans was strongly marked, and that before the end of the reign of his grandson it had almost disappeared."[28]

Since Macaulay's use of the *Ivanhoe* distinction becomes an expression of his horror at the possibility of being anything other than English,[29] it is ironic that this icon first became the basis of a fully developed historical theory through the work of the French historian Augustin Thierry. Thierry was born in 1795 and as a young man was influenced by St. Simon: he early formed the opinion that his ideal was "a government with the greatest possible amount of individual guarantee, and the least possible amount of administrative action."[30] Perhaps this interest attracted him to the question of the overall effects of the Norman Conquest of England.

In the early years of the nineteenth century, knowledge of this period, even among those who professed to be well educated, in most cases remained extremely slight. Of the first reviewers of *Ivanhoe,* both the *Blackwood's* reviewer and Jeffrey in the *Edinburgh* recounted in some detail the story of Ulrica and her enslavement by Front-de-Boeuf's father after the Conquest. Neither, however, noticed that this was an anachronism — which had he been aware of it, Jeffrey surely would have pointed out, since he questioned the historical probability of the entire book.[31] Similarly, Nassau Senior in the *Quarterly Review* questioned minor points of heraldry but failed to remark on the most glaring errors of chronology.[32] British knowledge of this period of history was clearly unsystematic. Thierry, the first historian to produce a full-length study of Britain in the Anglo-Norman period, was thus in a position to influence strongly the hitherto vague conceptions of the nature and spirit of this time.

Thierry's *Histoire de la Conquête de L'Angleterre par les Normandes* was first published in 1825; proof of its success is that four French editions had been issued by 1835.[33] As a conscientious historian, Thierry did his best to examine the contemporary sources of his history. But his organizing principle derived not from his study of the chronicles but from the recent novel *Ivanhoe.* From the structure of a romance Thierry developed a theory of the divisions of British society. Thomas Arnold had suggested that the language of the English rich and poor reflected Norman and Saxon vocabulary, but Thierry went much further in proposing that the distinction between Saxons and Normans was of paramount importance in understanding the course of English history. The discovery of this idea he freely ascribed to the Great Unknown:

for all those who, until recently, have written the history
of England, there are no Saxons after the battle of Hastings and the coronation of William the Bastard; a romance writer, a man of genius, was the first to teach the
modern English that their ancestors of the eleventh century were not all utterly defeated and crushed in a single
day. (Thierry 1:xxiv)

The political theory behind the distinction found in Thierry's study
derives from the old radical reading of the Conquest. The Saxons
had been a free and freedom-loving people; the Normans had been
the usurpers and the imposers of feudalism. But what Scott added
to this was a continued sense of Saxon identity. This sense is ab-
sent, for example, in a romance contemporary to *Ivanhoe*, Thomas
Love Peacock's *Maid Marian*. Here, following many of the traditional ballads, both Robin and Marian are Normans who fall afoul
of the law.[34] The struggle is one of freedom-lovers against statute-
makers, the independent-minded against those who seek to crush
independence. But it is not class against class, and certainly not
Saxon against Norman. In contrast, Thierry, following Scott,
believed that a fundamental division between the ideals and temperament of the Saxon commonalty and the Norman military
aristocracy had survived the Conquest and was a crucial factor
throughout the Anglo-Norman period — indeed, at one time Thierry
posited that it had continued until the English Civil War.[35]
    Thierry's reading of Anglo-Norman history had the advantage
of providing a schematic form in which events of the distant past
were not isolated and largely unmemorable facts but part of a
whole. At a time when divisions between rulers and ruled were
presenting fresh problems for Britain's new industrial society, any
theory that seemed to explain how the British nation had become
what it now was had relevance; and despite Thierry's original liber-
tarian intentions, the construction could be interpreted in at least
two ways. Either the radicals were correct, and the injustice of the
Norman Conquest still required reversal; or alternatively, the passing of time had itself created that reversal, the process of what

Turner had called "Norman graft on the Saxon stock" finally inject-
ing a new energy into the stolid virtues of the line of Alfred.

As the century progressed, many historians expressed their
dissent from Thierry. Even Scott, when he returned to the Saxon-
against-Norman motif in *The Betrothed*, avoided a serious theory of
racial characteristics such as that created by Thierry from *Ivanhoe*
and hinted instead that the only difference was a sense of difference.[36] *Ivanhoe*, however, uses the Saxon and Norman distinction
not only as a comic texture but also as a crucial part of its deep
structure; and inspired by Scott, Thierry had suggested a relevance
in the distinction between Saxons and Normans that had a reality
even in the writings of those most anxious to refute it. Indeed, once
the icon was presented to readers, it became a crucial part of historical interpretation.

The Influence of Ivanhoe: *Carlyle*

Thierry's reading of *Ivanhoe* had impelled the
Saxon-against-Norman motif in an avowedly ideological direction,
but the possibility remained of taking it still further — much further
than Scott might have chosen. Scott's famous opening observation
in chapter 7 of *Ivanhoe* — "The condition of the English nation was
at this time sufficiently miserable" — is usually cited as strong evidence that consciously or subconsciously, in exploring the divided
England of the 1190s, Scott could not but make use of his sense of
the divided England of the Regency. Jeffrey was, then, both right
and wrong in remarking that *Ivanhoe* was "just" a romance. He was
wrong in that through the mediation of Thierry, *Ivanhoe* made a
major contribution to the way in which British readers saw patterns
in medieval history; he was right in that the personal and social
crises of the world of *Ivanhoe* transcended the period setting and
had a relevance to Scott's own world. The conception that the past
only lives in relation to the present, and that the present can only

be understood in relation to the past, received its most masterful treatment from another Scot who had the benefit of knowing both Thierry's history and *Ivanhoe*, Thomas Carlyle.

As Fredric Jameson has argued, intentionality is not necessary to produce a political reading of history.[37] Scott is noteworthy for his denial of the political through his insistence on the stance of a gentleman-editor. Carlyle, in contrast, confronts the political directly. This is not to claim that Scott is in effect less political than Carlyle — yet Jeffrey would surely not have read *Past and Present*, for example, as "just" a biography. While Scott seems almost afraid to take the Saxon-against-Norman motif to the declaredly racial level of Thierry, Carlyle uses it as a direct means of exploring what he calls the "Condition-of-England Question." Scott's adopted persona of a gentleman-editor had compelled him to edit his own responses to social problems. Carlyle, in contrast, is a toiling editor, who needs to show his involvement in what his work unfolds to the reader. Two of Carlyle's publications, *Chartism* (1839) and *Past and Present* (1843), make use of the Saxon and Norman construct and show the direct influence of Thierry and Scott — but with the declared objective of providing serious social analysis.

Chartism was Carlyle's response to the massive petition of 1839, through which many working people expressed their desire for political involvement. They had come to the realization that the longed-for 1832 Reform Act, far from uniting the country, had merely caused a different form of division. Before 1832, the working classes and the middle classes had had common grievances; to the poorer members of society and their sympathizers it now seemed that the wealthy and middle classes were uniting against them. The laboring population suffered most from fluctuations in the economy: minor slumps might leave them without work and facing only the alternative of the workhouse and at the same time raise the already artificially high price of wheat, and hence bread. Carlyle was aware that the condition of the Irish poor was even worse. When Carlyle uses the word Saxon in *Chartism*, then, it has a precise meaning. Saxons are for Carlyle the ordinary British people (he seems to include the English and the lowland Scots), as opposed to the Irish — and implicitly, as opposed to the ruling classes where actions have repudiated their shared humanity.[38] One connotation of Saxon is thus emblematic and similar to its connotations in *Ivanhoe*. Being Saxon may partly be an accident of race, but it also determines a particular way of life.

In Carlyle's conception, however, nothing is quite this simple. The Saxons are the English, but not according to Thierry's distinction in the *History of the Conquest*. In *Chartism*, the author of the "strange rhapsodic *History of the Teuton Kindred*," Professor Sauerteig,[39] draws attention to Thierry's "ingenious Book, celebrating with considerable pathos the fate of the Saxons fallen under that fierce-hearted *Conquistator*, Acquirer or Conqueror, as he is named."[40] Although Carlyle chooses to leave undetermined exactly where he identifies with Sauerteig, we may assume that he agrees with the Teutonic historian in implying that such sympathy is misplaced: if the Saxons were degenerate enough to be overthrown, then the coming to power of a more vigorous people is no reason for regret. Reginald Horsman, indeed, claims Carlyle as "the first great British writer to view Saxon triumphs as being clearly a product of racial superiority."[41] Carlyle classifies the Saxons as Teutons, members of the Germanic race.[42]

In addition to Carlyle's choice of a "Teutonic" narrative voice in Sauerteig, *Chartism* proceeds to make an important statement revealing Carlyle, a major influence in bringing German writings and thought to British readers, as the precursor of the later students of "Teutonism." Scott's Normans show some indication of being French. He mentions their more refined sensibilities, their less-developed sense of integrity and loyalty, and their commitment to Roman Catholicism. But through Sauerteig, Carlyle, who admires the Normans for their energy and self-assertion, claims them as Teutons, the true heir of the god-hero Odin. He rejects the notion that "the conquerors and conquered here were of different races" and concludes that "the Normans were Saxons who had learned to speak French" (*Chartism*, 44–45).

The Norman Conquest hence assumes a significance very different from the old radical view, and modified from that of Scott and Thierry. It was, in fact, not unjust but just, since it brought forward the men best equipped to lead. The "old Saxon Nobles" had little to offer, but

> a new class of strong Norman Nobles, entering with a strong man, with a succession of strong men at the head of them, and not disunited, but united by many ties, by their very community of language and interest, had there been no other, *were* in a condition to govern it; and did govern it, we can believe, in some rather tolerable manner, or they would not have continued there.[43]

Like Scott and Thierry, Carlyle believes that the Normans had a definite identity that survived as a distinct entity for more than a century after the Conquest. The difference is that this is a Teutonic identity and not a French one. The Normans were "noble," moreover, not by birth but by virtue of being "strong" Teutonic men. By naming this chapter "Mights and Rights," Carlyle can deliberately suggest that the two are indeed equivalent. In direct opposition to Thierry's reading of history, where progress is achieved by a Saxon revolutionary undercurrent working against the power structure, for Carlyle, the creation of a vigorous new power structure itself is a source of social improvement. If might is right, then to be strong is to be just, and Carlyle assumes that if this had not been accepted, the Norman regime would have collapsed. He therefore adds: "Conquest, along with the power of compulsion, an essential universally in human society, must bring benefit along with it, or men, of the ordinary strength of men, will fling it out" (*Chartism*, 25).

Carlyle's *Chartism* is such a difficult work that most early reviewers merely commented on the obscurity of the style and added their own opinions on the half-solutions to the "Condition-of-England Question," education, and emigration.[44] To notice that Carlyle himself avoided a central question of the time, the status of the Corn Laws, was easier than articulating a direct response to *Chartism*. Some contemporaries read the work simply as a tract in defense of the movement: in *Alton Locke*, Charles Kingsley imagines that some Chartists, such as his own creation, the well-read activist

Mackaye, both believed in Carlyle and in the Chartist cause.[45] In actuality, working-class activists such as the Chartists probably knew little about Carlyle's writings, and the price of a pamphlet such as *Chartism* (which initially cost five shillings) does not suggest that such a readership was ever intended. Above all, in its presentation of the Normans, *Chartism* strikes at the basic assumptions of the Chartist claims of Saxon rights.

King John hence has a symbolic part in *Chartism*. The name of the Chartist movement, with the five points they were attempting to achieve, recalls the Magna Carta.[46] The Chartist movement has been associated with the beginnings of true workers' movements as opposed to liberal reform movements of the middle classes.[47] Chartism was undoubtedly evidence of a newly politicized working class. But the Chartists were still drawing upon the old radical myth of Anglo-Saxon England and visualizing themselves as within a historical tradition. One Chartist poem included the lines:

> Oh, where is the justice of old?
> The spirit of Alfred the Great?
> Ere the throne was debas'd by corruption and gold,
> When the people were one with the state?[48]

They were not claiming new rights, or even natural rights; they were reclaiming old rights with the ultimate end of felling King John and ending the domination of the Normans — the propertied classes — through the grant of a new Magna Carta.

In contrast, Carlyle rejects this view of the Normans. Although Carlyle himself accepts the symbol of the Magna Carta, having in *Sartor Resartus* described the chance or fortune that preserved one copy from the tailor's shears,[49] his Normans, as the embodiment of "Might," cannot be the deniers of "Right." While the Chartists are calling for an end of the domination of the new Normans, Carlyle contends that England actually needs new Normans whose authority is not based on inheritance but on merit. Such a possibility is explored further in a work partly set in the reigns of King Richard and King John, *Past and Present*.

Carlyle's concern for the condition of England did not, as did that of many of his contemporaries, disappear with the passing of the immediate crisis of 1839. In 1843, inspired by a long-forgotten medieval biography, he put aside his edition of Oliver Cromwell's correspondence to produce, in what was for Carlyle remarkably rapid time, *Past and Present.* In his own metaphysical language, Carlyle re-creates the world of *Ivanhoe* by first developing the theory of the relation of past and present from the icon made possible by Scott. Carlyle uses an even more ancient Saxon analogy to express the problem of England, describing the nation's internal struggles as a continuance of the ancient "savage fighting Heptarchies."[50] England has returned to the brutality of the Saxon world before Alfred the Great, and only with the coming of justice can the petty kingdoms — by which Carlyle surely means both regional and social divisions — be made into one.

In *Past and Present,* the three races of *Ivanhoe,* Saxon, Norman, and Jew, are again seen, as Carlyle explores Scott's divisions of medieval society through the mediation of a work actually written in the age of Richard and John, the *Chronicle of Jocelin of Brakelond Concerning the Actions of Abbot Samson at the Monastery of Bury St. Edmund's.*[51] In Carlyle's portrayal, the Jews fare worse than in *Ivanhoe,*[52] but continuing the Teutonic stance of *Chartism,* he further refuses to draw a clear distinction between the merits and demerits of Saxons and Normans. Abbot Samson's biographer Jocelin is said to be a "natural born Englishman" and a "Norman Englishman" (*PP,* 102). The setting of the tale is in an abbey devoted to St. Edmund, a Saxon saint; and Carlyle is anxious to trace a sense of history back to Saxon times. But the time is a double time. First, it is that of our own familiar world, in which old women, Saxons and Chartists both, protest bitterly at the tax collector. But although Carlyle claims Jocelin as his major source, he interprets his data by means of the icon provided by Scott and Thierry. Hence simultaneously it is the world of *Ivanhoe,* governed by an implicitly Norman feudal aristocracy. Using Scott's creation Gurth as the metonymic representation of the English working class, Carlyle argues that in the age of Richard and John, social injustices existed, but that "even a Gurth born thrall of Cedric lacks not his due parings of the pigs he tends."[53] In the Norman world, then, laissez-faire is replaced by strong, involved government: the working man is not left to starve.

Carlyle's reworking of *Ivanhoe*, although acknowledging some of the problems of the medieval period, nevertheless shows some variation from Scott's version. The instance of the choice of Gurth the thrall as the typical working man is in itself a idiosyncratic reading, since Scott implies that for all his faults, Cedric was a better-than-average master. Carlyle is justified in suggesting that Scott's novel implies an advantage for Gurth. In belonging to Cedric, Gurth had an identity that the rootless factory workers of the 1840s lacked.[54] But even then, Scott's presentation does not support Carlyle's claim that although the serf has been pitied "by Dryasdust and others," he had "at least the certainty of supper and social lodging when he came home; Gurth to me seems happy, in comparison with many a Lancashire and Buckinghamshire man, of these days, not born thrall of anybody! Gurth's brass collar did not gall him: Cedric *deserved* to be his master" (*PP*, 235). Carlyle's main point, that working people of his day were in a wretched condition, is undoubtedly true. Yet to see Gurth's world as providing an alternative is to misread *Ivanhoe*, for Gurth's collar in *Ivanhoe* does gall him; in fact, he secures his release from it at the first possible opportunity. Nor does Scott seem to imply that Cedric deserved to be Gurth's master, the Saxon aristocracy being portrayed as in severe decline, in contrast to the Saxon peasantry's more enduring spirit. Despite his disagreement with Thierry, Carlyle is actually accepting his interpretation by presenting Gurth the Saxon not as Scott's creation but rather as representative of the English laboring class. Carlyle's reading of paternalism finally proves more gloomy than that of his model. Scott hints in his presentation of Gurth that the faithful can achieve freedom. Carlyle suggests that the achievement at least of what the Chartists conceive to be freedom — personal representation — of necessity destroys the paternalist sense of belonging.

In *Past and Present*, although the setting is contemporary with *Ivanhoe*, the sense of identity provided by the Saxon nobility has been replaced by the more divisive structure of Norman aristocracy and Saxon subjects. Following Jocelin, Carlyle recounts how Samson showed his magnanimity of spirit and appropriate sense of political involvement by supporting Richard's faction against John (*PP*, 152). On the other hand, Samson refused to allow the rich shrine of St. Edmund to be stripped to help pay for Richard's ransom.

John's visit to the Abbey of St. Edmund is also mentioned: Carlyle, who receives little help in this episode from Jocelin, returns to *Ivanhoe* and imagines what Scott's John would have inevitably become a few years later: a "blustering, dissipated human figure, with a kind of blackguard quality air, in cramoisy velvet . . . tearing out the bowels of St. Edmundsbury Convent (its larders namely and cellars) in the most ruinous way, by living at rack and manger there" (*PP*, 106). King John's visit to the abbey confirms the traditional picture of his self-indulgence and lack of generosity. None of the abbey's minor interactions with the royal Normans, indeed, depict the rulers in a favorable light. Just as Scott had found true Saxons in the common people rather than in the declining nobility, Carlyle suggests that the true Teutonic spirit is found not in the kings, but rather in individuals such as Samson. Within the abbey, great political and economic questions must be solved — and solved they are, because unlike the world outside it, the abbey finds the ideal system of government in the man who deserves to rule and in the people who acknowledge his right.

In *Chartism* and *Past and Present*, Carlyle thus destroys the neat division between brutal Norman and loyal Saxon, oppressor and subject people, suggested by Thierry's schematized reading of Scott. But the implications of Carlyle's use of the Saxon-and-Norman motif are of major importance in the development of the Victorian self-image.

First, Carlyle repeats Professor Sauerteig's suggestion that both the British aristocracy and the common people can claim a Teutonic heritage. Whether Abbot Samson himself is a Saxon or a Norman is less important than that he asserts the strength of Teutonic manhood or than the power of a social order that grants to each class such as it needs and deserves. Samson is thus more clearly a representation of Teutonic aristocracy than are King Richard and King John, since his right to rule derives from merit. Whether Carlyle would have appreciated being informed that the practical implementation of his ideas would be the introduction of a republic must remain in doubt. Carlyle's writings are simply not practical, and reviewers of *Chartism* were more inclined to see him as a Tory than as a revolutionary.[55] In fact, both these works, while socially critical in their satire, may also be said to be celebratory, drawing attention to the enduring qualities of the greatest of the English.

But the second point to be made regarding Carlyle's insistence that the Normans were "Saxons who had learned to speak French" is that such a claim demonstrates a deliberate blindness to what for most British people made the Normans different — a factor also underestimated by Thierry. Scott had utilized the emotional power of references to the Roman Catholic church. In *Past and Present* Carlyle is polemically using a religious work to argue that religion is unimportant. Carlyle came across Jocelin's Chronicle in a Camden Society publication, and indeed, the editor John Gage Rokewood's decision to publish the manuscript may be connected with the English mixture of repulsion and fascination regarding monks. At a time of a new serious interest in the Roman Catholic tradition, Rokewood may have considered that he was providing insight into the real workings of English monasticism. Rokewood, who died shortly before the publication of *Past and Present,* was himself the son of a Roman Catholic baronet and received a Jesuit education; his family property was located in the region of Jocelin's narrative.[56] Had he lived, he would almost certainly have been horrified at Carlyle's use of his research.

The possibility was now occurring even to some of the more committed factions of the Church of England that in the process of the Reformation, the humane aspects of the Christian religion had been lost. Scott perhaps presented only a quasi-Gothic view, and the medieval church need not necessarily have consisted of self-seeking opportunists like Prior Aymer, monstrous villains like the Templars and Hospitalers, or greedy abbots who deserved to be robbed by Robin Hood. The Roman Catholic architect Augustus

Welby Pugin had been assuring them of such since the introduction of the Utilitarian-influenced New Poor Law by contrasting the lack of compassion of the workhouse system with the Christian charity of the medieval monasteries.[57] Since the condition of the poor during the 1840s was a cause for serious concern, the monastic alternative was increasingly attractive; and Rokewood's edition of Jocelin's Chronicle, while hardly presenting an ideal world, nevertheless depicted a community that finally succeeded in overcoming its major administrative problems.

Carlyle, in contrast, shows little interest in the religious possibilities of the medieval world. His focus is not upon reviving a form of Christianity, but is instead upon rediscovering the heroic potentials that the age of materialism has ignored. Carlyle rejects the possibility that a new ideal can be found in Roman Catholicism. In the midnight hour of Britain's crisis, the apologists for the Roman Catholic faith hold out the shadow of something that never was. Carlyle endeavors to oppose to this the flesh-and-blood reality of a hero such as Abbot Samson. But for all his acute sensitivity to the signs of the times, Carlyle shows less consciousness than Scott of the strength of feeling on the subject of religion, and his seemingly purposeful avoidance of one of the crucial questions of the 1840s leaves this aspect to other writers.

Young England and Roman Catholicism

In denying both the romance of medieval times and the place of religion, Carlyle was acting against an interpretation of history that he himself had helped create. The concept of the "Two Nations" of Scott and Thierry contributed to the conservative Young England movement. Admittedly, this was more directly the descendant of a chivalric medievalism that owes comparatively little to the Teutonists and that would be carried on by Charlotte Yonge in *The Heir of Redclyffe* and other novels; but the picture of medieval England created by Scott's realization of the age of Richard and John is another strong influence.

The key English work reflecting this revived interest in chivalry and knightly behavior is Kenelm Digby's *Broad Stone of Honour*. By focusing a series of discussions of gentlemanly conduct around figures who represent the crusading spirit, Digby seeks to instill a new sense of noble conduct and of charitable religion — his studies of the medieval period prompted him to convert to Roman Catholicism — into the young gentlemen of England. Richard Coeur-de-Lion, whom he portrays as an example of "a hero, and of a religious monarch,"[58] is consequently more idealized than in *Ivanhoe*, and substantially more so than in *The Talisman* (1825), where Scott's jaundiced depiction of the Crusades contrasts sharply with Digby's sense of a glorious adventure.

The Broad Stone of Honour combines the tradition of Renaissance courtesy literature with an unquestioning belief in the values of the Crusaders and knightly conduct. Digby's best-known novelistic influence was on the young Benjamin Disraeli. Indeed, *Tancred* (1847) bears the name of one of Digby's four key heroes — the Crusader-king of Sicily who was, significantly, a Norman. True to his name, Disraeli's Tancred sets off on his own crusade, although everything does not end as tidily as Digby had imagined.[59]

Disraeli's novels are more strictly in the chivalric tradition than shaped by a belief in authentic history, yet *Sybil; or, the Two Nations* (1845) reveals a fascination with origins real and illusory that includes awareness of the Saxon-and-Norman contrast and the sense of a divided nation as presented by Carlyle. Disraeli, however, further considers the topic Carlyle ignores, the place of religion.

Sybil first introduces the reader to the "Norman" world of the landed aristocracy. "Normanness" is the establishment of right within the propertied class, and Disraeli initially appears to be satirizing the belief that Norman blood is the sign of nobility. The hero Charles Egremont's family is descended from a stock "more memorable than illustrious" who, upon gaining a fortune, had claimed Norman descent.[60] The "great Norman peer" Lord Fitz-Warene de Mowbray is in actuality descended from a favorite of George III, and his ancestry was later "discovered at Herald's College" (*Sybil*, 84; 2:7). Yet Disraeli does not entirely reject the place of "blood":

these upstart Normans are contrasted with a true Norman nobleman, "a younger son of the most ancient Norman family in
England." The Reverend Aubrey St. Lys is "distinguished by that
beauty of the noble English blood, of which in these days few types
remain; the Norman tempered by the Saxon; the fire of conquest
softened by integrity; and a serene, though inflexible habit of mind"
(*Sybil*, 110; 2:11). St. Lys and the Roman Catholic Sybil give two
meanings to Carlyle's idea of Norman "right": they are both rightful
property-owners and morally superior.

Set against the supposed Normans are the Saxon workers
whose will to survive is their final resource against exploitation.
(Disraeli, incidentally, does not suggest that they are all exploited
directly by the Normans; his vision of English society has its own
version of the Saxon Plugson of Undershot, except that in Disraeli's world the achievement of property necessitates the denial of
one's Saxon ancestry.) Queen Victoria is hence monarch of two
nations, the rich and the poor (*Sybil*, 73; 2:5). The figure of Queen
Victoria is important to the two-nation structure since she is the
heir of the Norman kings and of the chivalric world, and is by birth
half-Saxon. According to Disraeli:

> Fair and serene, she [Victoria] has the blood and beauty
> of the Saxon. Will it be her proud destiny at length to
> bear relief to suffering millions, and, with that soft hand
> which might inspire troubadours and guerdon knights,
> break the last links in the chain of Saxon thralldom?
> (*Sybil*, 50; 1:6)

In the society presented in *Sybil*, the task for a queen, even a
queen with the racial mix of Scott's reconciling characters, may be
a large one, for the poor are portrayed as neither attractive nor
noble. Unlike the Christian Normans, the Saxons are by nature
pagan, as their home confirms: "Wodgate, or Wogate, as it was
called on the map, was a district that in old days had been conse-
crated to Woden, and which appeared destined through successive
ages to retain its heathen character" (*Sybil*, 160; 3:4). In contrast to
the elegant Norman names of the landowners, these people bear

such blunt Saxon names as Diggs, Toddles, and Prance when they have names at all — a privilege not granted to Devilsdust.[61] Like Carlyle, Disraeli suggests that in order to escape from their misery, the poor will need strong leadership. Where he differs is in concluding that they primarily need a sense of religion like that advocated by Sybil and St. Lys.

Kenelm Digby had deplored Thierry's reading of history, which he described as a "caricature of the conquest of England," unfairly disparaging both the Normans and Roman Catholicism.[62] In contrast, Disraeli's Sybil and her father are depicted studying "a fine book . . . though on a sad subject," *The History of the Conquest of England by the Normans* (*Sybil*, 170; 3:5). Sybil's greyhound, significantly named Harold, has announced the arrival of Egremont, also significantly using the alias of Franklin.[63] When Sybil suggests that the reason why Egremont/Franklin has not read the book — obviously Thierry's — is that he cannot be as interested in it as they (implicitly poor Saxons) are, her father replies: "It must interest all, and alike, . . . for we are divided between the conquerors and the conquered." Although we are supposedly in the world of Young England, Disraeli utilizes his readers' sense of an icon, his structural framework revealing itself as drawn from Thierry and ultimately from Scott.

Acknowledging the existence of the Two Nations as a survival from Saxon and Norman times, however, does not imply that a solution to the problem has been found. Like Carlyle, Disraeli suggests that society may be improved by individuals displaying true nobility, such as Sybil Gerard, the heir of the Valences.

Sybil's interpretation of her world is shaped by distinctions between Saxons and Normans. When she discovers that Franklin is an Egremont, she assumes that he must be "a Norman, a noble, an oppressor of the people, a plunderer of the Church — all the characters and capacities that Sybil had been bred up to look upon with fear and aversion, and to recognize as the authors of the degradation of her race." But just as she misreads the significance of the false Norman name, Sybil is also incorrect in dismissing Egremont's argument that natural leaders of the people exist (*Sybil*, 266; 4:5). The people's chosen liberators, the brutal Bishop Hatton and the tormented Stephen Morley, cannot prevent the children of Woden from plundering the "modern castellated building" known as Mowbray Castle (*Sybil*, 384; 5:11). Mowbray Castle, an apparently Norman symbol of power, is a sham, the true heir to the estate, the real Norman, being none other than Sybil's father. Sybil, then, proves not to be a poor Saxon but a noble Norman leader; and her belief in justice and charity represents the hope of Young England.

That after all her protestations Sybil is demonstrated to be the most truly Norman of all has been seen by some critics as an unsatisfactory conclusion to the problems addressed by the novel.[64] Two nations, after all, prevail even more than in, for example, *The Betrothed*, where the young people of mixed racial origins represent hope for the future. But while Patrick Brantlinger has strong grounds for observing that "Disraeli is so in love with irony that he allows it to undermine even the central thesis of *Sybil*,"[65] the novel maintains at least a tenuous hold on a romantic theory of natural aristocracy. Just as Carlyle's Cedric deserved to be Gurth's master, and Samson deserved to be Abbot, so Sybil deserves to be the natural leader of the people. Her claim is instinctively recognized by the Saxon "Dandy Mick" Radley, who, like his ancestor Gurth, risks all to ensure the preservation of the deeds that will reinstate his natural mistress. The solution to social problems cannot be found in rioting, strikes, or Chartism; but in abiding by the text chosen by Aubrey St. Lys: "Fear God and honour the King."

This solidly conservative conclusion indicates that Disraeli may well have judged the tastes of the public more soundly than did Carlyle. In the question of the importance of race, Disraeli and Carlyle show features in common. Finding nobility in character rather than in race may have been acceptable in Scott's time; but both Disraeli and Carlyle's writings indicate a more consistent identification of the racial with the symbolic character. In this world, the application of traditional racial characteristics as an expression of character, as in the case of Scott's portrayal of Richard and John, is not sufficient. Sybil must be a Norman by temperament, blood — and religion.

Whereas Carlyle seems deliberately to have deemphasized the place of religion, Disraeli realized that the topic was at the center of

public interest. Disraeli's optimistic conclusions concerning the An-
glo-Catholic revival (interestingly modified in *Tancred*) may not necessarily have been entirely popular with those members of the
established church who regarded Roman Catholicism as a threat.
Still, *Sybil* presents a novelistic expression of the question side-
stepped by Carlyle, the part of religion in the assessment of Saxons
and Normans. This aspect was to be developed further in the writings of a novelist and historian who is now little read, but who was
very popular in the 1850s, Charlotte Mary Yonge.

The writings of Charlotte Mary Yonge (1823–1901), or Aunt
Charlotte as she became in countless publications for children, are
currently less secure within the literary canon even than those of
Disraeli. Yet Yonge's writings deserve consideration here since
they helped further popularize a reading of the Saxon-and-Norman
myth that was simultaneously conservative while applying a theory
of race to representative figures such as Richard and John. Yonge
addressed her novels and historical narratives principally to children and would probably have been horrified had she realized her
affinities with two other influential groups. First, she provides a
link between historically based medievalism and the idealized Gothicism of the Pre-Raphaelites. Second, Yonge may also have unin-
tentionally contributed to Liberal ideas of the 1860s. Drawing on
the oppositions created by Scott and Thierry, Yonge presented her
own very definite ideas about what England and the English should
be like, and the wide circulation of her writings surely made some
small contribution to the formation of the imperialist image towards
the close of the nineteenth century.[66]

Hence although Yonge's writings are moving towards the
Gothic medievalism that does not form a part of this study, they
have a place here since they combine elements of documentary history with chivalric idealism. Her fascination with the knightly period was clearly influenced by *Ivanhoe*,[67] but her own portrayals of
King Richard and King John also demonstrate Yonge's taste for
chivalric medievalism in the tradition of Kenelm Digby. Yonge's
books reveal how a strongly Conservative, High Church writer
could make use of part of the Saxon-and-Norman myth.

In her earliest and best-known novels, Yonge explored on a

domestic level some of the ideas found in Disraeli's novels of high society. For Yonge was consciously very much a small-town maiden lady, whose task in life was to help those around her, both rich and poor, become better Christians. As Christabel Coleridge's biography of Yonge, which contains some autobiographical writing, reveals, Yonge was proud of her family history. She believed that her family had been loyal supporters of Charles I and had always fought for "Church and King,"[68] and she described herself in her old age as "a Catholic, but not a Roman Catholic."[69] Yonge's ideal England was one where the charity of the Middle Ages continued to survive, but where the church was emphatically English.[70] The cultural imperialism of her writings, however, is not entirely the result of a sense of certainty; it is also a response to the fear that radicals and liberals were destroying the old ways. Yonge lived all her life in comparative comfort in rural Otterbourne, near Winchester, and it is easy to detect a certain myopia in her belief in the traditional balance between the paternal aristocrats, the charity of the church, and the worthy and grateful poor. Hence while lacking the satirical bite, Yonge is doing something very similar to what Disraeli attempted in *Sybil.* In all her writings, birth is important in shaping character.

Yonge's first novel, *Abbeychurch; or, Self-Control and Self-Conceit,* depicts the leading family of a rural neighborhood who invest money and energy in building a new St. Austin's Church, a Gothic structure that simultaneously recalls the conversion of the Saxons. (Obviously, the intention is once again to convert the Saxons, the pagan poor who with High Church teaching might appreciate their place within a larger social structure.) In this world, the greatest danger to society is a denial of history. At the Mechanics' Institute, the haunt "of Chartism and Socialism, and all that is horrible," chivalry is dismissed as a "barbarous institution" at odds with a "civilized and enlightened age."[71] Yonge overturns this statement by characterizing the Saxons as barbarians who need the ruling influence of Norman religious chivalry.

From the first, then, Yonge espoused the values of chivalry. Her best-remembered novel, *The Heir of Redclyffe* (1853) was a sensational success. With its Gothic and knightly sensibilities, it was the favorite novel of the Pre-Raphaelites — although as Yonge reveals in a later novel, the admiration was not mutual.[72] The hero, Sir Guy Morville, may seem impossibly idealized. This should not be mistaken as bad writing by Yonge, one of whose strengths, indeed, is the plausible portrayal of children. Sir Guy is perfection because Yonge believes that in a Christian society the ideal can exist in a human being — or at the very least, is worth presenting as an example to others. Sacrificing his life to save his cousin's soul, Guy is, of course, a Sir Galahad figure, akin to the Arthurian medievalism of the period. But he also has historical definition. Impeccably well-born, he is descended from a leading Norman family — in fact, from Hugh de Morville, generally described as the least culpable of the four knights who murdered Thomas Becket.[73] Guy's Normanness is extremely important. Although there are various hints of Saxon Christianity in Yonge's novels, in terms of character her main sympathy lies with the aristocrats, the Normans. Georgina Battiscombe has remarked: "In her novels, the noblest heroes are always those of unimpeachable ancestry, though sometimes . . . they have fallen sadly from their high estates. In plain English, Charlotte was a bit of a snob."[74]

In fact, Charlotte was clearly a lot of a snob. But this presentation of her characters involves a strong sense of race. Yonge believed that Normans should guide and Saxons should follow. In her essays collected under the title *Cameos from English History* she informs her young readers that even in the present, Norman energy is detectable "among their descendants, a certain proportion of the English nobility, and the population of Normandy and of Yorkshire."[75] Aunt Charlotte further asserts:

> Without the Norman aristocracy, and the high spirit of chivalry and adventure thus infused, England could scarcely have attained her greatness; for though many great men had existed among the unmixed Anglo-Saxon race, they had never been able to rouse the nation from the heavy, dull, stolid sensuality into which, in this day, an uncultivated Englishman is likely to fall. (*Cameos*, 51)

This passage takes us back to the characterization of Athelstane in *Ivanhoe*. Yet Yonge's history was not merely a retelling of *Ivanhoe*, since she also used Palgrave's *Normandy and England*, almost certainly the major source for her novel of 1854, *The Little Duke, or Richard the Fearless*. A retelling of the story of the youthful adventures of a tenth-century duke of Normandy, *Richard the Fearless* reveals an important factor in Yonge's admiration for the Normans. Richard is not portrayed as French, but of Northman stock, and his noble character, shaped by the trusty Danes of Bayeux, proves infinitely superior to the faithless French.[76] Yonge was always shocked at the slightest hint of liberalism, but in this she reveals the flexibility of the Saxon-and-Norman myth: even the staunchest Tory, supportive of Norman aristocracy as opposed to Saxon egalitarianism, is eager to claim a part in the Teutonic heritage.

In *Cameos from English History*, Yonge sketches her own portraits of King Richard and King John with none of Scott's ambivalence as to Saxon and Norman characteristics. As an ardent supporter of chivalry, Yonge never questions the justice of the Crusades. Her Richard's character is flawed by "his unbridled temper," but he is brave, daring, and chivalrous, and passionately attached to "his own chosen and long-loved lady, Berengaria of Navarre" (*Cameos*, 233). Although as we have noted, no nineteenth-century writers seem to have considered the possibility that Richard might be homosexual, Richard as the model husband, whose "chivalry was all on fire" when his bride was insulted by the king of Cyprus, appears to be Yonge's own invention. If Richard was an ideal knight, then he must have an ideal lady. In the presentation by Yonge, Richard becomes a very simple character, driven only by his chivalrous feelings: he is, in fact, *Ivanhoe*'s Richard without Scott's realization that a hero of romance may be "brilliant" but may at the same time be "impractical."

King John appears in a series of three of Yonge's Cameos. Having established John's loathsome character by describing him as murdering his nephew Arthur of Brittany with his own hands, Yonge shows how his actions were opposed to the good of England, and how both Saxons and Normans — whose separate existence at this time she never doubts — united against him.

In the Protestant tradition, Yonge regards John's conflict with the pope as his one opportunity for glory. But unlike the early Protestant historians, she sees his failure not as his "tragedy" but as his "shame." She argues that John should have listened to the people of England and continued to resist the pope: instead, he bound England more than ever to the power of Rome.[77]

Yonge's assumption that the people of England instinctively opposed the Church of Rome is in accord with most versions of the Saxon myth. When retelling the story of the Magna Carta, however, her sympathies for the Normans create a rather different perspective from that of earlier writers. John is neither Saxon nor Norman, but alienated from the two groups, who unite against him to reclaim laws that Yonge portrays as Saxon in origin but ratified by the Norman kings (*Cameos*, 272). Yonge seems unable to describe such reformers with the enthusiasm Liberals might muster. Yet clearly the idea of an Anglo-Norman aristocracy championing the rights of Church and People — always for Yonge in that order — with the dutiful support of the Saxon Commons, appeals to her. This is what should be learned from the story: not that the ordinary English should fight for their hereditary rights, but that they should stand behind the aristocracy, guided in its turn by the church.

The writings of both Yonge and Disraeli demonstrate that the Saxon-and-Norman myth in English interpretation is not simply that of the Norman Yoke. Perhaps the true heirs of Scott, Yonge and Disraeli mark the conservative parameters of how the idea might be used. Yet in many respects, they were writing against the liberal Broad Church mainstream who were to adopt the story of the Saxon and Norman past as particularly their own. When he wrote *Sybil*, Disraeli's sense of religion had apparently been flexible enough to allow him to imply that if "real" Normans were Roman Catholics, that was not necessarily bad, and quite possibly good. Yonge takes a slightly different path in suggesting that the aristocratic English, the heirs of the Normans, are ideally not Roman Catholic but English Catholic, secure in their national and Teutonic heritage but able to return to the Golden Age of medieval charity. For many Britons, however, Yonge's distinction between Catholic and Roman Catholic was not as clear. In their opinion, if the

Normans were indeed responsible for the introduction of Roman practices into England, the claim that they were as Teutonic as the Saxons lacked conviction.

Sybil presents an England in which the solution to the Two Nations question might be a new Norman Conquest. Yonge's vision implies that such a conquest would not merely be what Carlyle suggests, the reimposition of the leadership of the strongest Teutons, but the revival of aristocratic justice tempered by the factor that Carlyle had chosen to ignore, the Christian mercy of Catholicism. In identifying the literal blood-line of the Normans with Catholicism, Yonge and, far more consciously, Disraeli are exploring the most topical of hopes and fears concerning the stability of the relationship between religion and government. Consequently, a tension is confronted that could not affect Thierry: English ambivalence concerning the medieval traditions that Protestantism, with its conscious overthrow of history, denied.

Against this new interest in medieval society the opposing point of view, fostered by some of the clergy in the moderate, established Church of England, began to assume a more strongly Saxon self-identity in an attempt to reclaim history for Protestantism. The English Reformation, they argued, should once again be seen as a true "re-formation" of the pre-Norman church, returning to a a particularly accurate interpretation of the Christian religion. Scott's opposition between Richard and John was now no longer the ideal test case since it lacked this clearly racial dimension. In the 1840s' debates over Henry II and Thomas Becket, these two elements — that race was both literal and symbolic and that the Saxons were superior — forged a central focus for historical interpretation.

Chapter 4

The Threat to Religion: Henry II and Becket

While the construction of an opposition between Saxons and Normans in the reigns of Richard and John can be traced to a specific historical moment, the dispute between King Henry II and his archbishop of Canterbury Thomas Becket seems always to have prompted an urge to side with one party or the other.[1] Indeed, if the interpretation of one event in English history might be said to capture the changing "spirits of the ages," that one event would be the story of Thomas Becket's life and death.[2] In the 1840s, however, the question assumed a new intensity; and while various aspects of the eventful reign of Henry II — for example, his love for Rosamund and his relationships with his sons — remained of interest, interpretations of this conflict of the 1160s not only assumed a new significance but were also argued with far greater intensity. The beliefs, actions, and racial identities of both Henry and Thomas were seen as having a direct relevance to current crises in thought. Like Richard and John, the opposed figures provided a means of exploring the significance of being — or not being — English. But in this instance, the question of identity was associated more closely with the role of religion.

For readers consciously placing a value on fact, the story of the conflict between king and archbishop was both intriguing and frustrating: the quantity of documents seemed the ideal material of history, but the many miracles they recorded scarcely coincided with a concept of history as raw fact. More contemporary biographical material was written, and, of more importance, has survived, on Archbishop Thomas Becket than on almost any other medieval figure. As interest in antiquarian publishing grew, many of these documents were printed, some more than once. Some commentators were Roman Catholics, but most of those who expressed strong opinions on the story were ordained members of the Church of England. In their reverent regard for the materials, and particularly in their attempts to construct one coherent event from the mass of sometimes contradictory evidence, they frequently adopted the methodology of biblical scholarship.[3] In the late 1840s this attempt at the creation of objective history paradoxically became a means of assessing the rights and wrongs of the controversy. The question now assumed the form of Thomas Becket's racial origin, and the seven-hundred-year-old debate over which of the two factions was more justified was reenacted in the quarrel over whether Becket was a Saxon or a Norman.

Henry II and Thomas Becket before 1846

The skeleton facts of the dispute between the king and the archbishop were more familiar to nonspecialist readers than most events in medieval history. Thomas Becket was initially appointed chancellor by Henry II, who ruled England and large tracts of France. Henry's violent fits of temper were well known to nineteenth-century readers, as was the story that he had kept a favorite mistress, Rosamond or Rosamund, in a secret labyrinth.[4] Perhaps the majority would have concurred with Southey's statement: "With many weaknesses, and some vices, Henry II was an able Prince."[5]

Henry found his match, however, when he appointed his chancellor Thomas Becket archbishop of Canterbury. Becket soon became involved in several conflicts with the king, particularly over the question of clerical legal privileges. The refusal of each party to find a compromise deprived Becket of the support of his fellow bishops, and from 1164 to 1170 he was exiled from England. In 1170 he returned; but the breach with Henry remained unhealed. A new conflict with the bishops — Henry had had his son crowned the Young King by the archbishop of York, which Becket interpreted as a challenge to his primacy — led to another series of excommunications. After some angry words by the king, four of his courtiers — Reginald Fitzurse (who had some personal connection with the archbishop), William de Traci, Hugh de Morville, and Richard Brito — killed Becket in Canterbury Cathedral.

But Becket was never forgotten. A cult of St. Thomas of Canterbury sprang up with remarkable rapidity, and within a few years of his death, miracles of St. Thomas, including the healing of blindness and leprosy, were not only being reported but also carefully investigated and recorded by the monks.[6] However implicated in Becket's death, Henry decided to bow to the general feeling. The cult of Thomas was sanctioned by the king's grief; by a rapid canonization; and by popular witness. Thomas was, then, both an official and an unofficial saint: recognized by secular and ecclesiastical authority, but also a favorite of the ordinary people. The power of the Becket legend is attested to not only by interest shown in England, but also by writings from countries as diverse as Italy and Iceland.[7]

Since so much of his life was spent in direct or indirect confrontation, from the very beginning Becket's story was presented in oppositional terms.[8] Until the Reformation Thomas of Canterbury was a symbol of martyred sainthood, infinite compassion, and the triumph of the church over secular authority. For these very reasons, Becket, like King John, underwent a drastic historical reappraisal during the English Reformation. As recorded by the medieval chroniclers, Becket may have been a saint; but he had presumed to assert the power of the Church — and the pope — over that of the king. His death had provided an excuse for the papal faction to tighten its control over the independent-spirited English Christians. In Henry VIII's reign, the jeweled shrine of St. Thomas at Canterbury was destroyed.

As in the case of King John, the new official view of St. Thomas was expressed by John Foxe in his influential *Actes and Monuments*. Foxe sarcastically characterizes Becket as "our English pope-holy martyr" because: "If the cause make a martyr, as is said, I see not why we should esteem Thomas Becket to die a martyr, more than any others whom the prince's sword doth here temporally punish for their temporal deserts." Foxe argues that execution would have been more appropriate "to teach all Romish prelates not to be so stubborn."[9] Any claims to spirituality in the story are dismissed as mere popish lies. Foxe's Protestant history presents the Becket story as a contest of temporal power in which the pope, the archbishop, and the king of France deliberately conspire against the English state as represented by Henry II.

This version of the story retained official sanction until the mid-eighteenth century, when Hume characterized the conflict in reference to the "genius of the age." Henry II was, at least in his conflict with Becket, a ruler ahead of his time, while Becket, although probably sincere, was "a prelate of the most lofty, intrepid, and inflexible spirit, who was able to cover to the world, and probably to himself, the enterprise of pride and ambition, under the disguise of sanctity, and of zeal for the interests of religion . . ."[10]

George Lord Lyttelton's verdict was similar in another work of the 1760s, his major biography of Henry II. An intense admirer of the king, Lyttelton consequently sees Becket as a man who abused his natural ability by becoming the English representative of the cunning policies of the pope. Lyttelton believes that the possibilities offered by his position were too tempting for a man of Becket's talents.

In response to Lyttelton's work Joseph Berington produced a new study of the conflict that made no profession of supporting the established view. Berington's *History of the Reign of Henry II* was published in 1790. The author writes as a Roman Catholic and a professed supporter of Charles James Fox, who, he hopes, will help bring about Catholic emancipation. Of Lyttelton he writes, "The horror of popery, which in some is a real malady, had disordered his judgment."[11] In his eagerness to identify the moderate Roman Catholic church with political reform, Berington concedes that in England at least, papal supremacy is inappropriate: "Had providence given Becket to his country, but a few years later, we should have seen him, opposing with main fortitude the wild pretensions of Rome, and at the end of the barons, wresting *Magna Charta* from the tyrant son of Henry" (Berington, 237). This interpretation is interesting since it opposes the standard post-Reformation English view of Catholicism as reactionary and opposed to constitutionalism. But of even more importance, Berington's book is the first to explore the possibility of opposing historical readings, some of which might be in contradiction to the "official" view.

The 1820s saw a number of such unofficial readings of the Becket story. For Augustin Thierry, the quarrel between king and archbishop was a key example of the central Saxon and Norman opposition he had developed from *Ivanhoe*. Unlike earlier "philosophic historians" (perhaps he is thinking of Hume), he believed that Henry and Becket's "mutual hate" was based upon race.[12] Henry was a Norman, and Becket, "the weaker and more unfortunate of the two," was a Saxon — the first Saxon to hold high office since the deposition of Stigand by William the Conqueror. In his rise to power, Thierry argued, Becket had succeeded in ingratiating himself with the Anglo-Normans. Upon his appointment to Canterbury, however, Becket had "laid aside his rich vestments, disfurnished his sumptuous house, broken with his noble guests, and made friends with the poor, with beggars, and with Saxons" (Thierry, 2:60). Consequently, the Normans saw him as the new embodiment of Saxon power: "The sons of the companions of William the Bastard thought the soul of King Harold had descended into the body of him whom they themselves had made primate" (Thierry 2:62). Henri Martin and Amadée Thierry, the editors of the posthumous tenth edition of Thierry's history, explain that although Thierry's work was repeatedly revised, the historian refused to change his mind about Becket.[13] Since *The History of the Conquest* first appeared, however, more definite proof had come to light that Becket was not a Saxon, but a Norman.

Thierry's desire to find in Becket a significant instance of the icon he had found in *Ivanhoe* forced him to make uncritical use of his sources. Several contemporary lives of the saint had been written by Becket's friends, and four of these accounts were printed as a compilation in Paris in 1495. This *Quadrilogus*, however, contains in addition to the information gleaned from eye-witnesses some other later material — and the story of Becket's origin is a good example.

The *Quadrilogus* first notes that Thomas was the son of Gilbert, surnamed Beket (the spelling favored by Thierry), and Mathilda, citizens of London of unimpeachable family and fortune. But following this is a second much longer story of how, after being captured by Saracens while on pilgrimage to Jerusalem, Gilbert became acquainted with the daughter of the Saracen admiral and told her about Christianity. When he escaped, she followed him to London, and despite knowing only the English words "Gilbert" and "London," she managed to find him. After consultation with six bishops, the Saracen princess was baptized and wedded to Gilbert. Through visions she learned of the future blessedness of her child, who proved to be Saint Thomas. Thierry quotes this story from the Paris *Quadrilogus* in his notes, and comments: "Such, according to the narrative of some ancient chroniclers, was the romantic origin of a man destined to trouble in so violent and unexpected a manner the great grandson of William the Conqueror in the enjoyment of his power" (Thierry 2:53).

Thierry was not alone in accepting this story as, if not the literal truth, then a possible truth. Sharon Turner had stated: "Becket was the son of a respectable citizen of London, and of a Saracen lady, whose adventures might be classed with the tales of romance, but that, after the crusades commenced, human life became a romance, and society was full of wild enterprise and improbable incident."[14] Turner, who adds that the idea of a saint having a "Mahomedan mother" is almost too strange not to be true, apparently would like to believe in the story; and the versions of it circulating in the Middle Ages (for example, in one of Thierry's favorite sources, the versified chronicle of Robert of Gloucester) suggest that it was well known.

In accepting the *Quadrilogus*, Thierry was merely following the example of most other historians — Berington and another Roman Catholic historian, John Lingard, being notable exceptions — at a time when consultation of original sources was still generally impracticable.[15] The difference between Thierry's reading and that of the earlier historians, however, was that in keeping with his belief in the distinction between Saxons and Normans not ending with the Conquest, Thierry insisted that Thomas was not merely born in England but was a Saxon. A few years later some English historians had also begun to refer not to Becket the Englishman, but to Becket the Saxon.[16]

Also published in 1840 was George Darley's *Thomas à Becket: A Dramatic Chronicle.* This was written as a five-act play, although Darley, an Irishman, apparently did not envisage its performance. But he did draw on the distinction between Saxons and Normans. In an early scene, Morville, one of the assassins, calls Becket "This son of a Saxon truckster, Gilbert Becket, / And a bought Moorwoman!"[17] Morville is portrayed as Norman-French, as is William de Traci, who is given such lines as "Allons, mes enfans!" (*TBDC* 1.3). Richard Brito, in contrast, is here said to be a Saxon (perhaps his name suggested "Briton" to Darley, although most commentators suggest that its meaning was "Breton"). Brito maintains that if Becket is an enemy, the cause is not his race: "Was Alfred the Great Saxon or no? tell me that. And was he only fit for a hogherd, a tender of bristled sheep? Did Alfred lack genius or learning?" (*TBDC* 1.3). Darley seems here to be adopting Scott's image of the Saxon swineherd, but at the same time, through the person of Brito, he finally rejects Thierry's contention that the prime motivation was racial conflict. The theme is only one of many in the drama, but nevertheless, Thierry's idea is resumed in Becket's dying boast to de Traci: "I have an arm as stout/ As any stalking Norman of them all!" (*TBDC* 5.2).

These two productions of 1840, however, mark the end, at least in Britain, of the brief unchallenged ascendancy of Thierry's interpretation of the Becket story. No sooner was Thierry's history recognized and known—to the extent that Disraeli's Sybil could find in it a true expression of the condition of England—than followed serious attempts to bring public attention to the scholarship disproving that Becket was a Saxon. When after 1841 the book became widely available in English translation, Francis Palgrave considered it necessary to attempt in the October 1844 *Quarterly Review* a correction of at least some of Thierry's "very doubtful views."

Why Palgrave was uncomfortable with Thierry's reading is not immediately apparent, for he seems to have accepted many of the most important assumptions, even conceding: "May it not even be asserted, that, from Thierry, we have learnt to appreciate the importance of investigating the internal stratification of society?"[18] On the other hand, he warns his readers that "Thierry does not give us English history, but the opinions which he chooses to engraft upon English history." He further accuses Thierry of insincerity in his sympathy for the Saxons on the basis that France was currently persecuting the Algerians: "Can he [Thierry] glory in the achievement of the Marechal, exterminating the swarthy Kabyles, and really lament the subjugation of the fair-haired Anglo-Saxons by the Conqueror?"[19]

To equate Thierry's personal opinions with those of the French government is somewhat unfair; yet the implied question of why as a Frenchman Thierry wishes to identify with the Saxons is not unreasonable. In Palgrave's opinion: "He is not congenial to the Anglo-Saxons; he pleads their cause, but he does not think with them. An advocate for the Anglo-Saxons, he is not an Anglo-Saxon advocate; their griefs were not his griefs."[20] In contrast, another French historian, Jules Michelet, follows Thierry's story of Thomas Becket as Saxon but shows little of Thierry's sympathy for the Saxons.[21] Still, Thierry, who was too young to have participated in the initial French republican fervor but who had shown sympathy for republican ideas, may have been expressing his own sense of social malaise. Unlike Michelet, Thierry wrote his book before the deposition of Charles X. At this time, he could scarcely advocate old-style republicanism, nor was he a supporter of the Napoleonic ideal. He nevertheless resembled Michelet in searching for a historical perspective not centered upon a cult of personalities or great men, but rather on a united sense of identity. As Edmund Wilson has remarked, before a Marxist analysis of identity based upon economics, what was most available was an analysis based upon race.[22]

For the young Thierry, then, Saxons and Normans may have

provided an example of class struggle, in which Becket represents the common identity of the underclass. For British readers some fifteen years later, after France had undergone a change of government that gave more power to the middle classes, such an interpretation of Thierry's thoughts was no longer available. Palgrave, who had made a conscious decision to identify himself as British and a member of the Church of England, was frankly suspicious of a Frenchman (Thierry was now a part of the ruling regime in France) who seemed so strongly opposed to the Normans. Palgrave's underlying thoughts are perhaps more complex than a simple assumption that if Thierry is French, he must of necessity approve of France's Algerian policy, and thus could not sympathize with an oppressed people — for the conception of the Saxons as an oppressed people was an icon largely of Thierry's making. Something was wrong with Thierry's reading; but Palgrave, who characterized Becket as not merely a Londoner but a cockney,[23] did not have the available data to confront it.

The first real challenge came as a response to John Allen Giles's edition of many of the Latin biographical sources concerning Becket for the Fathers of the English Church series in 1845. For the first time, Giles did not merely reprint the old editions but returned to the manuscripts. The following year, Giles published a two-volume work, *The Life and Letters of Thomas à Becket, now first gathered from the Contemporary Historians.*[24] The accessibility of more authoritative records concerning Becket prompted a new demand for a reconsideration of his historical position. Among the most vociferous of Becket scholars was James Craigie Robertson, later to be the editor of the monumental Rolls Series edition of Becket materials. Already in the 1840s, Robertson, then a vicar in the Canterbury district, was arguing the necessity of a reconsideration of documentary evidence; and Giles's work provided him with new materials. Seemingly unaware that Lingard had already quietly shown rejection of the tale, Robertson loudly challenged Thomas's Saxon birth in the Church of England's *Church Review* in 1846, where he pointed to the contradictions in contemporary sources: Becket "was, indeed, soon involved in quarrels with various nobles, but this was not from any enmity of Saxons against Norman, or of one class against another; but because *individuals* interfered with what he regarded as the rights of his see."[25] Other historians followed. The Anglican moderate Henry Hart Milman, for example, insisted in his *History of Latin Christianity:* "It was not as a Saxon, but as a Saint, that Becket was the object of unbounded popularity during his life and idolatry after his death."[26]

Could one be a Saxon and a saint? For some years, the question was to remain controversial. In 1859, John Morris published an account of *The Life and Martyrdom of St. Thomas Becket, Archbishop of Canterbury, and Legate of the Holy See.* Morris, a Jesuit, insisted that his sympathy with his subject was entirely justified by historical documentation.

> Every one will look for the most entire sympathy with him [Becket] and his cause in the following pages, and the writer cordially acknowledges that he entertains, and is proud of, this feeling. At the same time, he hopes that no one will think that because the Saint, whose life he has ventured to write, is hero in his eyes, he has recorded one word that he did not consider to be completely borne out by the ancient authorities.[27]

This assertion of historicity was too much provocation for Robertson, who responded with his own full-length biography of Becket. Here he reemphasized:

> It was not for the protection or for the elevation of the oppressed Saxons that Becket laboured: it was not to mitigate the barbarous punishments which in that age were usual, and perhaps necessary: it was to establish for his own class a superiority over all other men.[28]

By Becket's "own class," of course, he implies the clergy and the status of the ecclesiastical courts. Soon afterwards Charles Kingsley informed Cambridge students: "Becket, fighting to the death against Henry II, was not, as M. Thierry thinks, the Anglo-Saxon defying the Norman. He was the representative of the Christian

Roman defying the Teuton."[29] But by 1863, when Kingsley made this statement, the question was already changing: Becket's race was not so important as what he represented. When Walter Farquhar Hook published his *Ecclesiastical Biography* in the 1840s he had carefully followed the story of Becket's Saxon-Saracen birth.[30] Fifteen years later, in his *Lives of the Archbishops of Canterbury,* Hook merely alludes to the Saxon-and-Saracen story in a footnote with the observation that the Saxon myth is "now universally exploded."[31] The discomfort apparently felt by Palgrave in assessing Thierry's version of the Becket story could now be articulated by the simple statement that Thierry was factually wrong.

In twenty years, then, between the first widespread recognition of Thierry's history in 1840 and Kingsley's somewhat belated statement at Cambridge, Becket, formerly a Londoner, had become a Saxon, and was now again characterized as a Norman. The remaining question is why at this particular time the establishment of Becket's racial identity seemed so important.

The Becket Controversy in the 1840s

The urge to refute Thierry's claim that Becket was a Saxon suddenly manifested in British writings of the 1840s was almost certainly a consequence of a national crisis of confidence. As we have seen, the economic difficulties of the 1840s that formed the basis of what Carlyle had called the "Condition-of-England Question" prompted various proposed solutions; and the solution most emphasized was a new — or revived — sense of religion.

This, then, was the element missing in Thierry's reading of English history. Thierry ignored a dimension peculiarly English: the problematic relationship between the English church and the past that stemmed from the English Reformation. From the time of the establishment of royal supremacy over the church in England, the story of Henry II and Thomas Becket had been read almost allegorically. The conflict between King Henry and his former chancellor Thomas could only recall to English minds the conflict between Henry VIII and his chancellor Thomas More: the former Thomas had been made a saint by the pope and the latter Thomas was widely regarded as a Catholic martyr who had refused to recognize the king's supremacy over the church — and implicitly the national rejection of papal authority in England.[32] John Foxe's observation that Henry II would have done better to have executed Becket according to law surely implies an association of ideas with the later Henry and Thomas.

Thus most British writers make some juxtaposition between the two incidents. William Cobbett, for example, wrote his *History of the Protestant "Reformation"* shortly after Thierry published his *History of the Conquest*. Here he mentions Becket when describing the consequences of the Reformation: Becket's name was "especially . . . venerated in England, where the people looked upon him as a martyr to their liberties as well as their religion, to having been barbarously murdered by ruffians sent from the king, and for no other cause than that he persevered in resisting an attempt to violate the Great Charter."[33] Cobbett characterizes the church as the protector of the constitution, and the constitution as the protector of the poor, and thus implicitly connects Becket with the Saxon myth. (The reference to the "Great Charter" is presumably not an anachronistic mention of the Magna Carta but a reflection of the belief that the 1215 document was merely a reassertion of the Saxon constitution.) But his Henry II "preparing to rob the Church" has a strong resemblance to Henry VIII. Surviving documents suggest that Becket was worried by Henry II's attempts to obtain church revenues, but disputes over money seem to have been more a symptom than a cause of the quarrel. When Cobbett presented the idea that Becket might have been a champion of rights other than those of his ecclesiastical position, few people considered the implications. When, however, a similar view was espoused by Roman Catholics and members of the High Church party, the political implications of a reassessment of Becket necessitated a serious consideration of the potential significance of the story.

The first major claim for the restored status of the former saint came in the posthumous publications of Richard Hurrell Froude. Froude died in 1837, and in 1838–1839 his friends John Henry Newman and John Keble edited and published his works — including *The History of the Contest between Thomas à Becket, Archbishop of Canterbury, and Henry II, King of England*. Based principally on letters in the Vatican Library, the book attempts to show that contrary to the official view, Becket's transformation from chancellor to archbishop did not cause a drastic change in his behavior, and that while Becket may not always have been the ideal medieval ecclesiastic, he was a consistently good man. Further, the introduction argues that a key point of contention, Thomas's insistence on separate ecclesiastical courts, was at that time quite justified. Speaking pointedly to the High Church party of modern times, the introduction adds: "The high-church party of the twelfth century endeavoured as much as possible to make common cause with the poor and defenceless."[34]

Froude translated the letters in this collection, but how much of this introduction was his and how much was Newman's is not known. Newman's involvement, however, suggested that the choice of subject was polemical. If the degradation of Thomas Becket was symbolic of the Reformation, then this fragmentary work might be construed as an attack on the established church in England itself. The group of young scholars centered on Oriel College at Oxford who from the mid-1830s had made themselves known through the series Tracts for the Times presented a new threat to many evangelical and Broad Church adherents. New movements in the Christian church may seem always to justify themselves by a claim to return to origins, but the Tractarians were particularly forceful in reemphasizing the ritualistic inheritance and the possibility that the Church might again regard itself as "Catholic" — a Church Universal for all people that could bond together the Two Nations.

The *History of the Contest* never makes the claim that Becket was a Saxon. But the growing interest in the Roman tradition shown by the Oxford movement fueled the arguments of those identifying with the Broad Church that if this group was intent on reviving St. Thomas of Canterbury, that saint must represent not

Englishness but otherness. Indeed, a contemporary French work, the first part of Michelet's *History of France,* makes the claim that even if Thomas was a Saxon and supported the rights of the conquered, the cause that he championed was also that of "France and Christianity."[35] Suspicion of the Tractarians was further reinforced by Newman's 1841 publication of *Tract Ninety,* in which he made a Catholic reading of some of the Anglican church's Thirty-Nine Articles. The tract is dated on the feast of the conversion of St. Paul, and perhaps English readers were reminded that from the Catholic perspective, they might still be foreigners in need of an apostle. In the opinion of many of his contemporaries, Newman was simply not thinking as an Englishman, and the English church forced him into spiritual exile until what the church establishment itself had made inevitable finally occurred. Newman publicly identified himself as a Roman in 1846, at almost the same time that Giles and Robertson identified Thomas Becket as a Norman.

Two biographies of Henry II's archbishop published in 1859 were hence deliberately confrontational. Both claimed historical accuracy, but in their very titles they expressed their differences. John Morris, a Jesuit canon of Northampton, proclaimed Thomas Becket a saint and martyr and, further, a "Legate of the Holy See," ratified by the papacy. James Craigie Robertson, by this time an Anglican canon of the Canterbury district, called his book simply *Becket, Archbishop of Canterbury,* ignoring the question of sainthood.

But clearly, works such as Morris's were threatening to the concept of official history. The solution for the Broad Church party was to search again for "facts." The most direct statement about the use of facts as the key to understanding the reign of Henry II is of a somewhat later date, but perhaps already this kind of historical justification was needed. In his collection of materials relating to the itinerary of Henry II, R. W. Eyton noted: "Facts; simple facts; where they were accomplished; when they were accomplished; who accomplished them; and what was said as to how they were accomplished at the time of their coming to pass; these are the primary and most essential elements of pure history."[36] Eyton's belief that facts can be "simple" and history "pure," and that in compiling records of events he can be impartial, may be seen as unusually naive.

Yet Robertson and his friend Arthur Penrhyn Stanley (the protégé of Dr. Arnold and later dean of Westminster), while appreciating the complexities and contradictions of the materials they were using, also believed that by the process of criticism such as that applied to the gospels, pure historical truth could be revealed.

In an essay first published in the *Quarterly Review* in 1853, Stanley retold the story of the archbishop's murder by synthesizing the various versions in Giles's edition of the documents. Stanley here makes some attempt to acknowledge Becket's good qualities, but in the edition that was frequently reprinted for the rest of the century, *Historical Memorials of Canterbury,* Stanley warns his readers of the tale's seductive qualities. While the eyewitness accounts reveal his courage and sincerity, those readers

> who, in the curious change of feeling that has come over our age are inclined to the ancient reverence for St. Thomas of Canterbury as the meek and gentle saint of holier and happier times than our own, may, perhaps, be led to modify their judgment by the description, taken not from his enemies but from his admiring followers, of the violence, the obstinacy, the furious words and acts, which deformed even the dignity of his last hour, and well nigh turned the solemnity of his "martyrdom" into an unseemly brawl. They may learn to see in the brutal conduct of the assassins, in the abject cowardice of the monks, in the savage mortifications and the fierce passions of Becket himself, how little ground there is for that paradise of faith and love which some modern writers find for us in the age of the Plantagenet kings.[37]

Stanley evidently considers that by stating the documentary "facts," he can create a history that can better withstand changing prejudices. Through a synthesis of the eyewitness accounts, an accurate picture can emerge — one that contradicts the romanticism of those who wish for a return to the Middle Ages.

What Stanley failed to appreciate was that the adoption of an antiromantic pose, and particularly the attempt to construct a coherent narrative from so many different versions of the same event, was itself interpretative. Two examples from Stanley and Robertson illustrate the dangers of the supposedly factual approach. Perhaps Stanley and Robertson did not deliberately misrepresent their sources. But both these subtle changes cast adverse reflections on what the two churchmen wished to discredit — namely, monastic Christianity.

The obvious approach to undermining the reclaiming of Becket as a good Saxon Englishman would have been to question his integrity and expose him as a hypocrite. But in the contemporary documents upon which his attackers laid such stress, Becket shows little evidence of the Gothic cunning so frequently associated by Anglican writers with Roman Catholicism. Indeed, Becket rather displays the dogged determination and lack of ability to compromise even superficially that was becoming characterized as a Teutonic trait. His alien qualities must thus be revealed in other areas.

Robertson's and Stanley's general strategy is hence not to question Becket's sincerity but to accept all the claims for his asceticism while clearly implying that such qualities are not within the English church tradition. First, Becket's adoption of the penitential garb he was wearing under his robes at the time of his murder is suggested to be un-English. Stanley notes that the haircloth was designed to be easily removed for Becket's "daily scourgings" and that the "austerity of the hair drawers, close fitted as they were to the bare flesh, had hitherto been unknown to English saints; and the marvel was increased by the sight — to our notions so revolting — of the innumerable vermin with which the haircloth abounded" (*HMC*, 116).

The phrase "to our notions" pointedly discourages identification with Becket: he practiced strange and unhealthy popish rituals and should not be associated with Victorian gentlemen of the present.[38] In Robertson's 1859 biography of Becket, the phrase becomes even more barbed: "a mortification, it is said, without example among the English saints."[39] Robertson here implies that he has a documentary source for the "English saints" statement — but although Becket's saintliness becomes the subject for apostrophe in two source-accounts, no mention is made of this being a particularly un-English practice.[40] Here is a further echo of Thomas Arnold's idea that English Christianity was more genuine and less sensational than that of other nations: even English saints act with moderation, and it is Becket's very lack of moderation that such commentators seem to have found so disturbing. As for Robertson's phrase "it is said," the suspicion arises that it stands on no better authority than Stanley's preconceptions of the English religious tradition: Robertson is, in fact, quoting his friend. But Stanley and Robertson are doubtless correct in surmising that reference to the vermin and scourgings would emphasize the idea that Becket was a man of his time, and not a man of all times.

Second, as Edwin Abbott pointed out, one other passage creeps out of the Victorian commentators and, if not into sources, at least into the Victorian conception of the sources. Stanley, prototype of the timid little Arthur of *Tom Brown's School Days*, insists on "the abject cowardice of the monks."[41] Some documentary basis can be found for the monks' fear. According to the eyewitness Fitzstephen, who has what may be termed an artistic approach to "facts" — he appears to have invented the storm that broke at Becket's murder — the monks advised Becket to go into the cathedral on the mistaken impression that the knights would not dare commit the sacrilege of murder in the sanctuary. Becket told them not to be afraid: "Most monks are more timid and faint-hearted than they need be."[42] This is my translation; Stanley translates: "'No,' he said, 'fear not; all monks are cowards'" (*HMC*, 95). That Becket called the monks cowards is not difficult to believe: the most credible accounts of his death involve shouting and strong language. But such a statement at a moment of high emotional tension hardly proves the monks "abject." Since Stanley apparently does not consider that Becket's "martyrdom" was entirely necessary, to blame the monks because they chose not to be "martyred" with him seems a little unfair. Moreover, Becket was not completely deserted: a visiting clerk, Edward Grim, was seriously injured in an attempt to shield him, and Fitzstephen also claimed that he and another monk did not run away.[43]

Later pains to stress that Grim, whose arm was nearly severed in his defense of the archbishop, was not himself a monk but a visitor from Cambridge, may be connected with this idea of monkish cowardice.[44] (Thierry, incidentally, had characterized him as a loyal Saxon, with no apparent textual authority.) Not only did Robertson and Stanley reject asceticism; the very vocation of monasticism was un-English. The celibacy insisted upon in the priesthood of the Roman Catholic church was a particular source of abomination to many in the Church of England. In the opinion of Charles Kingsley, the Roman holy orders were virtually equivalent to emasculation — and something of this feeling seems exhibited here. In *Tom Brown at Oxford*, written by Stanley's friend Thomas Hughes, the muscularly Christian hero is horrified to find that fellow students interested in Gothic church-architecture also hang their rooms with muslin curtains and have scent on the mantelpiece: the members of the Oxford High Church party of the 1840s are, in Tom's phrase, "man-milliners."[45] Since even High Church leanings were unmanly, monks could scarcely be true manly Englishmen — and in his conclusion, Stanley, apparently oblivious that this "fact" is largely his own invention, warns the British public of the danger inherent in believing otherwise.[46]

Becket's critics accept his asceticism and celibacy since that increases the sense of otherness, but the question of his personal ambitions is more problematic. If Becket's plot was to commit England more deeply to papal control, then he should display some signs of the traditional image of the cunning popish prelate: hence the interest in whether or not his presentation of himself as a priest following his acceptance of the archbishopric was genuinely inspired or a hypocritical posture.

Very few commentators on the story consider the possibility that Becket might have suffered from increasing mental instability, even though his conviction that he was being, as it were, persecuted for righteousness' sake, caused him to excommunicate those he saw as enemies of himself and Christianity. Catholics and Anglo-Catholics, notably Froude and Morris, were happy to detect a saintly consistency from early childhood, displaying characteristics that in Morris's summary appear somewhat similar to Teutonic virtues. From his youth, the saint showed "a singular love for truth; his heart ever full of compassion towards the poor and needy; with the gentlest spirit of condescension toward the timid and humble, yet showing an indomitable courage and will in resisting the oppressor."[47] Nevertheless, Lingard, even though generally sympathetic to Becket's claims for the church, notes:

> Gradually, his [Becket's] opinions became tinged with enthusiasm; he identified his cause with that of God and the church; concession appeared to him like apostasy, and his resolution was fixed to bear every privation, and to sacrifice, if it was necessary, even his own life to so sacred a contest.[48]

But most of Becket's admirers, such as Hurrell Froude, ascribe to him a consistency in character, while his opponents are inclined to deny him a conversion experience.[49] By the time that Stanley attempted to tell once and for all the story of Becket's murder, a simplification of historical interpretation had emerged. The first possibility was that the fiery King Henry, grandson of a Saxon, was the true English king, realizing that constitutional progress depended upon a national church free of Norman (and thus Roman) domination. His actions could thus be seen as an attempt to reconstruct the fabled Saxon church, controlled both by the king and by its own moderation.[50] Alternatively, Thomas Becket, a Londoner and a Saxon, represented the cause of justice both in religious and social terms and stood for the cause of English Christian justice against Norman tyranny.

The problem with the latter reading was that Becket ultimately had won. And while he may have withstood the Normans, he had forged closer links with Rome. Whereas Henry VIII's execution of his former friend Thomas More had been an expression of his domination over the church, after Becket's death Henry II had abandoned ideas of Reformation and had subjected himself to Romish penance. Rather than liberating the church, Henry II had bound it tighter to the Roman tradition through the blood of a popular martyr, and the martyred Saint Thomas guarded England's allegiance to the Church of Rome for three hundred years more. In the uncertainty of mainstream Anglicanism and what it could offer the English people in the 1840s, the attraction of Becket was perhaps understandably a danger. For three hundred years, as Stanley pointed out, Becket had been a powerful saint. For three hundred years more, he had been a charlatan — and now influential thinkers were seeking to reinstate him as a great Englishman. In the contemporary religious crisis, Thomas Becket — who for many people may have been Henry II's own Newman — was driven into exile from Oxford in 1846, but still with the possibility of a triumphal return. Not until it was appreciated that whatever Newman might have done to the state church he had not destroyed it could a less impassioned view of the twelfth-century archbishop emerge.

Later Interest in Henry and Becket

Whereas historians rapidly abandoned the theory that Becket had been a Saxon, the idea that the story still required its teller to take sides persisted in a number of creative works. By the early 1860s, several writers had already seized on the notion of a shared Anglo-Saxon heritage between Britain and the United States of America, and some American writers interpreted the Becket story in this light. Gideon Hiram Hollister's *Thomas à Becket, a Tragedy*, probably inspired by Milman's account in *The History of Latin Christianity*,[51] seems to have been performed only three times — and without success. In this drama, published in 1866, Queen Eleanor refers to "Henry's low-born Saxon chancellor, / Archdeacon Becket."[52] But the king reminds his court that he himself is both Saxon and Norman, and he is somewhat more sympathetically portrayed than is Becket.

In *Thomas à Becket: A Tragedy in Five Acts* (1863), the work of Alexander Hamilton (1815–1907), the historical parts of the absurd plot[53] are taken directly from Thierry. In Thierry's own words, Becket is said to be "this church priest, born for the torment / Of the Anglo-Norman race."[54] But Hamilton's is declaredly an American play, and Becket's preservation of the rights of his order as "the sole true friend / Of Liberty" is seen as a defense of Anglo-Saxon rights against an oppressive monarchy represented by the objectionable persons of Henry and Eleanor. The dying Becket's pronouncement prophesies the revival of the true Anglo-Saxon line in America:

> Ye Norman Lords, here dies the Anglo-Saxons' hope;
> To rise hereafter in a far Western Land,
> Whence lies the sun, with Freedom's glorious rays,
> It shall illumine all the wide, wide, World.
> (Hamilton, 106)

If Hamilton's portrayal is at all representative of American opinion, the facts concerning Becket are seemingly of less interest than Thierry's theory of the Saxon heritage.

Similarly, in Britain, the possibility of Becket as Englishman seems to have once more become attractive when he was no longer identified with the Tractarians and with Newman himself. Since the threat to the established church now seemed less significant than during the 1840s, the conflict could again be seen in different ways. Freeman advanced one of the earliest arguments in favor of reconciliation in the *National Review* in 1860. In a survey of some of the Becket publications, he insisted: "If we wish fairly to judge of the right and wrong between Henry and Thomas, we must first of all shut our eyes to all modern controversies whatever."[55] Freeman's method of conciliation is to devote three pages to demolishing Thierry's "utterly untenable notion," principally on the grounds that although class divisions were strong at this time, the Saxon-Norman element was no longer relevant. The historian's confidence in advancing a reading that could claim both Thomas and Henry as Englishmen was based on the conviction that Thomas's cause finally did not prevail and thus did not thwart England's progress as a strong and independent nation.

Freeman then seems to advance what might now be termed a theory of alterity.[56] Becket "lived in and for his own age. To understand him thoroughly, one must first thoroughly know what that age is."⁵⁷ As a plea for a more systematic understanding of medieval times, this makes sense. But the argument that the situation of those times was interesting, but different, from the present is surely only an attempt to see the story of Henry and Becket as something other than a prefiguration of the tribulations of the Victorian church. Certainly, a few years later, when he wrote *The History of the Norman Conquest*, Freeman is again associating past and present and looking for a personal involvement in the Becket story. Here Freeman seems more eager to claim Becket not as different but as an Englishman and as a modern-style politician. Even if both Henry II and Becket had Norman blood, according to Freeman's definition, they could still be considered Teutonic; and in his reading, both men display Teutonic determination, as opposed to Roman suppleness. Freeman chooses to use the name Thomas of London, which emphasizes his belief that whether the archbishop was Norman by birth or not, the story of Henry II and Becket is evidence of the evolution of the English character and of a more modern approach to constitutional controversies. "Thomas," Freeman remarks, "born of Norman parents on English ground, thoroughly belonged, in spirit and feeling, to the land of his birth and not the land of his blood."⁵⁸

Freeman's comments come at the beginning of a new phase in studies of this topic, inspired by the Rolls Series publication of Robertson's nearly exhaustive collection, *Materials for the History of Archbishop Thomas Becket* (1875–1885). In his editorial remarks, Robertson, whose strong opinions on Becket were well known, stated that he would allow the materials to speak for themselves as unmediated history.⁵⁹ The impossibility of this objective is shown by the very title of the work, which states a thesis by omitting any mention of Thomas's sainthood. Moreover, Robertson is clearly uncomfortable with the miracle-stories, and, somewhat like Freeman and the church question, attempts to detach himself from them by presenting them "as illustrations of the manners and feelings of the time to which they relate . . ." (*Materials* 2:x1).

The question is whether for a nineteenth-century historian this level of detachment was possible. Three later writers who drew on

Robertson's collection of facts suggest that history does indeed demand emotional commitment. An essay by James Anthony Froude and dramas by Tennyson and Aubrey H. DeVere are distinguished from earlier works by a superficial lack of interest in whether Becket was a Saxon or a Norman — but identification with the roles of Henry and Becket in the conflict remains crucial.

The three works generally downplay crude racial categories. Froude, for example, casually remarks that Gilbert Beket's name "denotes Saxon extraction," without laboring the point. Yet at the same time Hurrell Froude's youngest brother makes what is probably the strongest statement of a conspiracy theory in all Victorian Becket studies:

> Among the earliest efforts of the modern sacerdotal party
> in the Church of England was an attempt to reestablish
> the memory of the martyr of Canterbury. The sacerdotal
> party, so far as their objects were acknowledged, aspired
> only to liberate the Church from bondage to the State.
> The choice of Becket as an object of adoration was a tacit
> confession of their real ambition.[60]

Although most of his contemporaries were looking for reconciliation, not further controversy, in their relative assessments of Henry and Becket, Froude even defends Henry's decree that all Becket's family and connections should be exiled, a pronouncement believed to have caused major loss of life. Froude's essay was published as a separate work under the title *The Life and Times of Thomas Becket,* and like his source Robertson he explicitly emphasizes the sense of difference of that time. Becket is set apart from the scientific Victorians through Froude's retelling of some of the more bizarre miracles of St. Thomas that entered the medieval martyrology. Perhaps anxious to dissociate himself from his own temporary identification with the Tractarian movement at Oriel College, where he had contributed to the series of English saints' lives, the younger Froude tells of the miraculous darning of Becket's undergarments by the Virgin, and of his absentmindedly turning water into wine.[61] Even after the supposed change in the new archbishop's lifestyle, Froude insists that this:

was not the religion of a regenerated heart, but a religion
of self-torturing asceticism, a religion of the scourge and
the hair shirt, a religion in which the evidences of grace
were not to be traced in humbleness and truth, but in the
worms and maggots which crawled about his body. He
was the impersonation, not of what was highest and best
in the Catholic Church, but of what was falsest and
worst.[62]

Perhaps even if the wounds inflicted on the Church of England by
Newman and his followers had partially healed by this time, Anthony Froude, whose life was shaped by his inability to believe,
cannot achieve historical detachment: he still has a personal grudge
against the saint in whom his dead brother and his friends had
believed so willingly.[63]

While Froude is anxious to present Becket as the outsider and
not a man for all times, the Catholic poet Aubrey Henry DeVere
uses the same availability of materials to reclaim Becket for the
British tradition. In *St. Thomas of Canterbury: A Dramatic Poem*
(1876) DeVere's characters mention a confusing variety of legends
concerning the origin both of Becket and of Henry and Queen Eleanor, as if, indeed, he has rejected the possibility of what R. W.
Eyton had called "facts, simple facts." Thomas stands principally as
champion of the "liberties of the native church," and in a passage
that reveals a major source to be Freeman's *Norman Conquest* it is
remarked:

> Thomas is English wholly — Saxon half,
> A scion of the ancient, healthful stock
> Which fell on Hastings' field; the first, moreover,
> Who for five reigns hath swayed Augustine's staff.
> King Harold, have thy joy![64]

But when DeVere mentions ancient rights, he is referring to the
independence of ecclesiastical authority, which he assumes to have
existed before the Conquest. Henry is thus the innovator and subverter of ancient customs. DeVere's St. Thomas is resolutely noble
and solidly English, talking of his "mother England" during his ex-

ile; and in the author's opinion his "single lapse" was his temporary agreement to the Constitutions of Clarendon.[65] The dramatic poem is long, earnest, and frankly not particularly interesting; but it does present an alternative to Froude's bitter condemnations.

The final, and most influential, product of this phase, however, is Tennyson's *Becket* (1879). Unlike the majority of the earlier Becket dramas, *Becket* was performed, apparently to some acclaim, in Britain and the United States. Henry Irving's 1893 adaptation gained popularity in its own right.[66]

To claim dramatic greatness for *Becket* would be an exaggeration. Yet Tennyson's play is of interest in its attempts to utilize rather than overlook the complexities in the relationship between Becket and Henry and thereby create a more disturbing juxtaposition between the historical moments of the story and its interpretation.

In the great emphasis on facts, Tennyson was criticized for his unhistorical combination of the two favorite stories of Henry II's reign, that of Becket's murder and that of Fair Rosamund. But perhaps by making no clear distinction between politics and personal feelings, Tennyson presents a more profound historical statement: facts never can speak for themselves. Tennyson hence takes Shakespeare as his dramatic model and focuses on the creation of character. The objective may make a refreshing change from the general assumption that if Thomas is good, Henry must be bad — unless if Henry is bad, then Thomas must be good. Nevertheless, the effect is uneven, partly because of Tennyson's use of source-materials, and partly because the themes of the play expand beyond the individual characters.

Tennyson's Henry is a bluff, impetuous man and hardly an intellectual match for Queen Eleanor. He believes that whereas an earlier pope had trampled on an earlier Henry, his task as a monarch is not to be controlled by Rome, but rather to have Rome under his control:

> I, true son
> Of Holy Church — no croucher to the Gregories
> Must curb her.[67]

Henry sets himself the laudable English task of correcting the relative positions of church and state; but as the play proceeds, Henry proves to have less control than he imagines over his people, his kingdom, and his own passions. The scene opens with a game of chess, but those who hope to control — Henry, Becket, Eleanor, Fitzurse — are persistently thwarted.

Becket equally is a sympathetic figure, and Tennyson perhaps understood his audience in portraying him not as an unworldly ascetic but as kind to animals (he nurses a poor man's dog), children, and the poor. He has a particular interest in the welfare of Rosamund, as if, like W. E. Gladstone, he sees part of his life's task as reclaiming fallen women. A good man, Tennyson suggests, may find himself in a disturbed world.

Most of the play seems more indebted to Tennyson's imagination and approximate knowledge of the more lurid tradition as preserved by Brompton than to close historical reading. Yet as Abbott notes, the play's depiction of Becket's murder is almost entirely derived from Stanley. Following Stanley's condemnation of the monks' "abject cowardice," Tennyson's Becket calls them "monks, not men," and adds, "Why should all monks be cowards?"[68] Rosamund's presence in the cathedral during the murder has been criticized;[69] but Morville is said in the narratives to have held back the crowds and Tennyson has him restrain Rosamund; perhaps here the audience — the crowd — is encouraged to adopt her view of the killing. The play ends with thunder and lightning, Tennyson adding in a footnote: "A tremendous thunderstorm actually broke over the Cathedral as the murderers were leaving it." This also Tennyson would have learned from Stanley, who follows Fitzstephen without questioning why Fitzstephen is the only eyewitness to mention the storm. But again, the confusion of Becket's death and the disturbance of nature seems to be part of Tennyson's vision. *Becket* presents a world where the political control of the chess game — shown in Henry's belief that through Becket the entire Church and State will be under his rule, and in the emotional control claimed by Queen Eleanor and Fitzurse — finally prove equally incapable of withstanding disorder.

Anthony Froude and Aubrey DeVere's readings of the Becket

controversy are unambiguous: the writers contradict each other, but each claims to know what the story is about. Tennyson's version shows a far less certain control — and what may in some respects be a dramatic weakness may also be more deeply revealing. Rather than constructing a historical escape, Tennyson comes far closer to Stanley's observation that there is little ground "for that paradise of faith and love which some modern writers find for us in the age of the Plantagenet kings." The world created in Tennyson's play, then, is not a paradise — but neither, it would seem, is the world of its creator. The Tractarians had seen the story of Thomas of Canterbury as a possible solution to the Condition-of-England Question; in Tennyson's version, even in the seeming refuge provided by Rosamund's bower, the dangers of the political world are ever close. The place of the flesh, through the entry of Becket, Eleanor, and Fitzurse, becomes also the place of the mind, and just as Becket enters the bower, so Rosamund finally enters the cathedral. Henry had hoped to compartmentalize his life. That the play concludes without Henry may seem a change in dramatic focus but also suggests that in this world of blurred distinctions, no one — not even the playwright — can retain ultimate control. The question of Saxons and Normans, then, underlies Tennyson's realization through his use of sources, but oppositions between the two races are not at the center of the play. Just as Carlyle had argued that Saxons and Normans must both be Teutons, Tennyson's Becket and Henry must finally both be English, for this imaginative version tacitly acknowledges what the historians chose not to see: that the position of neither man can be dismissed as alien and irrelevant to the audience's concerns.

Chapter
5

Romans
and Teutons:
William and Harold

When W. C. Sellar and J. B. Yeatman called their parody of English history *1066 and All That* on the basis that 1066 was one of the two dates that English people always remembered, it was not merely a humorous exaggeration.[1] As nineteenth-century historians remarked, the defeat of Harold's army by William, Duke of Normandy, on 14 October 1066 marked the last occasion on which England had been conquered. Freeman believed that

> it is from the memorable day of Saint Calixtus that we may fairly date the overthrow, what we know to have been only the imperfect and temporary overthrow, of our ancient and free Teutonic England. In the eyes of men of the next generation that day was the fatal day of England, the day of the overthrow of our dear country, the day of her handing over to foreign lords . . . till it was a shame to be called an Englishman, and the men of England were no more a people.[2]

For English radicals of the early nineteenth century, 1066 had symbolized a turning point — from a representative and just Saxon government to despotic Norman feudalism; from a society in which all free men had rights to one of barbaric reprisals; from a system conducted in the English vernacular to a legal system administered in French and Latin by foreigners disinclined to learn the native tongue; from a largely autonomous English church to a church controlled by a Roman pontiff not satisfied merely with entire domination of ecclesiastical matters but also determined upon forcing submission from the king himself. Freeman concurred in seeing 1066 as a turning point, although his statement specifically characterizes the Normans as the temporary conquerors of the English. The Conquest was an episode in a story that would finally achieve a happy ending.

Yet in a story with England as hero, at first sight the material and documentary evidence of the Conquest might seem less comedy than tragedy. Contemporary records such as William's famous Domesday survey and all the early chronicles, together with the pattern of landownership surviving into recent times, indeed support the claim that the Normans rapidly gained control of all but the far north of England. On the other hand, a belief in the strength of the Anglo-Saxon character prevailed. Englishmen, history proclaimed, were not readily defeated in battle and stripped of their most sacred rights of citizenship. But how could one battle fought six miles from Hastings in October 1066 have changed the structure of England? The question finally proved beyond the ingenuity of historians. Creative literature, however, found readier answers, and once again historical figures provided a means of exploring the problem. Some reason must have existed why Harold, the last of the Saxon kings, was killed by William, the first of the Norman kings; and that reason was explored most successfully in a literary, as opposed to a strictly historical, form.

Two literary works attempting to see in 1066 an image conforming with their assessments of the current status of England, Edward Bulwer-Lytton's *Harold, the Last of the Saxon Kings* (1848) and Tennyson's *Harold* (1876), each reveal in their titles a focus on the Saxons, the defeated race, as represented by a single personality. To these two influential views of the Saxons, a third and no more dispassionate work may be added, Freeman's *History of the*

Norman Conquest. Each is a tragedy, but the tragedy of Harold: the Conquest is finally not the tragedy of England.

Bulwer-Lytton's writing is often dismissed as laughably inept.[3] At times, Bulwer-Lytton admittedly seems to not to have relied on the discretion of his muse. But even were he alone in this fault, his works would still have a place in a consideration of nineteenth-century views of the Conquest, since his interpretation of the story influenced later versions including those of Freeman and Tennyson, and hence to some extent the "orthodox" reading of the 1860s.[4] Indeed, while Burrow's observation that the central volume of Freeman's *Norman Conquest,* devoted to Harold, is a "self-contained tragedy" is true, Freeman already had a model for this form in Bulwer-Lytton's novel.[5] In *England and the English* (1833), his slightly acidic portrait of the brave new world of post-Reform England, Bulwer-Lytton had rejected the Tory antiquarianism of Walter Scott as nostalgia that ignored the possibility of linear progress. For such writers, he observes, "an improvement is only imagined a return to some ancient and dormant excellence."[6] By the time of the composition of *Harold,* however, the Whig reforms seemed both an inadequate and an inhumane solution to social problems as enormous as the condition of the Irish and the urban poor, and Bulwer-Lytton shows himself more open to a historical analysis.

Harold is a particularly interesting example of Bulwer-Lytton's own theory of what a historical novel should be. Unlike Scott's approach, in which the adventures of his heroes usually have a tangential relationship to those of real-life figures, later historical novelists, for example W. Harrison Ainsworth in *The Tower of London* (1840) and Charles Kingsley in another novel set in the period of the Conquest, *Hereward the Wake, the Last of the English* (1866), often placed historically documented figures (that is, figures not invented by the novelist) at the center of their stories. Bulwer-Lytton makes his story of the last Saxon king a tragic romance. Yet although openly applying his own interpretation, he roots his story in the historical source-material available to him. The novelist, he claims, is more entitled to the use of hypothesis and human motivation, and may in these respects be able to construct a more convincing reading of a historical incident than falls within the limitations of the avowedly factual historian: "Where History leaves us in the dark — where our curiosity is most excited, Fiction gropes amidst the ancient chronicles and seeks to detect and guess at the truth."[7] The novelist's right to guess, then, may be a closer approach to truth than the historian's limitation to data.

Bulwer-Lytton saw this right as exercized in the novelist's interpretation of human motivation. The historical novelist could "illustrate the actual history of the period; and to bring into fuller display than general History itself has done, the characters of the principal personages of the time, — the motives by which they were probably activated . . . "[8] Yet the characters in the Conquest story were not necessarily those that a novelist might have chosen, particularly in the case of Harold.[9] For earlier historians, even Protestant historians such as Foxe, Harold's character had been uncomplicated. He was a usurper with no legal claim to the throne, and God had punished him for his ambition.[10] In contrast, for Liberal historians who accepted Macaulay's version of history — at least to the extent that they believed that the people retained the right to approve the king — Harold, chosen for ability rather than blood, was the ideal monarch. But if Harold was a hero who represented the best of the English race, why, then, did Harold lose and William not only win, but establish a lasting dynasty? Between them, the books provide three main answers, and each answer is connected to some aspect of the Teutonic myth.

The Decline from the Golden Age

The first possible reason for the fall of the Saxons conformed with the idea of historical progress: they deserved defeat and replacement by a more vigorous and purposeful race. That Anglo-Saxon England had a Golden Age under Alfred the Great was, as we have seen, accepted by the vast majority of those who showed any interest in the period. Obviously, however, the Golden Age rapidly passed, and the last of the line was Edward the Confessor.

Few nineteenth-century commentators seem to have admired Edward, and in Freeman's paean to English patriotism, he fared particularly badly. Edward, the son of Ethelred II and Emma, had been raised in Normandy. This was scarcely blameworthy, since had he stayed in England he would probably not have survived the reigns of the Danish kings who preceded him: on a rash visit to England, his brother was blinded by Harold I (Harefoot) and died as a result. What *was* seen as Edward's personal failing was his preference for all things Norman: the French language; Norman friends and fashions; and the Roman Catholic church. Edward plays an important role in Bulwer-Lytton's *Harold,* where his half-promises of the crown of England to both Harold and William strengthen William's claim yet are explicitly noted as unconstitutional: Edward states that he made a promise to William when he "knew not the laws of England."[11] Bulwer-Lytton's Edward speaks French and surrounds himself with Norman friends; but worst of all, he has accepted the Norman religious "fanaticism" without achieving saintly generosity.[12]

Edward's degeneracy is further revealed by his failure in a central duty of a king — the preservation of the bloodline; in this, Bulwer-Lytton's seeming caricature actually proves to be less extreme than the portrait sketched by the supposedly factual historian Freeman. Whereas for medieval biographers, Edward's lack of children was seen as evidence of his saintly self-control,[13] Freeman saw this as possibly an attempt to thwart the ambitions of the king's father-in-law, Godwin,[14] but asserting the superior morality of his own age, further remarked, "If this story be true, a more enlightened standard of morality can see no virtue, but rather a crime, in his conduct" (*NC* 2:47). Edward (Freeman preferred the spelling Eadward and ensured that a godson of his was christened in the Anglo-Saxon form) represents for Freeman the contamination of the free Teutonic spirit by Norman vices. His "real affections were lavished on the Norman priests and gentlemen who flocked to his court as the land of promise" (*NC* 2:29).

Many Victorians might have viewed Edward's interest in hunting as one of his more redeeming, or at least more English, features. Freeman, who opposed blood-sports and vivisection, strongly disagreed. He hence characterizes Edward's hunting as a Norman vice — and one that provides the opportunity for other Norman vices. While Harold is campaigning to rescue England from the Welsh, Edward is said to be in the company of Harold's brother Tostig, "enjoying the slaughter of unresisting animals" (*NC* 2:497). But Freeman is not merely criticizing hunting. He claims that "Tostig, rather than Harold, was Eadward's personal favourite. He was the Hephaistion, the friend of Eadward, while Harold was rather the Krateros, the friend of the King" (*NC* 2:384). Again, Edward's actions are selfish and "un-English," in the tradition of "royal favorites," which Victorian readers might have concluded from their knowledge of the reigns of Edward II and James I was not in the interests of the kingdom. The allusion to Plutarch's *Life of Alexander* is for a Victorian work a surprisingly explicit reference to what Freeman in his study of William Rufus was to call "the habit of the ancient Greek and modern Turk" and "the special sin, as the Englishmen then deemed, of the Norman."[15] In the idealized conception of the Anglo-Saxon king, Edward therefore failed at least on the counts of his religion and the form of masculinity expected of a good Englishman.

The advantage of ascribing these weaknesses to Edward was that the decline from the Golden Age need not be seen as absolute. The Anglo-Saxon Chronicle ascribes the defeat of the English to God's punishment for the sins of the people.[16] Yet this sense of collective guilt is undermined by the Victorian attribution of the degeneracy not to the Saxons in decline, as in Scott's reading, but to Edward alone. Instead, the fall from the Golden Age *was* the Conquest rather than an explanation of its cause. Another cause was needed, and a second possibility was to center the story on what Bulwer-Lytton called the "tragedy" of Harold.

Harold as Tragic Hero: The Godwins

Harold, the second son of Godwin Earl of Wessex, was born about the year 1021. Godwin's origins are obscure: chroniclers of later years described him as the son of a cowherd, an idea that some of his admirers accepted and some rejected. Tennyson's Harold, when taunted with the fact that his grandfather was a cowherd, responds that the old man was nevertheless a true Saxon who told him stories "of Alfred and of Athelstane the Great," thus reminding him of his national heritage.[17] Freeman believes that Godwin's father Wulfnoth was a "ceorl," not a peasant but a small landowner (*NC* 2:665). The reading of Godwin as a self-made man is compatible with seeing him as an English patriot. Godwin first came to a position of influence under the Danish kings and married a daughter of Cnut, although she was not necessarily the mother of his sons. He increased his family's prosperity under Edward, but not, Freeman insists, because they "held the King in a sort of bondage" (*NC* 2:31). This idea, Freeman maintains, is Norman propaganda even contradicted by William of Malmesbury, whom he elsewhere describes as a "lying affected French scoundrel."[18] Godwin's daughter became Edward's queen, while his sons rose to key positions in the kingdom. The medieval story that God had struck Godwin dead for falsely swearing that he was not a participant in Edward's brother's death was a problem for those who, like Freeman, wished to claim him as an English statesman. Freeman refuses to believe that a true Englishman could have been implicated in an act as savage as the fatal blinding of Prince Alfred, and ascribes the tale, recounted only in an appendix to his history, to monkish propaganda.[19] Godwin's role is important, and particularly important to Freeman, since he is portrayed as like later English patriots: a great man in debate like Hampden, who "distinctly asserted the right of every Englishman to a fair trial" (*NC* 1:520). More pointedly, he was also like W. E. Gladstone, unless Gladstone was like him. His position of distinction was not obtained by birth, nor by cunning, but by disinterested merit. When Gladstone became prime minister in 1880, Freeman exulted: "Surely Godwine has come back, and Simon [de Montfort] has smitten the foes at Lewes."[20] But Godwin is of further importance as the father of Harold.

History remains divided over the last Saxon king, Harold II, but many of the least contested facts about him are not in the true heroic vein. In the Norman chronicles, he is characterized as a fratricide and a usurper. The main charges against him are first, that he was not the true heir to the English throne; second, that he made an oath to support William's claim; third, that he was irreligious; and fourth, that he was avaricious like his father. To these might be added a somewhat obscure private life: he was betrothed to William's daughter, although he himself was older than her father; in his last years he married the sister of Edwin and Morcar, the northern earls; and his body was identified through "certain marks" by his lover, a woman named Edith.[21] He had no children by his surviving wife, but at least two by another relationship, Harold and Magnus, who after their father's death seem to have lived in Norway.[22]

Against all these may be set the claims for William: he was Edward the Confessor's promised heir and counted on Harold's support of his claim, ratified by the promise of his daughter. He rewarded his soldiers well, was a devout churchman, and most unusually for a prince of his time, was strictly monogamous.

To make Harold a hero, then, might seem difficult. But his defenders believed that Harold's first quality was patriotism. He had fought successful campaigns in Ireland and Wales and after his father's death assumed the earldom of Wessex. The charge of avarice was the one most easily dismissed: Harold did not distribute booty to his followers because he respected one of the most sacred rights of the English: their property.[23] The dismissal of other charges against Harold required an even more creative use of documentary evidence. Freeman has a simple solution to the standard historian's problem of the reliability of sources. Observing that both Thierry's *History of the Conquest* and Palgrave's *History of Normandy and of England*, the two most influential histories of the period before his own, fail in this respect, he remarks:

Both writers singularly resemble each other in a certain lack of critical power. Nothing in any period of history, above all nothing in the period of history with which I am concerned, is more necessary than to distinguish between the relative value of different authorities. (*NC* 1:vx)

This statement is superficially in accord with the view of objective history advanced by Freeman's German contemporary, Leopold von Ranke.[24] But in practice, Freeman's method of assessing the "relative values of different authorities" proves dependent on the assumption that Norman authorities are of less value than English ones. Although Freeman prefers the Normans to the rest of the French, he repeatedly claims that "the Norman writers never held truth to be of any moment when the relations of Normandy and England were concerned."[25]

That the basis of this statement is Freeman's racism is shown by his use of a "Norman" source, the *Ecclesiastical History* of Orderic Vitalis. Orderic was most probably an Anglo-Norman born in England in 1075. His first language was English, but at the age of ten he became a monk in the Monastery of St. Evroul in Normandy and never returned to England. For Freeman, this heritage made him superior to the average Norman, and he notes that the chronicler "fluctuates between his two characters of born Englishman and Norman monk" (*NC* 2:551). Freeman generally accepts Orderic's opinion on ecclesiastical matters but dismisses his justification of the Norman cause.

One does not need to be an ardent Teutonist to suspect that, at least in the question of who should be king of England, Orderic shows a Norman bias. The objective of the civil part of his history is to justify the Norman claim to England. William's battle at Hastings becomes for Orderic a form of divinely sanctioned revenge, not only for the duke himself but also for the many others whom Harold had wronged through his ambition.[26] For English patriots, Orderic might seem to be a worthless source — yet where his accounts appeal to them, such as in the story of Harold's virtuous brother Gurth pleading with him not to violate his oath by fighting in person at Senlac, they follow him as authentic.[27]

A similar application of race as a determinant of historical value in characterizing Harold is found in the use made of biographies of Edward the Confessor. In 1858, Henry Richards Luard edited three Lives of Edward the Confessor for the Rolls Series. All three versions tell of the great piety of the king, the miracles he performed in life and death, and some of his visions.[28] But while all imply that Edward was far from the most dynamic personality in his kingdom, the first two Lives, in Norman French, tell of the evil House of Godwin.

If the third Life, written in Latin, is what it purports to be, an offering to Edward's queen Edith, it would predate the Norman-French versions. Since Edith was both Edward's wife and Godwin's daughter, the tone is laudatory to both the king's and the queen's families, but the narrative focuses mainly on the Godwins. Having decided that the third Life is the earliest and the most English, Luard remarks: "On the whole, we may conclude that there is here a far more correct estimate of the character of Godwin than that given by Norman writers."[29] But if Luard is correct in believing this a contemporary work, the very fact that it is addressed to Edith surely means that every attempt will be made to present her family in a favorable light.

This document is important for Freeman, who accepts that it was written "within eight years" of the events it describes and frequently cites the authority of "the contemporary Biographer."[30] But Luard and Freeman ignore the obvious conclusion that if this writer's knowledge was so immediate, some points in the text must be deliberate suppressions of fact. Luard, for example, fails to note that Harold is here the eldest of four sons, whereas the Anglo-Saxon Chronicle specifically mentions that Godwin's eldest son Sweyn fell into disgrace for various misdeeds and later died on pilgrimage. By blaming Edward's archbishop of Canterbury, Robert of Jumièges, for the Godwins' exile, the biographer ignores what is recorded elsewhere, that part of the tension between Godwin and the king was due to the behavior of Sweyn. It is also known that Edward sent Godwin's youngest son Wulfnoth as a hostage into the safekeeping of William of Normandy — a standard practice of the age, but one demonstrating that even after their reconciliation a distrust remained between the two men.

Although the English historians saw these writings as having differing degrees of historical authority, elements of all became combined in the attempt to construct a consistent reading of the story of the Conquest. Orderic's evidence might seem rejected by Freeman and the others, but the story of the pleas of Harold's mother and brother Gurth before Senlac, which have a suspiciously conventional tone, are adopted as literal fact by Freeman and featured by Bulwer-Lytton and Tennyson. The Latin Life (BM Harley 526) is privileged despite the fact that the author deliberately glosses over the less attractive details of the House of Godwin.

All of these choices of fact affect the English reading of Harold. But the story of his oath to William, in which Harold seemed to contravene standards of English behavior, was the most crucial point in assessing his role as a tragic hero.

Harold's Oath

Harold's oath is central to the nineteenth-century vision of the Conquest as personal tragedy. Freeman might attempt to deny the significance of his hero's act, but the fact most uncomfortable to a nationalist reading of the conflict between Harold and William was unavoidable: that Harold made an oath, and he broke it.

Harold's oath did not assume tragic proportions only for nineteenth-century writers. The centrality of this act was pointed out by what is one of the very earliest versions of the story, the Bayeux Tapestry. The Bayeux Tapestry, actually an embroidery, is now one of the best-known pieces of evidence concerning the events of 1066 and immediately preceding. Its historical significance, however, was virtually ignored until the eighteenth century. Yet new interest in the embroidery prompted some historians, including

Freeman, to make a special visit to Bayeux in order to view it as historical evidence.

Almost certainly commissioned for the Norman city where it still remains, the embroidery may have been executed in England, but with the objective of creating a distinctively Norman interpretation of the events of the Conquest. Still, the main focus is on the story of Harold. As it now exists — perhaps the end has been lost, but the last surviving scene shows the chaos of battle after Harold's death — the tapestry tells the story of the fall of Harold in a clearly moralized form: Harold was false to his sacred oath, depicted in the central scene of the embroidery.

Yet this was less a tragedy than a morality tale, and Harold's nineteenth-century defenders apparently felt that more substance was needed to the story. The first possibility, which was adopted by Freeman, was to argue that Harold's original action may have been morally questionable, but that most of the blame must lie on the Normans. Certain problems, however, remain. When did this incident occur? Did Harold take the oath of his own free will or not?

In remarkable detail, the Bayeux Tapestry portrays Harold setting out on a sea voyage, apparently with a definite purpose.[31] The implied reason for his journey is that he is on an embassy between Edward the Confessor and his declared heir, William. Harold is portrayed as on friendly terms with William: the oath is given of his own free will and with full knowledge of what it entails.

The earliest English chroniclers do not mention Harold's oath, but Freeman cannot deny its existence, or that of the trip to William's court. In a short biography of William written for the Twelve English Statesmen series, Freeman observes: "We can hardly doubt that Harold swore some oath to William which he did not keep."[32] This event he places about 1064, but he remains reluctant to determine the purpose of Harold's voyage: again, he assumes that its outcome was accidental. Freeman does, however, follow the later English interpretation that Harold did not realize that a promise casually given was on the bones of the relics of Norman saints. The historian's rationalist English solution to this is twofold. First, oaths on the bones of the saints count for nothing, and he would think

worse of Harold if he took them seriously. Second, and most significantly, Harold could not promise William the crown of England,
since constitutionally, the crown was not his to give. Similarly, if
Edward had promised the crown to William, that too was unconstitutional. He hence concludes that "it is the honour of the Norman rather than that of the Englishman which is staked on its [the
story's] truth or falsehood" (*NC* 3:242).

Freeman's reference to honor (he defends Harold's honor in
thirty closely printed pages in an appendix to his *Norman Conquest*
[3:677–707]) points to an important problem for apologists for the
Saxons. Harold could scarcely be the ideal Englishman if he was
not true to his word. Freeman's strongest argument is thus that
Harold had no right to make such a promise. The best support for
this is the authority of the generally pro-Saxon Florence of Worcester, who notes that Harold was "elected by all the leading men of
England to the royal office."[33] Had Harold made an oath to William, he was acting in direct violation of constitutional practice; as
the servant of the English people, he was thus under a more solemn
obligation to break his oath than to keep it. Freeman does not,
however, have the support of Palgrave, one of the best-informed
authorities on the constitution. Palgrave states that since Harold
was not a member of the royal house, his election was in violation
of the constitution; and, moreover, that his end was punishment for
his ambition. After Stamford Bridge, Palgrave portrays Harold
"banqueting in festal triumph, with hands embrued in the blood of
a brother. . . . Harold was influenced by that obstinate, self-willed
determination, which leads the sinner on to his fate."[34] Palgrave's
Harold, indeed, not only resembles the traditional image advanced
by earlier historians but also bears a certain similarity to Shakespeare's portrayal of Harold's contemporary, Macbeth.[35]

Bulwer-Lytton and Tennyson, not surprisingly, are less interested in the constitutional logic of the question than in the psy-
chological implications. Ironically, it is not Freeman, with his
conviction that other nations may lie but the English do not, but the
fiction writers who are prepared to approach this question.

In an interesting alteration of the main source available to
him, that of the generally unsympathetic Palgrave, Bulwer-Lytton's

Harold is a true romantic hero, and later writers on the topic — not only the imaginative interpreter Tennyson but also the supposedly factual interpreter Freeman — acknowledged a debt to this reading of Harold's character.[36] Bulwer-Lytton's Harold travels to Normandy to release his youngest brother Wulfnoth and his nephew Haco, who have been held as hostages by William on King Edward's behalf. Harold's motivation is thus family centered. His decision to take the oath is also family centered: Wulfnoth exerts emotional pressure on Harold to accept so that they can leave, warning the free-spirited Saxon of the horrors of Norman imprisonment. In accordance with the later English version, Harold takes the oath without realizing that his hand is upon the reliquaries of Norman saints.

Tennyson's version, which was influenced both by Bulwer-Lytton and by Freeman, follows the same pattern. Spurred on by Wulfnoth and fearful of imprisonment and blindness, Harold agrees to lie and take the oath — only for William to reveal that he has sworn on "The holy bones of all the Canonised / From all the holiest shrines in Normandy!" (*Harold* 2.2). But although Harold rejects the superstition, he is not unmarked by breaking his oath. The cynical archbishop of Canterbury, Stigand, may have given Harold absolution for his action, but the old King Edward tells Harold: "Stigand is not canonical enough / To save thee from the wrath of Norman Saints." When Stigand protests that English saints can counteract them, Edward states that the Norman saints are "mightier than our own" (*Harold* 3.1). In the area of religion, England is to be temporarily overthrown.

Although Henry James correctly observed that Tennyson had "very frankly fashioned his play upon the model of the Shakespearian 'histories,'"[37] some of Tennyson's uses of what might initially seem the least innovative of stage conventions reveal an underlying anxiety similar to that found in *Becket*. Harold invokes the spirits of the dead to reveal his future. Harold's lover Edith provides a traditional mad-scene before expiring on his body. But the contents of these scenes disclose a fear that is genuine. Among the spirits that appear to Harold on the eve of the Battle of Senlac are the "Norman saints." Edith exclaims in her madness: "The Holy

Father strangled him with a hair / Of Peter . . ." (*Harold* 5.2).
Following Stigand's example, Freeman might scoff and say that
there is nothing in prophecies and superstition. Yet Tennyson's
play reveals a fear that the power of Roman Catholicism may be
real, and that it is this power by which England is to be overthrown. Like Henry II, Harold is fighting a religion hostile to the
English spirit.

But what makes this religion stronger than Harold is here implied to be his own sin. Harold's oath is crucial to interpretations of
the story of Harold and William because, as we have seen, from the
Reformation onwards the English had laid a special claim to a
greater commitment to truth than found in Roman Catholicism.
The Reformation question, "Thynke yow a Romane with the Romanes can not lye?" had recently been repeated in a new form by
Charles Kingsley: "Truth, for its own sake, had never been a virtue
with the Roman clergy."[38] John Henry Newman, to whom Kingsley
attributed the reconfirmation of this point of view, may be said to
have won the ensuing debate; but the nature of his response did not
entirely dismiss the implied opposition: Romans lie, but the English
do not. Harold, then, is not simply an eleventh-century warrior: he
becomes the representative of the English — and Anglican — gentleman, and in this role, integrity would be expected to be a crucial
part of his character.

For Tennyson, Harold's failure of integrity becomes a "tragic
flaw." Harold asks his brother Wulfnoth: "Is it not better still to
speak the truth?" But in living as a Norman hostage Wulfnoth has
grown accustomed to Norman ways and replies: "Not here, or thou
wilt never hence nor I." Harold still doubts but makes the oath that
he never intends to keep. Although on his return to England he is
absolved of his oath by the English bishops, Harold has still committed a sin against a truth that allows for no temporizing. The
absolute nature of truth cannot be rejected, and Harold's life is
marred from this point forward. Harold's personal tragedy hence
provides his audience with a moral example: even with the goal of
being true to England, one should never fail to act as a true Englishman.

Both Tennyson and Bulwer-Lytton end their stories with the

finding of Harold's body after he has been killed by an arrow in the eye.[39] The last representative of the old Saxon era is seen to have died perhaps partly because of personal ambition, but largely because his standards of integrity were too acute for the world in which he lived, and for the demands that he made upon himself. As such, the story is not entirely tragic. Had Harold lived now, the writers suggest, we could have accepted him as one of ourselves. And just as the overthrow of the constitution was temporary, so was the overthrow of the Saxon race personified in Harold.

In his search for Anglo-Norman narratives, Francisque Michel had discovered a medieval narrative suggesting that Harold had not actually died at the Conquest but had lived on as a hermit.[40] Although this story would seem to support claims that Harold had indeed been a champion to the English people, and was even remembered as a savior-king who might return, just as King Arthur was expected to return, nineteenth-century writers preferred to imagine Harold's survival not in the individual form of a priest, but in the general character of the English people. Bulwer-Lytton's novel concludes:

> Eight centuries have rolled away, and where is the Norman now? or where is not the Saxon? . . . In many a noiseless field, with Thoughts for Armies, your relics, O Saxon Heroes, have won back the victory from the bones of the Norman saints; and whenever, with fairer fates, Freedom opposes Force, and Justice, redeeming the old defeat, smites down the armed Frauds that would consecrate the wrong, — smile, O soul of our Saxon Harold, smile, appeased, on the Saxon's land! (*H/WBL*, 481; 12:9)

In the war between races, the Saxons won. But they won by the superiority of their moral code, and the old saintly fraud was defeated. Burrow correctly notes that this is a problem in a Whig conception of tragedy: in fact, a "Whig tragedy" is almost a contradiction in terms. The tragedy of Harold is rendered less poignant by the realization shared between author and audience that

England was to triumph in the end. Burrow observes that "in Whig history there are no important irrevocable losses: the long run compensates for all."[41] Perhaps, then, Harold became a hero neither for his achievements nor his failures, but merely because of the resonances suggested by his role as the last of the Saxon kings.

William the Norman

The third possible way to understand why the Saxons had lost in 1066 was to reconsider the role of William. Through the efforts of his admirers, Harold had been historically reassessed and was now considered a good king, conforming with the liberal theory that a king's primary right to rule was through the will of the people. But he had still been defeated by William of Normandy. The eighteenth-century radical judgment of William had been that he was a cruel tyrant: a ravager of the country, a wife-beater, a man who took his revenge in the form of mutilation—but above all, a subverter of the English constitution. By the late 1860s, when Disraeli's parliamentary reform act had extended the franchise to much of the middle class, commitment to this interpretation of William as the figurehead of the Norman destruction of the constitution was far less vocal. Palgrave had argued for the continuity of English law, and although the Teutonists dissented over the extent of the change brought about by 1066, many of them would have agreed that had the constitution ever been wrecked, it had now been restored. Freeman concludes in *The Growth of the English Constitution:* "Our present Sovereign reigns by as good a right as Ælfred or Harold"[42]—a statement based on the assumption that his own arguments for Harold's constitutionality had been generally accepted.

If, then, William was no longer interpreted politically as an evil usurper and bringer of tyranny, some reassessment of his virtues and vices seemed necessary. And the basis of this reassessment proves again to be the assumption that race affects moral characteristics. Whereas earlier in the century use of Saxon and Norman figures had been, implicitly or explicitly, socially critical, the later stress is not on capturing the essential nature of English society as a whole but rather on a less critical presentation of English society as composed of individuals reflecting a shared sense of identity. Yet almost as important as a comprehension of what this identity *was* became a sense of what it was *not*. If Harold had been reclaimed as a true English hero in personal terms, then William also might be less the representative of a political regime than the emblem of a personal code of conduct.

Writers as diverse in opinion as Freeman and Charlotte Yonge believed that William was one of the greatest men in English history. "In speaking of William the Conqueror," notes Yonge, "we are speaking of a really great man."[43] This is one point with which Freeman would have agreed. Freeman even asserted that the course of English history over the past eight hundred years was largely the result of "the personal character of a single man" — that man, of course, being William. Even William's keenest apologists, however, can scarcely ignore some of his bloodier deeds, such as his treatment of his hostages at the siege of Alençon. When the defenders of the city mocked William on the basis that his mother was a tanner's daughter, William tore out the eyes and cut off the hands and feet of his hostages and hurled the parts over the wall into the city. Freeman states: "Personal insult is always hard for princes to bear, and the wrath of William was stirred up to a pitch which made him for once depart from his usual moderation towards conquered enemies."[44] Granted that William's position as a bastard of Robert, Duke of Normandy, presented him with particular problems and dangers even in surviving to adulthood, a comment such as this, or the statement that William was so religious that he preferred to mutilate people rather than endanger their souls, seems strangely indulgent — particularly from a leading antivivisectionist.[45]

Liberals are more critical, though, when discussing William's treatment of his English subjects; and here an important distinction emerges in the consideration of his faults. Formerly, William had been the destroyer of the abstract, the English constitution. William was now seen to have deprived Harold of his throne and to have delivered English land and English people into the hands of his Norman vassals. The story of Harold's oath did not dilute the fact that Harold had been chosen king by the English people, and had "received, alone among English kings, the Crown of England as the free gift of her people, and, alone among English kings, died axe in hand on her own soil, in defence of England against foreign invaders" (*NC* 2:43). Harold's appointment was "the free choice of a free people," so that "never was there a more lawful ruler in this world than Harold."[46] William's violation of the English constitution, then, was in concrete, personal form. Harold was king by means of the constitution, and William subverted that constitution by destroying Harold.

In this lack of respect for English freedoms, William showed himself to be less a member of the "Teuton kindred" than a foreigner. Furthermore, William may have pledged himself to respect the laws of England — the constitution at least partly subjugating him — and similarly may have stressed the legality of his claim to the English throne; but William had despoiled England, which Harold was recorded as having refused to do. Even the enfranchised Victorian Liberals were not so removed from their radical predecessors that they did not recognize that the power of property was still largely in the hands of the Normans and that this was the work of William. For his admirers, William was not entirely alien. He was not as committed to England as Harold had been, but his qualities, notably courage and magnanimity towards his enemies (or at least a select few of them), could be seen as Teutonic: here was none of the Norman effeminacy seen in John and Edward the Confessor. On the other hand, William was not entirely a Teuton. He was also a Roman, and as such had forced England away from the path that the Victorians believed their nation was ultimately destined to follow.

In their imputed attitudes to religion and to codes of behavior, Harold and William most clearly reveal a contrast in which Harold is the Teuton and William the Roman. William is observed in all old histories to have had an unusual commitment to religion, not merely in principle but in orthodox attachment to the Roman Catholic church. As the characterization of Thomas Becket reveals, the tradition still commonly prevailed that in general tendency, Anglo-Saxon England was Roman Catholic but perhaps not entirely committed to Roman practices. Particularly in Bulwer-Lytton's *Harold*, Harold is seen to believe in the Anglo-Saxon church, and even to have a sympathy for the morality of the pagan religions. Harold's main link to the Teutonic religions is through the guardian of his lover Edith. Hilda, Bulwer-Lytton's own invention (although seemingly inspired by Scott's Ulrica), is an old Danish witch, with memory of past customs and illicit knowledge of the future. Harold's association with her suggests that the old ways of the northern peoples are only shallowly covered by the veneer of an unsatisfying Christianity.

Harold's commitment to a moral perspective further leads Bulwer-Lytton, however improbably, to depict him as a student of the classics. Bulwer-Lytton portrays an England in which the Saxon priests are ignorant and the Norman priests use cunning to control Edward and his people by superstition. In such a society, Harold stands as an exception in being guided in his religion by "common sense." A Victorian in advance of his age, Harold equates religion and good citizenship:

> He stood aloof from the rude superstition of his age, and early in life made himself the arbiter of his own conscience. Reducing his religion to the simplest elements of our creed, he found rather in the Heathen authors than in the lives of the Saints, his notions of the larger morality which relates to the citizen and the man. (*H/WBL*, 284–285; 4:1)

Harold, then, absorbs from the old Roman tradition what were seen as the non-Roman qualities of patriotism, fortitude, justice, and truth. The phrase "elements of our creed" here surely applies not to Christianity in general but to the assumed creed of the reader — a sensible, unemotive Anglicanism.

In Freeman's opinion, Harold was not irreligious, having a strong commitment to his patronage of Waltham Abbey. "No special lover of monks" (*NC* 2:413), Harold is said to have been "a deliberate and enlightened patron of the secular clergy. . . . In his eyes, even a married priest was not a monster of vice." Freeman notes that his search for foreign enlightenment directed him to Teutonic, not Roman, thinkers (*NC* 2:432). Such an attitude to religion was, Freeman concludes, "proof of his steady and clear-sighted patriotism." Harold is here again a Church of England man.

Like William, Harold is portrayed as having two main spiritual influences. One of these was the virtuous Aldred (also called Ealdred or Alred), archbishop of York. Aldred represents in most versions the best of the Saxon church — perhaps not well educated, but with a sincere regard for the welfare of the nation. In some documentary sources, Aldred is said to have crowned Harold. Bulwer-Lytton makes Aldred Harold's leading spiritual advisor, who assures him that breaking his oath is better than betraying England.

Harold's archbishop of Canterbury, Stigand, is a more controversial figure. Stigand seems to have been implicated in political intrigues with the Godwins in the 1050s; when the Norman Robert of Jumièges was driven out, Stigand succeeded to the primacy.[47] Bulwer-Lytton follows the Norman sources in making Stigand "the world-man and the miser" who scoffs cynically at the prophecies of the dying Edward as a sign of the old king's "dotage" (*H/WBL*, 424; 11:1). In contrast, Tennyson's Stigand is perhaps more matter-of-fact than merely a scoffer. He, not Aldred, absolves Harold from his oath, which certainly undercuts the spiritual value of the absolution. He is also a miser but gives Harold access to his treasure if needed against the Normans. Stigand thus proves that although he is fond of money, he is also committed to England. This is unquestionably derived from Freeman's opinion of Stigand. Freeman sees the "stout-hearted Englishman" as primarily a statesman and royal advisor, who will not allow religion to outweigh common sense. As such, he is also a "patriot." The story of Stigand has important associations with the story of Harold, for they were both the last of the Saxon lines, and all evidence suggests that the historical Harold and Stigand indeed worked together. What the Teutonists rejected was the traditional argument that they were unsanctioned rulers, replacing it with the contention that Harold and Stigand were more than men of their time. They were king and archbishop in conformity with the eternal English principles of a king with the approval of the people and a church with the approval of the king. Such an interpretation in its very nature cannot be medieval: like the nineteenth-century conception of Henry II and Becket, it is a post-Reformation reading of a medieval story. But the reading of history in the light of subsequent events was taken further in the consideration of William's relations with the church.

In contrast to Harold's spiritual advisors, whose first commitment is seen to be to England, the two men who represent William's religious opinions reveal a commitment to Rome. With the exception of his brother Odo, the warlike bishop of Bayeux, William's main spiritual guide was Lanfranc of Bec. Lanfranc was born in Pavia, Lombardy, and was one of the foremost scholars of an unscholarly age. None of the interpreters of this period question his ability. Nevertheless, Lanfranc was cast as a leading villain in the Norman Conquest. A champion of papal dominion, Lanfranc was the man who Romanized the Teutonic William and hence brought about the most feared conquest of England — the conquest of religion.

Theologically, Lanfranc was seen as in opposition to the moderate principles of English Christianity. But he was even more the link between Roman and Teuton in William's alliance with the pope. Through Lanfranc, his spiritual advisor and minister, William obtained papal sanction first for his consanguineous marriage to Matilda — the fiction writers imagine that Harold could not obtain such sanction for his own wedding to Edith — and later for his invasion of England. By means of Lanfranc's smooth negotiations, the invasion gained the status of not a usurpation but a crusade. Bulwer-Lytton visualizes Lanfranc proposing a deliberate destruction of the Saxons: like a devilish tempter, Lanfranc whispers in William's ear that if he negotiates with the pope, William will be able to "'behold the sun of the Saxon that sets evermore on England!'" (*H/WBL*, 435; 11:8). As a Roman, Lanfranc has no innate conception of freedom, but he does have a hatred of Saxon domination, and his plan here is phrased in both racial and religious terms. Lanfranc believes that he can bring about the permanent domination of Rome over the English. After the Conquest, he is to replace the Saxon Stigand as archbishop of Canterbury and thus assume a position where he can help William in the consolidation of his power. The Roman character of this coalition is shown by Freeman's sentence: "And truly William and Lanfranc ruled together in their island Empire as no Pope and Caesar ever ruled together in the Imperial city itself" (*NC* 4:348).

The Roman characteristics of the church supported by William are demonstrated to have "Romanized" his own disposition. William may be in broader outlines Teutonic, but he has the characteristic that Kingsley claimed the Teutons never succeeded in wresting from the Romans, namely, "cunning." Perhaps, then, Harold should indeed have been defeated by William — since William, as a Roman, could benefit from cunning, and Harold, as a Saxon, was tainting his own purity by using deceit. A telling episode occurs in the Battle of Senlac. Freeman notes: "In the Norman character the fox and the lion were mingled in nearly equal shares; strength and daring had failed, but the prize might perhaps still be gained by craft" (*NC* 4:487). Hence, unable to move the Saxon soldiers from their defensive position, William orders his soldiers to pretend to retreat. When the valiant but unsuspecting Saxons chase them down the hill, the Normans are at last able to breach the defensive wall. Bravery loses to cunning. The Northmen had learned a strong lesson from their stay in the land of the Romanized French — one which affected their language, their religion, and finally their characters.

The English writers' wish to find a Roman to blame for the shortcomings of the Teuton William may have caused them to overstate Lanfranc's part in shaping William's policy. And indeed, some Teutonists saw him very differently from Bulwer-Lytton's reading of him as the sly Italian priest of romance. Hook, who had seen Stigand as patriotic, also saw merit in Lanfranc: in Hook's opinion Lanfranc had, like a good Church of England man, seen his master not in the pope but in his king.[48] But again the fear of the influence of Romanism surfaces in the Victorian version of the Conquest. Most writers see Lanfranc as a wily Romanist and, above all, not as William's friend but as the loyal follower of Hildebrand.

Bismarck's famous statement of 1872, "Nach Canossa gehen

wir nicht" ("We will not go to Canossa"), reveals a long memory of the struggle between the Italian and German peoples even before their nations existed. But for the Teutonists, Canossa, where in 1077 Pope Gregory VII won submission from the German emperor Henry IV, had broader implications. Gregory VII, or Hildebrand, as British writers preferred to call him, personified to the nineteenth century the conflict between the Teutonic and Roman peoples.

Despite his Germanic name, Hildebrand was a Tuscan. He became abbot at Clugni, and later under Leo IX and Alexander II assumed internationally influential offices. Not until 1073 was Hildebrand to become pope himself, but both before and after his elevation he seems to have remained on amicable terms with William of Normandy — although the latter refused to give him entire control over ecclesiastical appointments. All of Hildebrand's actions and beliefs seemed to English commentators to have been directed towards laying the foundations for the modern papacy;[49] and most notably, as Henry II of England observes in Tennyson's *Becket,* he had humiliated Henry IV.

The last cause for resentment, forcibly expressed by James Stephen in his long *Edinburgh Review* article on Hildebrand (1845), suggests that English readers would identify more readily with the German emperor than with the Italian pope. Stephen observes that although the pope sternly demanded just actions by the rulers of Europe, he was indulgent of Norman oppression.[50] Stephen implies that Hildebrand recognized the Normans as his flock, the true children of the Roman church; the Normans and papacy unite to seek opportunities to oppress the Germanic peoples.

Thus characterized, Hildebrand makes an interesting entry into the story of the Conquest. In some versions, indeed, he becomes almost the mastermind behind a Roman Catholic plot. When describing how the two Italian priests, Lanfranc and Hildebrand, worked together, Bulwer-Lytton appends a note:

> It is curious to notice how England was represented as a country almost heathen; its conquest was regarded quite as a pious, benevolent act of charity — a sort of mission

for converting the savages. And all this while England was under the most slavish ecclesiastical domination, and the priesthood possessed a third of its land! But the heart of England never forgave the league of the Pope with the Conqueror; and the seeds of the Reformed Religion were trampled deep into the Saxon soil by the foot of the invading Norman. (*H/WBL*, 438; 11:8)

This reading was not entirely Anglican paranoia: the chronicle sources confirm that William's invasion of England had the pope's approval, most mentioning the papal banner borne by William's men. The chronicles do not, however, mention the involvement of Hildebrand. Most probably, as archdeacon of Rome, he was involved in the negotiations with William's envoys. And it seems that as Pope Gregory VII, he claimed some personal credit in having persuaded the pope to give his sanction to the Norman cause.[51] Yet the historians move into the murky world of popish plotting when W.R.W. Stephens observes that "Hildebrand had the sagacity to see that if the enterprise of William succeeded, England would be brought within the more direct influence of Rome. . . . The ecclesiastical even more than the political liberties of England were overthrown on the day when William conquered Harold."[52] The disciple and biographer of Freeman here portrays the Romans as deliberately having helped bring about the downfall of Teutonic freedom; and the ideal man to be seen as responsible for this farsighted plot was Hildebrand, enemy of the Teutonic nations. Given such an ally, William of Normandy could scarcely lose; given such an opponent, Harold, the champion of freedom in religion, could not hope to win. The invasion of 1066 brought Normans and Bretons into England, but it also brought Romans. Even Freeman, the historian most willing to acquit William of the charge of being Roman, believes that his Teuton hero helped introduce Romanism into England:

William came, as it might seem, to pour a new Latin and Celtic infusion into Teutonic England. He brought his Romanized Northmen and the Welsh of lesser Britain to

bear rule over Saxons, Angles, and Danes who had
never fallen away from their Teutonic heritage.[53]

The final judgment of William's character may be seen to rest on
this: so much as he was Teutonic, his actions might be excusable;
but so much as he was Roman, his actions required, and had received, the full vengeance of history. In the time of Thomas Paine,
judgments of William had depended on a moral interpretation of
human rights, but now the morality first depended on racial interpretation. A myth of politics, once sacred to radical reformers, was
becoming fixed as a conformist myth of racial identity.

A Dissenting Voice: Matthew Arnold

By the time of the *Norman Conquest*, the liberal,
patriotic, Broad Church tendency of the Teutonists was well established, and Freeman could expect to win some support for the idea
that the Teuton spirit had finally triumphed. Such a characterization of a period once again begs the question of whether a particular historical moment can have a distinct mood: whether, in fact,
there can be such a thing as a "spirit of the age." Of course, any age
will have its dissenting voices; the interest in the classics and the
strength of the English Catholics during this period demonstrates
diversity. One might note, however, that the Battle of the Books no
longer necessarily implied commitment to either ancient or modern
texts, but not to both. A Teutonist could also be a classicist: indeed,
Thomas Arnold is both the reviver of interest in the classics and a
key influence on the shaping of the image of a "true Englishman."
Martin Bernal has recently argued that for such thinkers, the idea
of ancient Greece was less threatening than the possibility of the
influence of non-Aryan cultures.[54] An interest in ancient Greece and
Rome, then, was not incompatible with a Teutonist point of view.
Similarly, even Roman Catholics, seemingly opposed to the Teutonists, were nevertheless drawn into a way of thinking that, while

implying a rejection of the interpretation of the Conquest advanced by the Liberals, did not contest the importance of this period of history.[55]

But was there still room for flexibility of interpretation? Charlotte Yonge had pushed interpretations of the Conquest perhaps as far as they would go in a conservative direction: it was left to Matthew Arnold to challenge whether historically based nationalism was really as much within the liberal tradition as Freeman and his allies claimed. The younger Arnold did not write specifically on the theme of the Conquest. His writings on Teutonism, however, deserve examination within the context of the Liberal-affiliated writers of the 1860s, since by not attempting to explain away the Conquest Arnold implicitly questioned his contemporaries' assertion of Saxon continuity. Arnold's stance demonstrates how a writer dissenting from the mainstream nationalistic liberalism of the period, even when challenging the limitations of the prevailing Saxon-and-Norman interpretation, nevertheless remained within the bounds of certain cultural barriers.[56] Question as he might the historical intepretation advanced by those he classed as "vulgar Liberals," Arnold never entirely escaped the burden of his own family and national history.

As we have seen, Matthew Arnold's father Thomas was a liberal churchman of generally Latitudinarian views, but one who did not reject the concept of a state religion. In some ways, indeed, in considerations of church and state, the state was more important to the elder Arnold than specific doctrines of the church. Matthew Arnold himself was not particularly interested in the church, but in his work as a school inspector, he was the servant of the state. In his writings on culture and education, the consideration of one of the questions that had preoccupied his father — what it meant to be a liberal Englishman — is clearly still important to him.

In *Culture and Anarchy*, Arnold is eager to dissociate his personal beliefs from those of the mainstream patriotic Liberals, the devoted Teutonists. The exact points of differentiation, however, are not perhaps as clear as is often asserted.

Born in 1822, Arnold was raised in a society in which a liberal characteristic was the admiration of all things German. As early as

1833, Bulwer-Lytton had drawn British attention to the advantages of the Prussian education system.[57] In the years that followed, the Prussian model of practical, nationalist education was increasingly quoted by Liberals as a positive example. In the preface to his 1868 study of Continental schools and universities, Arnold quoted Liberal (and also some Conservative) claims that the Prussian system was the best in Europe.[58] Conservatives might advance the values of Gothicism, which Liberals now saw as part of the spectre known as Rome; radicals such as George Grote might aspire to Athenian democracy; but mainstream Liberals rejected both these alternatives and, taking Germany as both a cultural parent and a contemporary model, claimed an indigenous, nonclassicist cultural base — a world in which, for example, a rough-mannered Teuton such as found in Kingsley's *Hereward the Wake* might be a hero. This was a rejection not perhaps of the values of paternalism, nor of idealistic egalitarianism, but rather of the elitism of caste and intellect upon which they were based. Even when Frederick Furnivall and others attempted to make the English-language tradition part of the intellectual canon, their efforts were associated with a belief in popular education and a rejection of the privileging of Rome and the classical tradition introduced by the Normans.

Furnivall's efforts were partially successful: English works such as the *Canterbury Tales* have subsequently become studied as literature, in editions resembling those of classical texts.[59] But the literary canon has at the same time privileged the views of other Victorians: for example, John Ruskin, with his search for stability in the Gothic Middle Ages, and Matthew Arnold himself, with his quest for spiritual freedom through true culture. Perhaps in his own time, however, Arnold's conquest of the "Philistines" was less complete. His condemnation of Philistines may now be better known than the attitudes he was criticizing. But two important considerations should not be overlooked. First, unless those attitudes had had real substance, Arnold would scarcely have expended his creative energy in opposing them. Second, the very act of opposition forces Arnold himself to consider where precisely he stands in relation to prevailing ideas. And though he may hold himself apart, he cannot entirely separate himself from the Liberal view of history.

The word "Philistine" may suggest an ancient Middle Eastern tribe; in Arnold's use of the word there is a strong association between "Philistine" and "Anglo-Saxon." "Philistine" was used in Germany in the early nineteenth century to denote those who had not received a university education and who tended to practical opinions — in many ways, the reverse of "romantic."[60] Carlyle used the word as a consciously German borrowing in his early writings, including *Sartor Resartus*.[61] In Arnold's essays, Philistinism assumed a slightly different significance. He first discussed the word in his 1863 essay on Heine, observing that it "must have originally meant, in the mind of those who invented the nickname, a strong, dogged, unenlightened opponent of the chosen people, the people of the light."[62] In *Culture and Anarchy* Arnold proceeds to divide the people of England into Barbarians (aristocrats), Philistines (the middle class), and Populace (the working class).[63] While Arnold shows some concern for the state of the Populace, his principal mission is to consider the role of the middle class. Arnold is not, of course, speaking of the entire group, for he concedes that in some individuals "humanity" triumphs over environment. Rather, he is exposing the petit-bourgeois attitudes that are most strongly associated with Anglo-Saxonism.

Arnold's main attack is on the complacency of the Philistines, previously the topic of "The Function of Criticism at the Present Time." Quoting Charles Adderley — a Conservative — who had asserted that the "old Anglo-Saxon race" was "the best breed in the whole world" (*PWMA* 3:272), Arnold pauses to reflect upon a girl called Wragg who had killed her child. As Arnold points out, her name sounds solidly Anglo-Saxon (one might compare her to Scott's insignificant Saxon, Higg of Snell), yet culture has not yet advanced to the point where such Anglo-Saxons are treated as true human beings. If this is the height of achievement of Anglo-Saxon culture, clearly there is still something to be desired. Arnold urges that instead of glorying in limited and material achievement, culture should embrace a wider tradition and form a basis for criticism that "regards Europe as being, for intellectual and spiritual purposes, one great confederation, bound to a joint action and working to a common result; and whose members have, for their proper outfit, a knowledge of Greek, Roman, and Eastern antiquity . . . " (*PWMA* 3:284).

As much as Arnold is justified in attacking complacency in a country that clearly still has many social problems, this final solution — study of the classics — may suggest that Arnold chooses to maintain intellectual elitism. A society in which everyone has the opportunity to study the classics is not, of course, inconceivable. In all his writings on education, however, Arnold implies that different kinds of education are appropriate in a society with class demarcations: young Bottles, the son of the wealthy middle-class manufacturer in *Friendship's Garland*, does not gain "humanity" through sharing in an aristocrat's education.[64]

We might further question Arnold's association of these ideas with the Protestant Dissenters from the Church of England. Dissent was admittedly probably strongest in England among the middle-class city people who were prospering through manufacturing and trade during the middle years of Victoria's reign.[65] But at least in its literary expression, the main propagators of the myth of the great Teutonic heritage were nominally or actively within the Church of England, Freeman and Kingsley providing obvious examples.

But even if not all were Dissenters, Arnold is probably right in noting that the rank-and-file support for this kind of nationalism was most common among the non-Normans, the middle classes dependent on Britain's industrial and colonial progress. Hence, although on intimate terms with some of the more "muscular" Liberal spokesmen such as Thomas Hughes, Arnold advanced himself as a true Liberal, distinct from the "vulgar" faction.

Yet perhaps the vulgar should not be seen as a faction, but rather as the true test of the prevalence of Teutonism. Despite all the interest shown in the past, nineteenth-century Britain had never become a society in which Anglo-Saxon texts were best-sellers, or where ordinary families would describe themselves as part of the "Teuton kindred." The historically based nationalism of the Liberals — the assumption not based on the reading of history as much as on an acceptance of the myth of an enduring English spirit — reveals itself in much-read novels, in poetry and the visual arts,[66] and in the popular press. Arnold's concern is hence directed towards these Liberals, who read the popular journalist George A. Sala's articles in the *Daily Telegraph* and supported a belligerent Anglo-Saxonism.[67]

In "My Countrymen" (1866),[68] Arnold again questioned the imperialism that caused Britons to believe they were the first nation in the world, and that prompted them to describe themselves as Anglo-Saxons. Even though Arnold is already using something of the ironic tone developed further in *Friendship's Garland*, he is surely both playing with the middle class's image of itself and also confronting the possibility that there may be some cause for self-importance when he states: "Of course if Philistinism is characteristic of the British nation just now, it must in a special way be characteristic of the representative part of the British nation, the part by which the British nation is what it is, and does all its best things, the middle class" (*PWMA* 5:6).

Arnold, however, places a limit on the importance: England is only part of a broader cultural tradition. The possibility that Britain might not be greatest nation on earth would scarcely discourage the nationalist mood. The Philistines, Arnold notes, claimed the successes of what was probably in reality the leading world power, the United States, as their own — their justification being a belief in not a common Western tradition, the tradition of Moses and Homer, but rather a common Anglo-Saxon race.

In *Friendship's Garland* itself, essays in letter-form that appeared in the *Pall Mall Gazette* between 1866 and 1870, Arnold introduces the figure of Arminius, Baron Thunder-ten-Tronckh. Arminius might at first seem to be like Carlyle's Professor Sauerteig in *Chartism*. But rather than expressing Germanic exclusiveness, Arminius's inquiring spirit gives Arnold the chance to detach himself and ask questions that an Englishman, blinded by familiarity with his society, would not think to ask. Arminius represents what Arnold believes to be the true German spirit, distinct from the aggressive Anglo-Saxonism of the vulgar Liberals. He enables Arnold to express his disquiet at such statements as Goldwin Smith's suggestion in the *Daily News* that Britain should support a strong Prussia and that the two countries should "combine to curb France"

(*PWMA* 5:39). Arnold's observation that "wherever I go, I hear people admiring the letter and approving the idea" may be a humorous exaggeration of the numbers of the Philistines; but it simultaneously expresses his concern that the enemies of criticism and culture may become the general face of British liberalism.

Through adopting an ironic voice more Teutonist than Arminius, a true German liberal — Arminius, for example, and not Arnold, calls Goldwin Smith a "fanatic" — Arnold satirizes the current ardor for Prussia. For example, Arminius's remark that even Napoleon III had a certain sense of *Geist* is footnoted: "The indulgence of Arminius for this execrable and unsuccessful tyrant was unworthy of our geat Teutonic family. Probably, after Sedan, he changed his opinion of him" (*PWMA* 5:9). Arnold, in the role of editor, is posing not as a liberal critic but as a Philistine Liberal party member.

In the second part of *Friendship's Garland* a young disciple of Sala's style of journalism recounts how the fictional Arminius has been ignobly killed by a stray shot at the siege of Paris, a victim of the contest between French and Teutons. He is buried, more out of a sense of duty than love, by the "young lion," whom he calls the "rowdy Philistine," and "three English members of Parliament, celebrated for their ardent charity and advanced Liberalism" (*PWMA* 5:348).[69] This may be Arnold's means of conceding that his ideal German, one who read philosophy in quest of *Geist,* was sacrificed to the Prussian military ideal — Arminius dies blessing Germany, not Prussia (*PWMA* 5:347). Arminius, representative of European philosophy, is the victim of petty nationalism, functioning as a concession on Arnold's part that the "warfare" against the Philistines had not been entirely successful: sometimes, Goliath wins.

It was not, then, philosophy that England was seeking through the Prussian connection. As Arnold sadly notes in *Culture and Anarchy,* the pragmatic English middle classes were encouraged to despise the classics as merely "a smattering of the two dead languages of Greek and Latin" (*PWMA* 5:87). Similarly, in their turning to Germany, they failed to acquire the intellectual philosophy that Arnold himself admired.

Does this mean, however, that Arnold's stance was entirely

distinct? In fact, both the Philistines and Arnold were looking to tradition for a national identity. The nationalist Liberals found this in the myth of the shared Germanic past; Arnold found it in the tradition of a shared culture. But both were looking for a sense of unity on which the state could be founded. For all his rejection of the middle-class Anglo-Saxon myth, Arnold is perhaps not so far from the persona of the narrator of *Friendship's Garland* after all. He might push at the boundaries of the liberal identity that his father had helped create, but in revealing its vulgarity he also revealed its strength. The sense of identity that claimed both Harold and William as part of the Teutonic heritage may have had its origins in scholarship, but it was fueled by popular acceptance, and against this chosen identity more sophisticated thought could propose an alternative — but could scarcely impose it. By the 1860s, indeed, the Saxon-and-Norman myth had lost much of its richness of possibility. Once a pattern for an ideal, it was now the confirmation of a pragmatic system of values.

Chapter
6

The Conquest
Reversed:
King Alfred
and Queen Victoria

On Queen Victoria's Diamond Jubilee in 1897, Poet Laureate Alfred Austin recalled how at the coronation sixty years earlier:

> with grave utterance and majestic mien
> She with her eighteen summers filled the Throne
> Where Alfred sate: a girl, withal a Queen,
> Aloft, alone![1]

Austin was the second laureate in succession to bear the name of the Anglo-Saxon king: the given name of Alfred, now comparatively rare in Britain, became very common in Victorian Britain.[2] Doubtless, Tennyson's reputation after the publication of *In Memoriam* in 1850 contributed to the name's popularity; but apparently showing an early consciousness that Alfred was a king to be emulated, Queen Victoria had already named her second son Alfred Ernest Albert in 1844. About the same time, Arthur and Harold began to grow in popularity as given names, as if the names of ancient British heroes were now as acceptable as those of saints.

Names were merely one expression of the idea that Victoria was the occupant of the throne of Alfred. But her role as the ultimate reverser of the Conquest, symbolizing both progress and a return to the Golden Age, was perhaps more clear from the perspective of 1897 than it had been at her accession. The personal impact of Victoria and her family was a vital part of the sense of Anglo-Saxon heritage: in them, the personal linear inheritance from Alfred became public property.

Victoria's Family

Victoria's very person reinforced the Saxon identity. Whereas the line of English monarchs had been assumed Norman, the accession of the Hanoverian kings had increased interest in a shared Germanic tradition. Victoria inherited Hanoverian blood from her father the duke of Kent, the eldest among George III's sons to have surviving legitimate issue. But additionally, Victoria's mother, Victoria Mary Louisa, was the sister of Leopold, Duke of Saxony, who became king of Belgium upon that country's separation from Holland. Victoria, then, was Saxon in the ancient and modern sense.

The young queen's marriage in 1840 to Albert, second son of the duke of Saxe-Coburg-Gotha, was not initially a popular choice. British policymakers recognized the part played in the marriage by Victoria's German advisors, notably Baron Stockmar, and doubted whether an obscure and not especially wealthy German prince was a suitable match for a monarch.[3] Albert moreover failed to gain popular favor during his lifetime, his influence over the queen prompting fears of foreigners behind the throne. But by 1848, Victoria was already being presented as the reviver of the timeless qualities of the Saxon race. Disraeli had observed in *Sybil* that "fair and serene, she has the blood and beauty of the Saxon."[4] John Mitchell Kemble remarked that during the unrest throughout Europe in 1848–1849:

On every side of us thrones totter, and the deep foundations of society are convulsed. Shot and shell sweep the

streets of capitals which have long been pointed out as
the chosen abode of order: cavalry and bayonets cannot
control populations whose loyalty has become a proverb
here, whose peace has been made a reproach to our own
miscalled disquiet. Yet the exalted Lady who wields the
sceptre of these realms, sits safe upon her throne, and
fearless in the holy circle of her domestic happiness, secure in the affections of a people whose institutions have
given to them all the blessings of an equal law.[5]

Kemble's book, which as Burrow has pointed out seeks Saxon origins for the same kind of continuity emphasized by Macaulay's directly contemporary history,[6] bears the title *The Saxons in England*.
In her person, Victoria is seen to embody all the ancient institutions
of the Anglo-Saxons, while her fair-haired, blue-eyed family, far
from alien stock, are literally "the Saxons in England."

After Albert's death in 1861 the suspicions concerning his
"Germanness" were forgotten as the nation shared in Victoria's personal devastation. The awkward foreigner who had been a figure of
ridicule in *Punch* became the representative of a new kind of Englishness.[7] Victoria was not the first monarch to cultivate the identification of her country with herself. Elizabeth of England and Louis
XIV of France, both also long-reigning monarchs, had adopted similar personas[8] — and while Alfred the Great may not have had such
a concept of nationhood, later English commentators had seen him
as the representative of Saxon England. But if Alfred had symbolized the spirit of the Anglo-Saxon Golden Age, in a strange reversal
Victoria drew the spirit of the nation into her own: her personality
was reflected in the entire nation.

In the decade following Albert's death many complaints were
made at Victoria's withdrawal from public life,[9] but popular opinion, at least as represented by newspapers and municipal art, began
to accept Victoria's personal image of Albert.[10] The association of
Albert with the mystical figure of King Arthur inTennyson's *Idylls
of the King* is a well-known story encouraged by Victoria's own children.[11] Tennyson had, of course, had a long-term interest in Arthurian legend, and several of the *Idylls* identified with Albert long

predated his apotheosis. Still, Prince Albert had expressed his admiration of the *Idylls* the year before his death, and Tennyson's dedication of the 1863 version to the memory of the Prince Consort was interpreted by some commentators as encouraging a comparison of Albert to Arthur. Swinburne even remarked that the poem might more properly be called the "Morte D'Albert."[12] Tennyson himself was uncomfortable at the direct comparison and revised his lines on the Prince Consort, "And indeed, He seems to me / Scarce other than my own ideal knight," to conclude, "my king's ideal knight," to avoid such direct comparisons. It was, however, too late.[13]

But Albert was also a Saxon warrior. Even the qualities ascribed by Tennyson to Albert in the dedication to the *Idylls*, which include conciliatory diplomacy, unbiased judgment, and patronage of the arts, suggest that Tennyson's ideal of a prince included qualities traditionally and historically associated with Alfred. Indeed, when in 1897 Walter Besant attempted to describe Alfred, he used Tennyson's description of Albert.[14]

Victoria's own consciousness that she had lost a Saxon consort is indicated by her choice of portrayal in a statue of Albert and herself, which she commissioned from William Theed the Younger for Windsor Chapel. Acting on the suggestion of Victoria and her daughters, Theed represented Albert as an Anglo-Saxon chief making his farewell to Victoria, portrayed as a Saxon queen. The inscription, from Goldsmith, suggests that Albert was "Allured to brighter worlds, and led the way."[15] From this point, Albert was to function in the Victorian world-picture not as the graceless foreign consort of the queen, but as an ideal example of Teutonic manhood.

Victoria's children strengthened the Germanic link throughout Europe. Her eldest daughter, Victoria, married Crown Prince Frederick Wilhelm of Prussia; their eldest son, the future Kaiser Wilhelm II, was known as Victoria's favorite grandson. The Prince of Wales married Princess Alexandra of Denmark in 1863, a union that some Teutonists saw as a repetition of the pre-Conquest rule of both Saxons and Danes. In *Hereward the Wake*, Charles Kingsley even refers to a genealogy of Princess Alexandra that traces her descent from the Viking rulers of England — and even more improbably, from the daughter of the last Saxon king, Harold.[16] (Presumably, no one remarked that Scott had ascribed a similar lineage to Athelstane in *Ivanhoe*.) The heirs of Prince Albert Edward and Princess Alexandra, then, were derived from the stock of both great Saxon hero-kings, Alfred and Harold. Prince Alfred Ernest Albert was adopted as heir to the Duchy of Saxe-Coburg-Gotha. Alfred married a Russian princess, and Tennyson's marriage ode recalled the wedding of the last Saxon King Harold:

> Fair empires, branching both in lusty life!
> Yet Harold's England fell to Norman swords
> Yet thine own land has bowed to Tartar hordes
> Since English Harold gave its throne a wife.[17]

Tennyson was presumably alluding to a tradition recorded by Lappenberg that Harold's sons married into the Russian royal line, but Princess Maria Alexandrovna might have been forgiven for believing that her husband himself was descended from Harold, not from Harold's conqueror.

Others of Victoria's children strengthened associations with Hesse, Schleswig-Holstein, and Battenburg. To some extent, these choices were dictated by the long-term national policy of not allowing marriage with Roman Catholics, which ruled out alliances with Spanish royalty and the family of Napoleon III.[18] Clearly, however, these marriage-alliances between the royal houses of Britain, Germany, and Denmark were intended to create a bond between the Teutonic nations — the alliances with Russia doing little to allay Victoria's suspicions of the tsar.

Through the queen's family, then, a Teutonic statement was made. More than ever before, the monarch's family was seen as the representative of the people; and in this case, history indeed seemed to be cyclic, in that once again England was ruled by Anglo-Saxons. This sense of identity created by the infusion of new German blood was strengthened by the claims of science. The emblematic figures of Victoria and family were complemented by developments in language theory suggesting that the German link was not merely revived in the nation's ruling dynasty but inherent in every speaker of

English. Just as Victoria's family represented the entire Germanic family, so the English language was part of the Germanic family of languages.

The experiences of Kemble, Thorpe, and other British scholars in the field of Germanic studies had proved that, until the 1850s at least, most of their compatriots, and even those who claimed an interest in the past, had little enthusiasm for language studies.[19] Despite their missionary zeal, however, throughout the century comparative philology was dominated by Germans. Although Kemble and Thorpe had advanced similar theories some years earlier, not until the 1860s did the subject attract non-specialist interest in Britain.

Then in 1861, the German scholar F. Max Müller delivered a series of lectures to the Royal Institution in London. Müller had come to England as a young scholar under the patronage of Baron Bunsen, who had also had a share in giving Britain Prince Albert. He taught Sanskrit and comparative philology at Oxford and by 1861 was professor of modern languages. Müller's lectures, published under the general title of *The Science of Language,* encountered a British public so new to the idea of language as a science that Freeman's friend George Cox, writing in the *Edinburgh Review,* claimed that the "Ptolemaean theory of the universe was not more completely set aside by the system of Copernicus, than all previous conceptions of grammar and speech by the new-born science of language."[20] As a science, language could be compared with others such as geology and evolutionary biology, which, in Burrow's words, "were all concerned with the reconstruction of states no longer directly observable, by means of classification into stages and the postulation of laws or sequences of development."[21] For example, a fossil may be the only material evidence of a geological epoch whose role in the evolutionary process must be deduced. In a similar manner, surviving linguistic resemblances among the Sanskrit, Greek, Romance, and Germanic languages were seen to be evidence of a ommon heritage and a clue to a race whose existence was also a matter of deduction. Language was hence, in Müller's words, that "which connects ourselves, through an unbroken chain of words, with the very ancestors of our race."[22] That race, Müller asserted, was the Aryan, or Indo-European, which had possibly originated in the Caucasus and had spread their influence throughout Europe. In the writings of early philologists such as William Jones, similarities in linguistic forms and myth had been seen as proof of how much all peoples had in common.[23] Yet in Müller's time, attention became focused not on universal origins — indeed, as Martin Bernal has pointed out, the possible contributions of other cultures were ignored[24] — but on the specific origins that explained the Germanic peoples. Within the Aryan group, which included the Romance and Slav tongues, Anglo-Saxon was a part of the Teutonic, or Germanic subgroup:

> The language of England may be said to have been in succession Celtic, Saxon, Norman, and English. But if we speak of the history of the English language, we enter on totally different ground. . . . To the student of language English is Teutonic, and nothing but Teutonic. . . . The grammar, the blood and soul of the language, is as pure and unmixed in English as spoken in the British Isles as it was when spoken on the shores of the German ocean by the Angles, Saxons, and Juts [sic] of the continent. (*SL*, 68–70)

Müller bases his claim on the objective proof of grammar:

> The single *ð*, used as the exponent of the third person singular of the indicative present, is irrefragible evidence that in a scientific classification of languages, English, though it did not retain a single word of Saxon origin, would have to be classed as Saxon, and as a branch of the great Teutonic stem of the Aryan family of speech. (*SL*, 75)

This statement is obviously extreme, devaluing the significance of vocabulary; yet the theory of the Indo-European languages is not here in question. The use made of Müller's theories by other writers, however, requires examination.

Müller emphasized the Germanic family as indicated by language but was reluctant to involve language-theory in support of racism and, particularly, as a justification for slavery. Nevertheless, Müller's arguments *were* interpreted historically and politically. They provided the justification for Kemble's assumption that the history of the German tribes in Europe was also the history of the Saxons in England: here at last, after Kemble's death, was what Tennyson had prophetically described as "iron-worded proof."[25] Müller's grammar statement further suggested that settlers in England between Harold and Victoria could be regarded as a deviation from the "real" English race: grammar proved the English Teutonic.

Linda Dowling has argued that the new linguistic science "raised a spectre of autonomous language — language as a system blindly obeying impersonal phonological rules in isolation from any world of human values and experience — that was to eat corrosively away at the foundations of a high Victorian ideal of civilization."[26] In terms of the English conception of a literary tradition, this may be true. But the autonomous nature of language also seemed to provide proof beyond historical interpretation — "iron-worded proof" of origins that came not from the historian but from science itself. While literature felt a loss of direction, fact was given new encouragement, and the English nationalists, Freeman among them, seized upon Müller's pronouncements with eagerness.

Freeman had published an expanded version of two lectures in 1872 under the title *The Growth of the English Constitution from the Earliest Times* — a clear association of political institutions with an evolutionary model. Then in 1873 Freeman read a series of lectures to the Royal Institution, to which he gave the title *Comparative Politics*. These were, in Freeman's words, "an attempt to claim for political institutions a right to a scientific treatment of exactly the same kind as that which has been so successfully applied to language, to mythology, and to the progress of culture."[27] Freeman points out that comparative philology "teaches us facts about which no external proof can be had, but for which the internal proof, once stated, is absolutely irresistible." Acknowledging his debt to Müller, he then proceeds to do what his exemplar had been careful to avoid and uses philology as a model for political theory. Freeman sees points in common between all Aryans — the "Greek, Roman, and Teuton" — but his belief in the self-governing powers of ancient Aryans is so great that his focus inevitably returns to the Teutons "on either side of the German Ocean and on either side of the Atlantic." Of these he claims that "we" — the English — may "boast ourselves as the truest representatives."[28] Freeman justifies this assertion not because of the "purity" of linguistic inheritance (he assumes without question that a Teutonic language is more pure than one with a "Romance infusion") but because "our own is, beyond all doubt, the one which can claim for its political institutions the most unbroken descent from the primitive Teutonic stock" (*CP*, 45).

Freeman's reasoning leaves some cause for skepticism. His proof of the political connection is philology, but he simultaneously claims that politics is a stronger proof than language — which would seem a difficulty if the original political institutions are only proved by the linguistic analogy. Yet even if in Freeman's presentation these arguments are in an extreme form, similar ideas permeate British constitutional thought of the period. Probably the most influential work on the English constitution — indeed, it was a standard text for the rest of the century — was William Stubbs's *Constitutional History of England*, first published in 1866. Stubbs expresses ideas similar to Freeman's in more complex terms. The English, he claims, "are a people of German descent in the main constituents of blood, character, and language, but most especially in connexion with our subject, in the possession of the elements of primitive German civilisation and the common germs of German institutions."[29] According to Stubbs, the three main factors influencing the growth of the constitution are "the national character, the external history, and the institutions of the people." He concedes the complexity of the relationship: "The national character has been formed by the course of the national history quite as certainly as the national history has been developed by the working of the national character" (*CHE* 1:1). But like Müller and Freeman, Stubbs confirms that essentially, in their language and characteristics, the English are the same people as they were before the Norman Conquest.

The resulting change in terminology is not always recognized, even by modern scholars, to be polemical.[30] About this time, some scholars, led by Freeman, began to use the term "English" rather than "Anglo-Saxons" to describe the pre-Norman inhabitants of England and "Old English" or simply "English" to describe the language. The argument that the term "Anglo-Saxon" has no historical basis and that writers of the period used the word "Englisc" to describe their language and people is, of course, true. But a reversion to these terms implies that what happened to the English and their language in the intervening eight hundred years was in both Müller's linguistic sense and in a national sense irrelevant. The Saxons were truly English; the other occupiers of England were merely incidental.

Müller's arguments on classification could also be applied in a wider sense than he had intended. The philologist had noted:

> The object of classification is clear. We understand things if we can comprehend them; that is to say, if we can grasp and hold together single facts, connect isolated impressions, distinguish between what is essential and what is merely accidental, and class the individual under the general. This is the secret of all scientific knowledge. (*SL*, 17)

Müller was hence offering scientific support to two crucial claims. First, he suggested that classification was an aid to interpretation: the knowledge that a historical figure was a Saxon or a Norman was a guide to understanding that person's actions and character. Second, such an interpretation implied that to understand the individual through the general was scientific. What, then, were Saxons and Normans? They were not what they had been for Scott, a structural device; they were a scientific means of classification. Müller claimed that in Teutonic languages, the third person singular of the present indicative had an S-ending; the English language had this ending; therefore English was a Teutonic language. Such an argument, even if ignoring the significance of vocabulary, was not unreasonable. The question was whether the statement could be

applied to human characteristics, particularly those with moral implications.

For example, the analysis of Thomas Becket had implied the
syllogism: a characteristic is Norman; Becket possessed that characteristic; therefore, Becket was a Norman. Such a syllogism
ignored the crucial questions of how it was known that a given
characteristic was Norman; whether it was exclusively Norman;
and why if "pure fact" was possible, different historians judged
Becket's possession of this characteristic differently. Rather than
seeming complex and obscure, Becket's motives when seen through
the "scientific" method seemed easy to understand. Science, in fact,
fictionalized him as a product of his classifiers. This was not, of
course, entirely incompatible with fictional characterizations; but
Ivanhoe had implied a similar framework without the need of scientific justification.

More seductive still was the reversal of Müller's theory of
classification. If Saxons have specific qualities, and the English
were Saxons, then they too could claim those qualities. A basis for
identity was provided beyond simple identification with the hero of
the novel. In the present, Victoria's family provided a Saxon model;
history continued to provide many others from the Saxon past.
Harold, for example, was now not merely a hero with whom to
sympathize: he was the representative of the characteristics of a
race, and others who saw themselves as members of that race could
also lay claim to such characteristics.

The King Alfred Millenary

On 22 January 1901, Queen Victoria died.
The year 1901 had a special significance, since it had been chosen
some years previously as the date on which to celebrate the thou-
sandth anniversary of the death of Alfred the Great.[31]

As we have seen, some parallels had been drawn between
Prince Albert and King Alfred. Yet Victoria herself was also a

"type" of Alfred, an idea which was exploited during her Diamond Jubilee celebrations in 1897. The year before the jubilee, the poet laureate had written a dramatic poem called *"England's Darling."*[32] Although by his preface Austin appears unaware that earlier poets had written on the theme, his drama strongly resembles the Alfred plays of a century earlier—both in structure and literary merit. The compliments to its dedicatee, Alexandra, Princess of Wales, are scarcely subtle. Edgiva, who marries Alfred's son and is presented as the mother of the English race, is the daughter of a Dane—like Alexandra, a Danish princess. Her husband, the high-spirited and careless Edward, recalls (Albert) Edward, Prince of Wales. And although the parallel is less specific, this places Queen Victoria in the role of Alfred—bringer of peace, forger of justice, and universal educator.

One change is made, though, from the eighteenth-century Alfred plays. In *"England's Darling,"* the quality most stressed to be English is that of "truth-telling." Edward does not distinguish himself by his behavior during the play. But Alfred, placing the same emphasis on truth as Victoria's biographers insist that she did,[33] says of Edward:

> He is my son, and never, since he learned
> From Saxon mother this our Saxon tongue,
> Or spake or thought untruth.
>
> (*ED*, 59)

The English language, then, may itself be conducive to plain speaking. Another repeated theme of the play is Alfred's interest in translating books into English. Latin may be the language of learning, but Alfred's tongue is the language of truth.

"England's Darling" ends with the observation that what Saxon England lacks "is learning":

> And every English boy must read and con
> The Chronicle of this his cradle-land,
> Growing apace and nigh upon our time,

That tells him whence he came, and what those did
Whose deeds are in his veins.

(ED, 80)

This desire not to forget the heroic past of England contained
within one's very blood, combined with the success of the Diamond
Jubilee, cemented a determination to celebrate Alfred's millenary.
The people of Wessex were particularly eager. In the words of another Alfred, Alfred Bowker, mayor of Winchester (King Alfred's
capital city):

> Since it is acknowledged that the English-speaking
> people, after the lapse of a thousand years, still derive
> great and incalculable benefits from Alfred's indefatig-
> able work, his splendid achievements, and the example of
> a life wholly devoted to the welfare and improvement of
> his people, it was felt that the memorial to the "hero of
> our race" should be worthy not only of the city [of Win-
> chester] and neighbouring counties, but also of the Anglo-
> Saxon race.[34]

An enthusiastic group took up the project, and the queen herself expressed approval. Royal patronage was deemed important.
During the speeches in favor of the proposal recorded in Alfred
Bowker's commemorative volume *The King Alfred Millenary*, the
bishop of London reemphasized Victoria's heritage: the English

> might surely feel proud to consider it an absolute fact
> that our history had gone on since the days of Alfred till
> now, and that the sign and token of it was that the blood
> of Alfred still ran in the veins of her most Gracious Maj-
> esty Queen Victoria. (*KAM*, 13)

During a period of sixty years, in which other European countries
had undergone major changes in government, and the government

of Britain itself had gradually changed, Queen Victoria had provided continuity of leadership. Alfred, though, made her part of a thousand-year dynasty.

Bishop Creighton's statement is characteristic of the Alfred Commemoration Committee in ignoring the Norman Conquest. The emphasis was on continuity and on reconciliation: United States citizens were invited to participate as part of the shared Anglo-Saxon heritage. Perhaps with more goodwill than appreciation of the possible implications of the figure of "Alfred, hero of our race," representatives of the Roman Catholic church and the chief rabbi of the London Temple also gave the project their support.

In 1899, the committee published *Alfred the Great: Containing Chapters on His Life and Times*, with the object, its editor (once again Alfred Bowker) announced, "of diffusing, as widely as possible, public knowledge of the king's life and work." The book was prefaced with "The Spotless King," a poem by Alfred Austin that reminded readers: "Through the distance of a thousand years / Alfred's full radiance shines on us at last."[35]

Sir Walter Besant, panegyrist of Victorian progress, contributed a long introduction to the work. To celebrate the Diamond Jubilee, Besant had written *The Queen's Reign and Its Commemoration 1837–1897*, an illustrated work focusing less on the queen herself than on "the transformation of the people" during the period.[36] Besant believed that "the people" had grown more more dutiful, better behaved, and more contented. Yet even this self-proclaimed believer in Victorian progress combined linear with cyclic models of progress by noting that the Victorians were now achieving on the same level as their Anglo-Saxon forebears. For example, "the woman who sews now," says Besant, "sews more beautifully, turning out work more equal to that of her ancestress, the Anglo-Saxon lady."[37]

Besant, who had also written a short life of Alfred intended for wide circulation through The Library of Useful Stories, makes several other extreme claims. A strong anti-Norman (he had assured the readers of his Diamond Jubilee volume that the House of Lords should not be accused of containing Normans), Besant comments that the quicker witted Norman despised the Saxon as slow of understanding. Perhaps: but the Saxon proved himself in the long-run far more capable of enthusiasm, of loyalty, of patriotism, of sacrifice, of all those actions and emotions which spring from the imagination and produce forces united and irresistible. Remember that the whole of our literature is Anglo-Saxon; none of it is Norman. No Norman literature was produced on this our Anglo-Saxon soil.[38]

Besant stresses that "in a word, the Anglo-Saxon of the ninth century was in essentials very much like his descendant of the present day" (*AG*, 9). But above all, Alfred led the way: "Alfred is, and will always remain, the typical man of our race — call him Anglo-Saxon, call him American, call him Englishman, call him Australian — the typical man of our race at his best and noblest" (*AG*, 37). Alfred is thus for Besant both ideal and typical — a model to which all Anglo-Saxons can aspire.

Alfred's morally-exemplary nature continued to be emphasized by the Commemoration Committee. The ceremonies arranged for September 1901 included pageants, parades, and lectures and centered upon the unveiling of the great Alfred statue in the city of Winchester. Sculpted by Haco Thornycroft, the statue portrays Alfred holding a sword with its point downwards, drawing attention to the the cross of the handle: with his crowned helmet and shield, Alfred suggests military strength but not aggression.

The death of Queen Victoria some months earlier, which might have undermined enthusiasm for the event but for the coincidence of the dates 901/1901, caused the royal focus to be directed towards the new King Edward VII, to whom the commemoration volume was dedicated. During the celebrations, news came of the death of the United States President McKinley, shot by an assassin eight days earlier; and consequently the closeness of the Anglo-Saxon races in their triumphs and sorrows was a keynote of the celebration. Alfred Bowker, speaking in his role as mayor of Winchester, even termed the president's death a "great loss to the whole of the civilised race" — the definite article clearly implying that only one civilized race existed.[39]

The main speaker at the unveiling ceremony for the memorial statue of Alfred was, appropriately enough, the earl of Rosebery, British prime minister and, as leader of the Liberal Imperialists, himself one of the last of his race. At this time, Rosebery had a strong reputation as an orator, and his address doubtless conformed to expectations. In the presence of international dignitaries and two thousand schoolchildren, Rosebery, whose speech was also printed in Bowker's 1902 volume, saw Alfred's triumph as "a question of personality." His five great attributes were first, "his absorbed devotion to duty"; second, "he was the first Englishman of whom it is recorded that he never knew when he was beaten"; third, he had "the supreme quality of truth, frankness, candour, an open heart; his word was his bond"; fourth, "he was a man, a complete man"; and finally, "he was a king, a true king" (*KAM*, 109). Rosebery concluded by imagining Alfred as like a British Aeneas, being shown the destiny of his race. He would have seen "the first dark hour in which his kingdom and race should be overwhelmed by a Norman invasion, of which the iron should enter the English soul — not to slay, but to strengthen, to introduce, indeed, the last element wanted to compose the Imperial race."[40] Alfred might also have seen his country's progress: "the little Saxon fort developed into a world-capital and a world-mart, inhabited by millions of the crowded and distressed, but familiar with comforts unknown to a Saxon prince" (*KAM*, 111–112). Rosebery evidently envisages Alfred congratulating himself on his children's progress. But the King Alfred Millenary seems even more an exercise in national self-congratulation. Efforts were made to keep the celebrations inclusive in race and caste: an admission charge was only made for a dramatic reading by Sir Henry Irving (from Tennyson's *Becket*). Nevertheless, the ruling classes were firmly in control, unthreatened by the version of Alfred that they had created. Alfred was no longer the symbol of social criticism, representing what England had once been and might be in the future: rather, Alfred represented England in contemporary glory. The English people might still learn from the example of Alfred, but the example was now dutiful support of social structures. In Alfred, then, might be seen the history of the Liberal party, from moderate radicalism in the late eighteenth century to tired imperialism at the beginning of the twentieth. The Alfred Memorial still dominates Winchester, but perhaps less as a commemoration of the ninth-century king than as a relic of the nineteenth-century imperial dream.

Saxon Superiority

In 1850, the young Edward Freeman had written:

> We have conquered, we have conquered,
>   Though not on tented plain,
> And the laws and tongue of Alfred
>   We have won them back again,
> The boasted might of Normandy
>   For aye is laid at rest,
> But the name of Saxon freedom
>   Still warms each faithful breast.[41]

At the time of that writing, the outcome of this bloodless reversal of the Conquest was perhaps still not quite certain. By 1901, however, at the King Alfred Millenary celebrations, the Saxons could afford to be generous, knowing that their defeat had been avenged.

The millenary showed the self-styled Saxons at their most benign, the stress on "our race" being partly tempered by a solid belief that unity was healthy. The cost of unity, however, was a loss of complexity. Whereas formerly the relationship between Saxons and Normans had constantly been redefined and reevaluated, the icon now demanded a wholehearted identification with the Saxons and acceptance of their superiority over the Normans.

Rosebery's address at the King Alfred Millenary showed how easily the Saxon ideal could be combined with imperialism. Alfred the Great, after all, is said by Asser to have sent envoys throughout the known world, even to India. By 1901 the concept of Saxon superiority was an integral part of the British myth of origins. As during Victoria's reign Britain's position as a world power continued to increase, the queen's image as a similar bringer of peace and culture had also been emphasized. Victoria was formally appointed empress of India in 1876, while British influence, already predominant in Australasia, continued to expand in Africa. From time to time, Britons asked themselves why they, a small island people, had been favored — or burdened — with the task of ruling the world.[42] "The welfare of the Teutonic race," asserted Charles Kingsley in 1863, "is the welfare of the world."[43] Interestingly, although Kingsley inclined to the opinion that "the hosts of our forefathers [the Teutonic tribes] were the hosts of God," the solution that it was the will of God or of fortune was not often deemed satisfactory. The favor of a sensible English God might be part of the answer. Above all, though, Anglo-Saxons had the favor of race.[44]

Yet even the concept of the favor of race needed a mandate. The mandate of fiction, of course, was found in Scott, and not only in *Ivanhoe*. In *Count Robert of Paris*, for example, Hereward the Varangian is physically and morally superior to the decadence of Byzantium. In structural terms, "we" remained superior to "they." Thirty years later, convinced that the English were the Teutonic tribes as opposed to the Romans, Kingsley asserted of the declining Roman Empire: "Thus the Romans were growing weak. If we had lost, so had they."[45]

To the later Victorians, however, the mandate of science seemed more secure. Parallels of evolutionary theory (particularly a crude interpretation of natural selection) with the development of languages in fact suggested no radical departure from the novel-structure. But the hero surviving to the end was now justified by what the racists who called themselves Social Darwinists chose to label the "survival of the fittest."[46] Harold's defeat was merely temporary. Roman cunning might periodically thwart Teuton frankness, but finally history proved Teutonic superiority. The English were not merely an island people but representative of the best qualities of the ancient Germanic tribes.

With our knowledge of the direction that the concept of a pan-Germanic family was to take in the twentieth century, belief in Teutonic superiority can too easily be dismissed as the delusion of extremists of the far right. In nineteenth-century Britain, however, the idea of the superman might first have been introduced to speakers of English by Carlyle, but as Matthew Arnold noted, it had become increasingly associated with the Liberal party. The Whig reformers of the 1830s, whose political views were influenced by modified utilitarianism, had been insistent that no inherent distinctions existed between races. This was not to imply that they liked the French,[47] but rather that they believed personal characteristics to be acquired, not inherited. For example, Macaulay, whose father had attempted to bring the benefits of European culture to Sierra Leone, argued that once all races could be brought to think like Englishmen, then all sense of racial separation would end.[48]

Yet these Whigs were comparatively uninterested in the Germanic tradition. Later liberals showed a greater admiration of Germany and all things German. In this, the science of language seemed to give them support. In the biblical-creationist view of philology, the "original" language was generally assumed to have been Hebrew.[49] In contrast, Germanic philology, concentrating on Indo-European languages, implicitly placed Hebrew outside the "family," providing a convenient linguistic justification for anti-Semitism. Since peoples of non-Caucasian stock were considered barely worth mentioning, the Jews were particular targets, although many claimed humanitarian reasons for hating Turks. The idea was taken further in attitudes towards the Romance languages. Even though the "Romans" were part of the Indo-European "family," differences as opposed to similarities were stressed.

By the time of *Friendship's Garland*, Liberals were the most vociferous in support of the absolute mastery of the Saxons.[50] Saxon superiority implies Norman inferiority, and the Liberals were apparently uncomfortable with applying this to a struggle between classes. Instead, they found new Normans in the modern French. Of course, something of the long-standing mutual distrust between French and English, who were at war for much of the period between 1793 and 1815, had been a part of the Saxon-and-Norman opposition in Scott's novels. The faults of the French as conceived by the British, however, had undergone some change. First they had been presented by the early English Protestants as a Roman Catholic power, fighting against the true faith. But later the possibility arose that the supposed devotion to the pope was merely a grateful acceptance of the sanction of untruth. In 1852, the French president Louis Napoleon proclaimed himself his uncle's heir as Emperor Napoleon III. Reactions in Britain were mixed — Palmerston lost his position for congratulating him, although Queen Victoria came to accept the new emperor — but a poem by Tennyson demonstrates Saxon fear. Napoleon III is a liar, and the pope has sanctioned his lies: Britons are advised to "rise if manhood be not dead." Once again, manliness and being British are placed in opposition to popery and being French. Somewhat unconvincingly denying hatred for France as a whole, Tennyson proceeds to ascribe to Napoleon III Jesuitical untruth:

> We hate not France, but France has lost her voice,
> This man is France, the man they call her choice.
>> By tricks and spying,
>> And craft and lying,
> And murder, was her freedom overthrown.
>> Britons, guard your own! . . .
>
> Rome's dear daughter now is captive France;
> The Jesuit laughs, and reckoning on his chance
>> Would unrelenting
>> Kill all dissenting
> Till we were left to fight for truth alone.
>> Britons, guard your own![51]

Ironically, Britain was shortly afterwards to enter upon the Crimean War in alliance with France, and Tennyson's position as poet laureate perhaps made him quietly forget this poem. Yet socially, Tennyson's poem has a claim to interest in showing the mood of many Britons towards France. The debacle of the Crimean War did not help to endear Napoleon III's regime to the British, and both Napoleon III and Palmerston, who was seen as his lackey, were repeatedly caricatured in *Punch* and other popular publications.[52]

Freeman, writing as a Gladstonian Liberal, associated this hatred with conceptions of Saxon and Norman history. Freeman hated the French for precisely the reasons seen in Tennyson's poem: they disturbed the peace of Europe, they were Catholics, and unlike the Teutons, they were dishonest.

Ignoring the claims of *Friendship's Garland* to express true liberalism, the mainstream English Liberals therefore hailed the Franco-Prussian War as their own victory. One of the more curious responses to the dislike of Napoleon III was Thomas Hughes's biography of Alfred the Great. Hughes, like his creation Tom Brown, was born in the Vale of the White Horse traditionally associated with King Alfred; he notes that during an earlier major crisis in Europe — the revolutions of 1848 — Pauli wrote his history of Alfred as an example to the Germans and claims that he personally, writing at a similar time of crisis, will compare Alfred with Charlemagne.[53] Hughes's point is not subtle. Just as the Saxon king was a worthier founder of European — and world — institutions than the Frankish king, so the modern leaders of the Saxons can set an example to the new Charlemagne, Napoleon III.

In a similar mood, Freeman exulted in the Franco-German War of 1870–1871 (he preferred the name Franco-German to Franco-Prussian because he remained unsure whether or not he hated Prussians). W.R.W. Stephens recalls that Freeman "hailed the success of the Germans with the deepest satisfaction." Like Tennyson and the *Punch* writers, he projected this hatred principally towards the figure of "Louis-Napoleon, whom he regarded as an odious and criminal tyrant," but the war gratified him "because it humbled the pride and crippled the power of the French nation, which had for ages been the principal disturber of the peace of Europe."[54] More than thirty years earlier, a French counterpart of Freeman, Michelet, had expressed a similar opinion about the English: to Michelet, the English were the disturbers of the peace of Europe, who not only provoked violent conflicts but also claimed victories not wholly their own.[55] Michelet's hatred is distinct from Freeman's, however, in being conscious. French disunity gave a need for an object of hatred: in hating England, French people became France. Freeman, in contrast, displays less self-knowledge. In a letter to the *Pall Mall Gazette*, ironically also the publisher of many of Arnold's papers on liberalism, Freeman sought to explain his stance historically:

> The war on the part of Germany is, in truth, a vigorous setting forth of the historical truth that the Rhine is, and always has been, a German river. It is practically important to make people understand that the combined fraud and violence by which Philip the Fair seized Lyons, by which Louis XI seized Provence, by which Henry VII seized Metz, by which Louis XIV seized Strassburg, by which the elder Buonaparte seized half Europe, and the younger seized Savoy and Nizza, are all parts of one long conspiracy against the peace of the world.[56]

Freeman began to see Wilhelm I as a new William the Conqueror and even to identify himself entirely with the common Germanic cause. To his fellow historian Edith Thompson he wrote: "We must have Elsass back again, if not Lothringen," deliberately using the German forms of the names of the long-disputed territories Alsace and Lorraine.

Freeman's hatred, though, was not limited to the French: indeed, superficially it shows an irrationality. Gladstone's speeches on behalf of the Bulgarians, who were persecuted by their Turkish overlords in the period 1875–1878, were probably not merely a party propaganda exercise but also a sincere expression of concern for fellow Christians. Freeman's reaction to the "Bulgarian atrocities," on the other hand, concentrated itself in a hatred of the Turks (whom he suspected of particularly "unmanly" vices). But he also blamed the Bulgarian atrocities on the Jews — his references to "the Jew" generally being directed at Benjamin Disraeli, the Conservative prime minister whose "balance of power" policy in Europe, firmly supported by Victoria, required the survival not of those fittest to rule but of the Sick Man of Europe, the Turkish Empire.[57]

Freeman was vehemently opposed to vivisection and fox-hunting, and the irrationality of his likes and dislikes may seem further expressed in his comment about what creatures should be shot; in later life, he wrote to a friend: "I have a general notion that hares, rabbits, Turks, Jews, and Irish landlords would be well got rid of."[58] Why foxes and Bulgarians should deserve the doubtful favor of Freeman's protection is not clear. But Freeman's conception of the Aryan heritage seemed to him to provide a pattern of justification for his hatred of the Semitic peoples, among whom he classed the Turks, under the suspicion that shared blood was the reason for Disraeli's support for them. At the same time, as a Teuton, he continued to hate his "natural" enemies the "Romans," led at this time by the French. Thus although France's seizing of territory was unacceptable (Freeman seems to have overlooked Britain's own cooperation in France's annexations), British imperialism, given the moral superiority of the British people, was a duty. Whereas Virgil had ascribed the study of the arts to other races and domination to the Romans, the new empire assumed roles of both educator and legislator. Like Carlyle (perhaps surprisingly, Freeman did not appreciate Carlyle and he did not read many of his writings), Freeman believed implicitly in the Teuton ability to rule.

One of the stranger manifestations of this conviction of Teuton superiority was the question of the government of Greece. Somewhat prior to an interest in the Bulgarians, the Liberal party had declared a special concern with Greece. Some Liberals convinced themselves that thinking Greeks would prefer an English king. In October 1862, Freeman's friend George Finlay, who had lived in Greece since the War of Independence, wrote from Athens with an astonishing proposition. Finlay believed that the Greek people were "very generally" eager to have "an English prince, or a prince connected with England." One possibility was Victoria's son Alfred. But in Finlay's personal opinion: "The best thing the Greeks could do would be to elect Mr. Gladstone King."[59]

Gladstone himself did not take the suggestion seriously: in fact, he and his family were amused by the idea.[60] But Freeman

gave it earnest consideration. First, the British Liberals, having rejected Rome, felt a cultural affinity with Greece.[61] Further, the notion combined liberal ideals of kingship by will of the people, rather
than right of birth, with the understanding that an honest Englishman with a good knowledge of Ancient Greek was an entirely appropriate choice for governing a non-Teutonic nation.[62] The picture
of Gladstone as king of Greece may seem ludicrous. On the other
hand, many parts of the British Empire were ruled by administra-
tors far less able, who also justified their positions by the British
natural right to sovereignty and the stability of a thousand years of
Saxon history. When in the 1850s Freeman had written, "The
boasted might of Normandy / For aye is laid at rest," the claim was
not quite certain. Pierre Bourdieu has suggested that universally
accepted cultural traditions that have assumed an objective position
do not require assertion.[63] Whatever their subsequent reputation, in
their own time, writers of broader-than-nationalist perspectives
such as Matthew Arnold were largely unsuccessful in establishing a
heterodox position. Hence by 1901, superiority over France, no
longer in doubt, needed no further restatement. What needed assertion more than before, however, was a general sense of unity and
the value of imperialism.

Conclusion: The Saxon-and-Norman Legacy

By the beginning of the twentieth century,
even hardened English patriots (or Francophobes) could look be-
nevolently on the Norman Conquest. At most, it had given the English character the addition of determination. At least, it had not
prevailed against the essentially Teutonic nature of the English
race.

In the light of such a reading of the Conquest, and virtual
abandonment of the theory of the Norman Yoke, Alfred's role, and
the role of the Anglo-Saxons, required redefinition. No longer did

the Saxon world provide a contrast with contemporary events. Whether history was regarded as cyclic or progressive, the English of Alfred's time and of Victoria's reign were fundamentally one and the same. History, then, begins in the present, and its manipulation of the past provides the means by which the present can be understood.

But Alfred was now less than ever a myth. Statues in town squares are almost invariably of historical figures, and the centerpiece of the King Alfred Millenary, the eighteen-foot-high statue in Winchester, confirmed his solidity. The presentation of Alfred as a realistic warrior, indeed, made him almost more real than the representations of Prince Albert as knight of romance,[64] or Queen Victoria as bride of England on the "wedding cake" style of the slightly later Victoria Memorial outside Buckingham Palace. The statue of Alfred confirmed that the socially critical myth of one hundred years earlier had become a structure-affirming fact.

The novels of Scott and Disraeli had suggested two possible directions for British cultural identity. The struggle in each case was between two nations — the Normans and the Saxons. In *Sybil,* these "Two Nations" are unambiguously the rich and the poor. Normans and Saxons also represent rich and poor in *Ivanhoe.* But *Ivanhoe* also creates the possibility of the Two Nations as French and English, although without the entire certainty that the Normans are wrong and the Saxons right. Whereas Scott's novel presents the problem as a structure of fiction, the Liberals of the later part of the century had historicized it — largely without the consciousness that they were doing so. King Alfred was hence champion of all the Anglo-Saxon peoples without reference to class, and even, as Arnold's "My Countrymen" essay and the millenary celebrations suggest, without reference to national boundaries. He represented patriotic duty, perhaps primarily to England, but by extension to all who claimed Teuton descent. Even the inclusiveness of the King Alfred Millenary, then, was also exclusive.

Michelet had realized that to galvanize a force within was to project it without.[65] The English Teutonists, though, appear to have been incapable of acknowledging their hatred as the product of their own historical creation: they were too much products of that creation themselves. Michelet had said: "History, then, in the course of time, makes the historian much more than it is made by him. My book [Histoire de France] created me. The son made his father."[66] If the English Teutonists do not demonstrate such consciousness, that may in itself be proof of the success of their history.

Since, though, the Saxon-and-Norman opposition was by the end of Victoria's reign treated not as a literary opposition but as an actuality, it no longer provided a critical perspective or a flexibility of interpretation. History had become a more clearly defined world of heroes and villains than the fictional model it followed. The implications of the relationship, however, whether seen as the effect of the construct upon consciousness or the reverse, a cultural consciousness producing the construct, are of major significance.

First, the British, themselves following the historical precedents both of the Roman Empire and of the racial and moral superiority of the Teuton tribes that overthrew it, had set an imperial example. This example other European nations sought to follow. But the syllogism of generalized characteristics, leading to the conclusion that because of race, France would act in one way and Germany in another, caused Britain to reserve its suspicions for the non-Teutonic nations, particularly France and Russia. Reliance on the trustworthiness of the Teutonic kindred caused complacency concerning the ambitions of the German nations, of whom Prussia emerged as a clear leader in the 1860s. In this, Britain's queen showed royal leadership less according to party politics than according to a Teutonic theory. During the Balkan Crisis of the 1870s, Victoria's letters show that she was deeply concerned over the balance of power — at least as far as the question related to Russia. In contrast, during the Franco-Prussian War, while retaining some personal sympathy for the Empress Eugénie and her children, she had noted the advantages to Britain of a strong Germany:

A powerful Germany can never be dangerous to England, but the very reverse, and our great object should therefore be to have her friendly and cordial towards us. Germany ever since 1848 has believed us unfavourable to her consolidation and unity which was greatly strengthened by Lord Palmerston's strong anti-German feeling exhibited on the Schleswig-Holstein question, and on many other occasions while he advocated the Italian unity which was no political object for us, and for which the Italians were far less fit than the Germans. This grieved and distressed the dear Prince most deeply.[67]

Palmerston, often remembered as the archetypal Philistine politician, was in fact insufficiently nationalistic for his queen. Victoria easily accepts a generalized picture of Italian behavior and justifies her opinions through the Prince Consort.[68] And such opinions based upon stereotypes had a shaping influence on British national policy.

This is not to suggest that Britain should have, or could have, intervened to prevent the buildup of the German military machine before 1914. Britain's sudden outrage at German imperialism at this time, however, may be questioned on the basis that Britain had knowingly and even cynically supported the concept of a strong Germany since 1870.

Second, the Mouse's recitation in *Alice in Wonderland* with which this study began prompts the question of why within a specific cultural setting nobody questions how certain cultural traditions have survived the conditions that created them. The emphasis upon Anglo-Saxon loyalty and integrity is an interesting example. As early as 1848, Kemble had asserted the Anglo-Saxon respect for their leaders, while support for established authority was presented as patriotically English. But although this spirit of "dying for one's lord" is no longer a strong part of the British sense of cultural identity, the belief that the British are more truthful — or perhaps more averse to lying — than other nations is still prevalent. A societally induced value of a horror of lying is often treated as a racial characteristic, as though genetically the Anglo-Saxons are more inclined to truthfulness. Fredric Jameson observes that "in its generic form, a specific narrative paradigm continues to emit its ideological signals long after its original content has become historically obsolete."[69] An idea originating in a literary sense of "the Other"

—aliens, and particularly Romans, lie, but Teutons do not—has, almost like a tabu, survived its original cultural utility. Just as the Mouse's recital of the history of the Conquest in *Wonderland* is outside its context, so the contextual relevance for the values of a world-dominating power has been lost.

Yet there are still more disturbing implications. The Saxon-and-Norman opposition of the nineteenth century was a clear precursor of—even a contributory factor to—the racist excesses of the twentieth. Freeman's wholehearted commitment to the mythic history he created is beyond question, but very probably Adolf Hitler believed his own history also. The closeness of the opinions expressed by Freeman and Hitler is disquieting, yet Freeman's friend and biographer Stephens published Freeman's bigoted racial opinions evidently with the confidence that patriotic Englishmen—and even women—would agree with them and admire the late historian all the more.[70] And the myth of the Teutonic kindred even survived world war. Hitler, writing in the early 1920s, expresses astonishment at the (presumably Teutonic) "genius" of Edward VII, whose personal influence contributed to "Entente" with France, which was in Hitler's opinion "almost counter to natural interests."[71] A Germanic alliance with Britain still seemed possible to him, and Hitler may indeed have believed that Britain would be more reluctant to fight against "natural interests" for a second time. In the 1930s, after all, Britain had a large and vociferous fascist party who continued to ascribe to a crude theory of natural racial superiority.

Fascism in Britain today largely cultivates a working-class image.[72] Nevertheless, continued support, albeit by a small minority, for Germanic racial superiority in Britain (now dominated by the National Front and the British National party) finally reveals racism as a conservative construct, a solution to the problem of the Two Nations. A concept of "the Other" as another race diverts attention from the possibility that "they" may be defined in economic terms—another class. Even if in the present acceptance of this pattern of history must be at least in part a cynical social manipulation, the search for a historical construct, an understanding of the present by claiming the values of a mythic past, has proved stronger than the imperial power that it was adopted to explain.

Notes

Introduction

1. Carroll, *Annotated Alice*, 46–47.
2. Green ascribes the passage to Havilland Chepmill's *Short Course in English History* (1862), in *Annotated Alice*, 46.
3. White, *Metahistory*, ix.
4. Geertz, *Interpretation of Cultures*, 5.
5. Jauss, *Aesthetic of Reception*, 23–25.
6. Pierre Bourdieu has defined the *doxa* as "that which is beyond question and which each agent tacitly accords by the mere fact of acting in accord with social convention" (*Theory of Practice*, 169).
7. This is John Cartwright's central theme in many of his writings, notably *Take your Choice*.
8. While visiting the United States in 1881, Freeman wrote to a friend:

   > I told a man here my notions of citizenship, which were
   > these —
   > 1) Dutchmen, High and Low, at once [by which Freeman
   > means peoples speaking Germanic languages]
   > 2) Other Aryans in third generation
   > 3) Non-Aryans not at all.
   > And I find many in their hearts say the same, although they
   > make it a point of honour to let in everybody.

   (Quoted in W.R.W. Stephens, *Edward A. Freeman* 2:237).

9. Butterfield, *Whig Interpretation of History*, 131.
10. de Certeau, "History: Science and Fiction," in *Heterologies*, 200.
11. Michel Foucault has drawn attention to the assumption of the document as inert (*Archaeology of Knowledge*, 6).
12. For a discussion of the work of art as created within the constraints of particular social conditions see McGann, *Romantic Ideology*, 1–3.
13. Even contradictions of this fact, however, can be found. Jules Michelet states that William landed in Kent, not Sussex, and it is not merely a verbal slip: Michelet develops a theory of Kentish regional identity that even contributes to his reading of the Becket story (*Le Moyen Age*, 297).
14. Carr, *What Is History?*, 16.
15. See, for example, Geertz's listing of Kluckhorn's different definitions (*Interpretation of Cultures*, 3–4).
16. The problems of Butterfield's blanket interpretation are shown in the person of his principal example, Lord Acton. Acton did not see himself as exclusively British, and he was not Protestant.
17. Acton, *Study of History*, 2; 74.
18. For the sense of "difference" represented by the Other, see de Certeau's *Heterologies: Discourse on the Other*, and Wlad Godzich's foreword, in which he notes that "Western thought has always thematized the other as a threat to be reduced, as a potential same-to be, a yet-not-same" (p. xiii).
19. Hill, "The Norman Yoke," 57.
20. Lord Macaulay, *Works* 1:3.
21. Indeed, Hill cites Marchamont Nedham, author of *The Case of the Commonwealth of England Stated*, as one of the earliest proponents of the theory, although Nedham's conception of history as the rise and fall of successive civilizations is strictly cyclic.
22. Toynbee, *Study of History* 2:302.
23. Croker, *"Waverley,"* 360; italics are the *Quarterly Review*'s.
24. Lockhart, *Sir Walter Scott* 7:117–118.
25. In *Waverley*, for example, the hero retires to bed at the end of fourteen chapters. This is partly a structural motif — a new chapter implies a new day — but also gives Waverley solidity as a hero who requires food and place, picturesque or otherwise, to sleep.
26. Georg Lukács, *Historical Novel*, 34–41.
27. See White, "Narrativity in the Representation of Reality," in *Content of the Form*, 1–25.
28. Jauss, *Aesthetic of Reception*, 15.

Chapter 1

1. Foucault, *Order of Things*, 219.
2. White, *Content of the Form*, 27–28.
3. Christopher Hill's major examination is the 1954 essay "The Norman Yoke": he has discussed the topic further in *"The World Turned Upside-Down"* (1972). See also Reginald Horsman's *Race and Manifest Destiny* for a discussion of the Norman Yoke as interpreted by early American colonists.
4. Foxe, *Actes and Monuments* 1:5.
5. Haller, *Elect Nation*, 142.
6. Foxe, *Actes and Monuments* 1:xviii.
7. Hill, "Norman Yoke," 57.
8. Richard Verstegen, *Restitution of Decayed Intelligence*, 1.
9. For example, in *The Law of Freedom* (1651) Winstanley argues that the natural order of property and government was overthrown by William of Normandy who "took possession of the earth for his freedom and disposed of our English ground to his friends as he pleased, and made the conquered English his servants" (p. 297).
10. Hill, "Norman Yoke," 60.
11. Haller, *Leveller Tracts*, 58.
12. Somner, *Dictionarium Saxonico-Latino-Anglicum*. A prefatory poem signed "Johannis de Bosco Hodiensis" (John Wood Daly, perhaps?) describes how the "unletter'd swords" of the current "yoke" (the Republicans) show no interest in antiquities.
13. See, for example, Sir William Jones's ninth annual discourse, "On the Origin and Families of Nations" (1792), where Jones bases his theories of racial origins on linguistics.
14. See L'Isle's introduction to his *Divers Monuments in the Saxon Tongue*.
15. George Hickes discusses the interest of his studies in the dedicatory epistle to his "Grammar" addressed to his patron Sir John Pakington, and in the long essay to Bartholomew Shower "On the Usefulness of Northern Literature," both contained in his *Thesaurus*.
16. For Wanley's life and researches, see Wright, *The Diary of Humfrey Wanley*.
17. Elizabeth Elstob, *Rudiments of Grammar*, ix.
18. Shelton's book could be purchased in boards for eight shillings — expensive, but more affordable than the original massive work.
19. In the fourteenth chapter of his *Divers Monuments* L'Isle claims kinship with the Spelmans; he also acknowledges help from "my honourable friend Sir Robert Cotton." Sir Henry Spelman's grandson Sir Roger continued the interest in Anglo-Saxon antiquities to a third generation, helping William Somner to benefit from his family's endowment for Anglo-Saxon studies at the University of Cambridge.

20. John Petheram claims that Elstob's brother was Hickes's "nephew": the exact relationship, if any, remains a mystery (*Anglo-Saxon Literature*, 89–93).

21. Nichols, *William Bowyer*, 313.

22. The exact name used by these devotees to describe themselves is not clear. Samuel Kliger does not seem justified in claiming that they thought of their studies as Gothic. In his address to his young patron in his *Thesaurus*, Hickes remarks that he made Pakington a "PhiloSaxo," the nearest suggestion of a label.

23. "In hoc libro, qui Poeseos Anglo-Saxonicae egregium est exemplum, descripta videntur bella quae Beowulfus quidam Danus, ex Regio Scyldingorum stirpe ortus, gessit contra Sueciae Regulos" (Hickes, *Thesaurus* 2:219).

24. Kemble, *Beowulf* 1:xxviii.

25. Hickes, *Thesaurus* 2:279.

26. Ibid., 281.

27. Hickes, *De Utilitate Litteraturae Septentrionalis* [Epistle to Shower], in *Thesaurus*, e.g. 82–87. Subsequent references are cited in the text as *De Utilitate*, by page number.

28. See Kliger, *Goths in England*, 1–6.

29. At this time, the other option, that history should be seen as constant progress, is far less prevalent than some version of a myth of a past Golden Age, variously seen as the time of Tacitus' *Germania*, the reign of Alfred, or some other obscure historical period.

30. Foxe, *Actes and Monuments* 2:21.

31. MacDougall, *Racial Myth*, 20, 32.

32. Spenser, *Faerie Queene*, bk. 1 canto 1, stanza 65.

33. See Asser, *Asserius de Rebus Gestis Ælfredi*, xiv–xxvii, and also Kevin Kiernan's discussion of the manuscript.

34. Spelman's *Life of Ælfred the Great* was first published in a Latin translation thought to have been made by Christopher Wace and edited by Obadiah Walker in 1678. Walker evidently had some hand in it, since at least one presentation copy bearing his signature survives. Quotations are from Thomas Hearne's 1709 English edition unless otherwise stated.

35. "Outlines for Tragedies" in *Works of John Milton* 18:243.

36. Blackmore, *Alfred, an Epick Poem*, 339. Blackmore's sources appear to have been a few pages of the Latin edition of Spelman. He may also have used Higden's *Polychronicon*, which lacks the romantic adventures and like Blackmore's work names Alfred's father as Atolphus instead of the more usual Ethelwolf.

37. Pye, *Alfred, an Epic Poem*, 93.

38. Blackmore was writing on the assumption that his dedicatee, Prince Frederick of Hanover, as the eldest son of George I's son (the future George II), would eventually become the new King Alfred. The unfortunate Blackmore was wrong again: Frederick predeceased his father.

39. Knowles, *Alfred the Great*, dedication.
40. Thomson and Mallet, *Alfred, a Masque*, 8. This work was the basis of several later versions, including a 1757 opera by Thomas Arne.
41. The 1753 play follows Tindal's translation of Rapin-Thoyras directly in names: for example, the Danish leader is usually called Guthrum, but the playwright follows Tindal in calling him Guthurm.
42. Home, *Alfred, a Tragedy*, ix. As in the majority of cases, this is only a "tragedy" in the sense of being a serious drama.
43. Kliger, *Goths in England*, 112–113.
44. Horsman, *Race and Manifest Destiny*, 17.
45. Differing interpretations of the *Germania* are set out by T. A. Dorey, *Tacitus*, 12.
46. Robert Powell's full title was: *The Life of Alfred or Alured, the First Institutor of subordinate Government in this Kingdome, and Refounder of the University of Oxford. Together with a Parallel of our Soveraigne Lord, K. Charles.*
47. Ibid., 153.
48. Spelman, *Life of Ælfred the Great*, 158.
49. Ibid., 253.
50. Paine, *Common Sense*, 47.
51. Paine, *Rights of Man*, 41.
52. Catherine Macaulay, *Revolution in France*, 5–10.
53. Complimentary references to Alfred are included in a privately printed collection of six odes presented to Macaulay at a birthday celebration at Alfred-house, 2 April 1777.
54. Bicknell, *Life of Alfred the Great*, 196–197. Bicknell also wrote a play about Alfred, seemingly choosing to ignore most of the facts collected for his history.
55. Cartwright, *Take your Choice*, 119. I can find no evidence that Alfred ever stated that all Englishmen should be as free as their thoughts. Perhaps the idea was derived from Alfred's translation of Boethius, although the "freedom" there discussed is not freemen's rights but free will. It is even possible that Cartwright, or some unidentified source from which he obtained whatever information he had not gleaned from Rapin-Thoyras and law books, confused the free will granted to "angels and men" *("englum & mannum")* with free thought granted to English-men.
56. Ibid., 147.
57. For example, in 1797, when Parliament voted that electoral reform would "subvert" the constitution, Cartwright exclaimed in horror that "such language" could be allowed by the descendants of "divine, immortal Alfred" *(English Constitution*, 12).
58. Jefferson, *Writings* 18:42. See Horsman for more on the early American perspective.
59. Burrow, *Liberal Descent*, 17.

60. See Liebermann, *Die Gesetze der AngelSachsen* 1:655, note.
61. *Alfred* in *Works of John O'Keeffe* 4:264.
62. Spelman, *Life of Ælfred the Great*, 106.
63. In *De Utilitate* Hickes claims that Spelman's assertion is without authority and that he believes juries to be an ancient Germanic practice introduced to England by the Normans (*Thesaurus, 42; 50*). Interestingly, Wotton and Shelton, who summarized Hickes's *Thesaurus*, agreed with Spelman.
64. Rapin-Thoyras, *History of England* 1:45.
65. Hume, *History of England*, chap. 3; appendix.
66. Blackstone, *Commentaries* 3:349.
67. Austin, *"England's Darling,"* vii.
68. Dickens, *Child's History of England*, 25.

Chapter 2

1. Walpole writes with equanimity of such items as "a chimney-back which I had bought for belonging to Harry VII" (*Correspondence* 20:396).
2. Percy, *Ancient English Poetry* 1:xv.
3. As a point of comparison, the Nicols sales catalogue of the Roxburghe Library reveals that a Shakespeare First Folio sold for 100 pounds in 1812, while an illuminated Chaucer manuscript raised 340 guineas. Still, this itself proves that interest in medieval writings was growing, since the same Chaucer manuscript had been auctioned for only 5 guineas in 1799.
4. The Huntington Library copy of Ritson's *On the Abstinence from Animal Food as a Moral Duty* is hand-inscribed "Bears marks of incipient insanity," presumably because it suggests that humans are closely related to apes and advocates vegetarianism. Ritson was adjudged to have died insane while trying to prove that Christ was a fraud.
5. Levine, *Amateur and the Professional*, 177–178.
6. *Roxburghe Club, List of Members*, introduction.
7. Laing, *Bannatyne Club*, introduction.
8. Since several members of the Surtees family participated in the society, no mention was made of the forged ballads that Robert Surtees had sent to Scott with plausible explanations as to where he had obtained them.
9. The English Historical Society's aims are included in *Bede's Ecclesiastical History* (English Historical Society, "General Introduction," 1).
10. Wiley, *John Mitchell Kemble and Jakob Grimm*, 224.
11. According to Levine, only in London were less than 10 percent of the members of historical societies ordained clergy (Levine, *Amateur and the Professional*, 184–185).
12. Kemble, *Codex Vercellensis* 1:vi.

13. Evans, *Society of Antiquaries*, 236–237.

14. Thompson, *Surtees Society*, 102–103; 141.

15. For example, in the first two years of operation, the Roxburghe Club's only publications were reprints of the Elizabethan earl of Surrey's translation of the *Aeneid* and of a very obscure 1599 poem by Thomas Cutwode, which made little sense without annotations.

16. Nichols, *Camden Society*, iv.

17. Nicolas, *Historical Literature*. Nicolas's book specifically addresses the home secretary and asks for government action.

18. Garnett, "Antiquarian Book Clubs," 313.

19. Levine, *Amateur and the Professional*, 179–180. This figure, of course, does not include the Roxburghe and Bannatyne clubs, founded earlier.

20. Keynes, *William Pickering, Publisher*, 13.

21. According to Thomas Gray's "advertisement" for "The Fatal Sisters" and "The Descent of Odin," he attempted the experiment as part of a proposed history of English poetry (*Complete Poems*, 27–34).

22. ". . . (Poor Alfred! Pye has been at him too!)" was Byron's note to line 390 of "English Bards and Scotch Reviewers" (*Complete Poetical Works* 1:402).

23. Cottle, *Alfred, an Epic Poem* 2:137–145. Subsequent references are cited in the text as JC, by volume and page numbers.

24. See the article on Turner by Thomas Seccombe in the *Dictionary of National Biography*.

25. Sharon Turner, *History of the Anglo-Saxons (1836)* 3:286. Subsequent references are cited in the text as ST 1836 (for the 6th ed., the last of Turner's lifetime) or as ST 1799 (for the substantially different 1st ed., *History of the Manners*), by volume and page numbers.

26. According to Petheram, Thorkelin transcribed *Beowulf* in 1786. If Turner's statements are correct, England obtained an ironic revenge for the Viking destruction of Saxon learning when Thorkelin's work was destroyed by coastal bombardment at the Battle of Copenhagen (Turner, *Anglo-Saxons* [1836] 3:288). Kiernan's researches, however, suggest that Thorkelin and his helpers had transcribed the poem more than once by this date (*Beowulf Manuscript*, 98).

27. Kiernan ascribes part of Turner's confusion to a folio that had been misplaced when Thorkelin's second transcriptions were made in 1787 (*Beowulf Manuscript*, 136–137).

28. Grierson, *Letters of Sir Walter Scott* 12:221.

29. Coleridge refers to Turner's work in a list of well-known contemporary historians in "Letters on the Spaniards" (1809), but this is not conclusive evidence that he had read it (Coleridge, *Essays on His Times* 2:40).

30. Coleridge, *Collected Letters* 3:405. Turner was apparently suspected of repeating confidences concerning the 1812 quarrel between Wordsworth and Coleridge, probably as he heard from Southey at Longman's house.

31. Curry, *New Letters of Robert Southey* 1:270.

32. By his 1836 edition, Turner was aware that Werferth rather than Alfred himself had translated the *Dialogues* but apparently still thought Alfred personally reponsible for the *Pastoral Care* (*Anglo-Saxons* [1836] 2:91–92).

33. The change in Turner's opinions was evidently noted by some of his contemporaries, since H. H. Milman responded to Turner's letter to Murray complaining at the latitudinarian tendencies of Milman's *History of the Jews* with the observation: "For his character I have the highest respect, but should have valued his opinion on this subject more highly some twenty years ago" (Smiles, *John Murray* 2:299).

34. Yonge, *Abbeychurch*, 90; 128; 49. Austin is, of course, an alternative name for Augustine of Canterbury. The "delightful Norman Conquest" must be Thierry's: whether Yonge would have agreed with her heroine's opinion of it is questionable.

35. Palgrave, *Anglo-Saxons*, prefatory letter addressed to Anna Gurney.

36. Ibid., 158.

37. Palgrave, *English Commonwealth* 1:8.

38. Palgrave, *History of Normandy* 3:596.

39. Ibid., 617.

40. In *Parliamentary Debates* (Commons), 3d ser., vol. 2 (1–2 March 1831), col. 1201, for example, "property" refers to the qualification for voting, private possessions endangered by rioting, and even to the possibility that a seat in Parliament itself might be regarded as property.

41. Burke, "Roll of Battle Abbey," 31.

42. Palgrave, *History of Normandy* 3:480.

43. Bishop Richard Rawlinson (1690–1755) had endowed a chair of Anglo-Saxon at Oxford. The recipient had to be born in England, unmarried, without a doctorate, and not a fellow of the Royal Society or Society of Antiquaries; the maximum period of office was five years. These conditions, apparently dictated by Rawlinson for personal reasons, inevitably disqualified many of the most able candidates.

44. Conybeare, *Anglo-Saxon Poetry*. Some of the contents were reprints of contributions to *Archaeologia* (1812–1813).

45. Bosworth to Frederic J. Furnivall, February 1864, FU45, Furnivall Papers, Huntington Library, San Marino, Calif.

46. Dowling, *Language and Decadence*, 52–53.

47. The early date of *Beowulf* has been convincingly questioned by Kiernan, who sees the poem as an English representation of Danish culture — similar to Thorkelin's interpretation (*Beowulf Manuscript*, 62). The desire to see the poem as a link with German prehistory nevertheless continues: the New American Library edition of a recent translation of *Beowulf* by Burton Raffles describes it as the "earliest extant poem in a modern European language. It was composed in England four centuries before the Norman Conquest."

48. Kemble, *Beowulf* 1:xxix.

49. Prefatory letter by Kemble in Francisque Michel's *Bibliothèque Anglo-Saxonne*, 25.

50. Wiley, *John Mitchell Kemble and Jakob Grimm*, 50.

51. Ibid., 112.

52. See Gretchen and Robert Ackerman's *Sir Frederic Madden, a Biographical Sketch and Bibliography.*

53. Kemble in Michel, *Bibliothèque Anglo-Saxonne*, 45.

54. Garnett, "Antiquarian Book Clubs," 311. As Michel's *Bibliothèque* reveals, Garnett slightly underestimates the number of Anglo-Saxon texts published but is correct in noting that they were few.

55. Petheram, *Anglo-Saxon Literature*, 180.

56. Honey, *Tom Brown's Universe*, 8–10.

57. "The Social Condition of the Operative Classes" (1832), in *Miscellaneous Works of Thomas Arnold*, 407.

58. Thomas Arnold, *Modern History*, 17. The sentiments sound somewhat like Edward Freeman's; as a student at Oriel, Freeman was in attendance (Burrow, *Liberal Descent*, 157).

59. Arnold, *Modern History*, 30.

60. Stanley, *Doctor Arnold* 1:71.

61. Honey notes that of the estimated 1,500 to 1,600 boys who would have come into contact with Arnold as he taught Rugby's Sixth-Form, some 300 became Church of England clergymen; and 18 of 30 Sixth-Form boys in 1834 eventually became schoolmasters (Honey, *Tom Brown's Universe*, 27).

62. "A Plan of a Work on Christian Politics" (1827), in *Miscellaneous Works of Thomas Arnold*, 436.

63. Ibid., 78.

64. Strachey, *Eminent Victorians*, 210.

Chapter 3

1. Behlmer, *The Adventures of Robin Hood — Screenplay*, introduction.

2. In the preface to the 1830 edition of *Ivanhoe* Scott recalled the rhyme about an ancestor of John Hampden (a later English hero of the people) as:

> Wing, Tring, and Ivanhoe,
> For the striking of a blow,
> Hampden did forego,
> And glad he could escape so.

The rhyme as quoted by one of Scott's early readers in a letter to the *Gentleman's Magazine* in October 1820 gives the name as that of a real village, Ivinghoe; presumably Scott was recalling a garbled version. But his *Blackwood's* reviewer of January 1820 explains: "For the benefit of our fair readers, be it mentioned, that this word means, in Anglo-Saxon (and very nearly in modern German), the *hill of joy.*" This fair reader, who accepts the suggestion of Kenneth Cameron in *English Place Names* that "Ivinghoe" means spur ("hoe") of the people ("ing") of Ifa, is at a loss to account for the reviewer's etymology.

3. Scott's title for Cedric's father, Hereward of Rotherwood (as opposed to the usual name Hereward of Bourne or Brunne), and the placing of his estates in Yorkshire rather than East Anglia might seem to preclude the possibility that Scott intended that his Hereward should be identified with the Saxon hero. But Hereward was a far less well known figure at this time than after the work of Francisque Michel; and perhaps Scott did not notice, or chose to ignore, that Turner's account of the historical Hereward (*Middle Ages* 1:107) implies that he came from the Peterborough region. Prior Aymer mentions Cedric's pride in his "uninterrupted descent from Hereward, a renowned champion of the Heptarchy"—that is, the old Anglo-Saxon kingdoms of England (*Ivanhoe*, 26; chap. 2). Perhaps the wisest assumption is that as a Norman, Prior Aymer has his facts wrong, the Heptarchy having disappeared some four hundred years previously and the only famous Hereward being one of the time of the Conquest.

4. Although he only acknowledges Ellis, Scott almost certainly read the complete poem, which was edited by Henry Weber and issued by his own publisher Constable in 1808.

5. Richard's sexual preference, if he had one, is not clear in the contemporary sources; and the belief that he was undoubtedly homosexual is an interesting example of how a very modern conjecture has become incorporated into the body of "historical fact." Burrow describes Richard and William Rufus as Freeman's "homosexual kings" (*Liberal Descent*, 209), but whereas Freeman describes William Rufus explicitly and Edward the Confessor implicitly as homosexuals, his view of Richard remains unclear, and Burrow's apparent assumption that for Freeman chivalry implies active homosexuality must be questionable. See also chap. 5.

6. Scott, *Ivanhoe*, 464; subsequent references to this edition are cited in the text as *Ivanhoe*, by page and chapter numbers. Fragments of the manuscript of *Queenhoo-Hall* remain among Scott's papers but appear to have been edited by someone else—perhaps Joseph Strutt Jr. Possibly Scott oversaw the final revision.

7. For example, Macaulay's retelling of the history of this period is close to what he had read in Scott's novels. Scott's reading of history was seemingly acceptable to a liberal of the 1840s.

8. Logan, *Poems, and Runnamede,* 181. There may possibly be an association here with John Cartwright's insistence that Alfred proclaimed: "Every English-man should be as free as his thoughts," except that as a Scot, Logan prefers the word "Briton" to the narrower term "Englishman." The banning of this play is ironic, because it could easily be read as a plea for reconciliation between English and Scots. (Connolly, *Censorship of English Drama,* 79–80).

9. Wilson assumes that Scott's notes acknowledge Turner's *History of the Anglo-Saxons* (*Ivanhoe,* 589). Turner is inconsistent in his use of titles, and Wilson refers to Turner's *Anglo-Saxons* (1799–1805) by the title of a later edition. Neither of these cover the period of *Ivanhoe,* for which Scott's more direct source is probably Turner's *History of England from the Norman Conquest to the accession of Edward the First,* later incorporated into his *History of the Middle Ages.*

10. In addition to novels and poems on chivalric themes, Scott also wrote an 1818 "Essay on Chivalry."

11. Bale, a former Carmelite, shows much of a convert's zeal in his condemnation of the Roman church, and in this play, Verity, the chorus, asks, "Thynke yow a Romane with the Romanes can not lye?" (*King Johan,* line 2197). See also Fairfield, *John Bale.*

12. Turner, *Middle Ages* 1:408. Subsequent references are cited in the text as *MA,* by volume and page numbers.

13. Even when George III was plainly incapable of carrying out official business, Parliament was extremely reluctant to declare the Prince of Wales regent and debated at length what restrictions should be placed on his actions; this sug-gests that the prince was not held in highest trust by the body that had previously been obliged to find the means of paying his debts (*Parliamentary Debates,* 31 December 1810).

14. Charlotte Mary Yonge, also discussed in chapter 3, is one example of a Prot-estant historian who saw John as the betrayer of England.

15. Chandler, *Dream of Order,* 31.

16. Ibid., 37.

17. Joseph Ritson had researched Robin Hood as a historical figure and pub-lished a collection of ballads on the subject in 1795. Unlike some of his sources, he believed that his hero lived in the reign of Richard I and that his true identity was Robert Fitz-Ooth, a Norman baron.

18. George III was still alive at the completion of *Ivanhoe,* but it must have been obvious to all that his death would soon leave England in the hands of "Prince John." The Royal Marriage Question of 1820, when Whigs and To-ries supported respectively the queen and the king, shows the extent of the disaffection with George IV even before his "real" reign began.

19. Rebecca is, according to the *Blackwood's* reviewer, "second, we suspect, to no creature of female character whatever that is to be found in the whole annals either or poetry or of romance" (*Blackwood's Magazine* 6[1819]:263). Francis

Jeffrey called her "this delightful personage" and "the divine Rebecca" (*Edinburgh Review* 33[1820]:32,50). Jerome Mitchell has noted in his discussion of *Ivanhoe* in *The Walter Scott Operas* that in several of the operatic adaptations of *Ivanhoe*, wildly improbable plot devices are used to ensure that Ivanhoe marries Rebecca, not Rowena.

20. Jeffrey remarked that since the interest was in the situations, the author of *Ivanhoe* "might have incited equal interest in the adventures of Oberon and Pigwiggin" (*Edinburgh Review* 33:54).

21. White, *Tropics of Discourse*, 88.

22. Thackeray expressed this opinion first in "Proposals for a Continuation of *Ivanhoe*" (*Fraser's Magazine* 34 [1846]), then elaborated on it in *Rebecca and Rowena* (1850). Modern readers, and particularly women, may suspect that in fact Rebecca's fate was happier than Rowena's.

23. White, *Tropics of Discourse*, 88. White makes it clear that the narrative itself is not the icon, but provides the reader with the means of forming one.

24. Freeman, *Norman Conquest* 5:839. The dispute between the Saxon and Roman churches over the date of Easter is mentioned in *The Betrothed*, not in *Ivanhoe* as this statement would seem to imply.

25. Since the "historical" Hereward was not in England at the time of the Conquest, Cedric's statement casts even more doubt on the question of whether his father is to be identified with the famous Saxon warrior of that name.

26. Scott's imaginary editor of the Wardour MS., Laurence Templeton, seems to contradict this by stating in his letter to Dryasdust that the fabled document is "Anglo-Norman" (*Ivanhoe*, 531), but perhaps he means in period rather than in language.

27. See Wilson's note on chapter 1 (*Ivanhoe*, 549). The effect is actually closer to two generations.

28. Macaulay, *Works* 1:8–13.

29. Macaulay, who in spite of his Scottish name even when in Scotland emphatically denied being a Scot, prefers the name England to Britain.

30. Thierry, *History of the Conquest* 1:xvi. Subsequent references are cited in the text as Thierry, by volume and page numbers.

31. Jeffrey observes in his review of *Ivanhoe* that in this society "nobody could have survived — Rotherwood must have been burned to the ground two or three times every year . . . " (*Edinburgh Review* 33:53).

32. Senior, "Author of *Waverley*," 135. To be fair, Senior's intention is not merely to be pedantic: he wishes to suggest that the mistake in heraldry by "the Great Unknown" was also made by Walter Scott in *Marmion* and to leave the *Quarterly* readers to draw their own conclusions.

33. Two English translations of Thierry's *History of the Conquest of England* were made: by C. C. Hamilton (1825, reissued 1841), and the better-known version by William Hazlitt the Younger (1846). The book appears not to have been well known in England until the 1840s.

34. Robin Hood's name is given as "the noble Robert Fitz-Ooth, Earl of Locksley and Huntingdon." Peacock claimed to have written the story in 1818, before he knew of *Ivanhoe*; his principle source is clearly Ritson.

35. "Not content with metamorphosing the Cavaliers and Roundheads into Normans and Saxons, he carried the theory of the conquest, and subjection of the one race to the other, even beyond the reign of Charles I" (Thierry, *History of the Conquest* 1:xiii).

36. The racial conflicts in *The Betrothed* are complex to the point of confusion and take on comic proportions in the presentation of Eveline's elderly aunts, one Norman and one Saxon, resembling each other only in an anachronistic pride of race. Although the aunts are presented humorously, Scott emphasizes that neither Saxon nor Norman places Eveline's personal happiness above considerations of race. Her future and the future of England are finally found to lie only in marriage with the half-Saxon Damian, with which the novel concludes.

37. See Jameson, *Political Unconscious*, e.g. his discussion of "ideologemes" as units of cultural interpretation (pp. 185–186).

38. Carlyle believes that the ruling classes are also Teutonic but implies that the ordinary working people are those in whom the Saxon past is most evident.

39. *Chartism*, 44 (subsequent references are cited in the text as *Chartism*, by page number). What Carlyle intended to suggest by calling his professor the German word for leaven / yeast remains in doubt, but perhaps Kingsley read him correctly when in his own 1848 exploration of the "condition of England," *Yeast*, he finally explains that his words are "yeast — an honest sample of the questions which, good or bad, are fermenting in the minds of the young of this day, and are rapidly leavening the minds of the rising generation" (Kingsley, *Works* 2:229).

40. *Chartism*, 25.

41. Horsman, *Race and Manifest Destiny*, 63.

42. For the origins of the concept of Teutonism, see also ibid., 27–29.

43. *Chartism*, 24.

44. The *Monthly Magazine*, for example, supposedly reviewing *Chartism* in February 1840, says very little about Carlyle's ideas.

45. See chapter 6 of *Alton Locke* in *Works of Charles Kingsley* 3.

46. The Five Points of the Charter were in the second and third charters enlarged to six. These were: universal manhood suffrage; a secret ballot; equal electoral districts; abolition of the property qualification for MPs; payment for MPs; and annual parliaments. The first and sixth of these reflect a Saxonist belief in the *folcmote*, while the others are anti-Norman in aiming to undermine the basis of "Normanness" — property.

47. See E. P. Thompson's *Making of the English Working Class* for a discussion of Chartism's place in class-consciousness.

48. These lines, by William Hick and first published in the *Northern Star* in June

1841, were adopted by Christopher Hill as an epigraph to his essay on the Norman Yoke.

49. Carlyle, *Sartor Resartus*, 165.

50. *Past and Present*, 80. Subsequent references are cited in the text as *PP*, by page number.

51. The Camden Society text, published without translation, is called *Chronica Jocelini de Brakelonda de Rebus Gestis Samsonis Abbatis Monasterii Sancti Edmundi* (1840).

52. In Jocelin's narrative the Jews are characterized as bankers who not unreasonably expect their loans repaid: Carlyle transforms them into "horse-leeches" (*Past and Present*, 116).

53. The continued severe punishment of the poor for violation of the game laws even in times of hardship recalled to many observers the cruel Norman forest laws — under which large tracts of land became private property — and also the flaunting of these laws by Robin Hood. Reference is made to forest laws in *Ivanhoe*, and also in *Sybil* and *Yeast*.

54. One of the more interesting responses to Carlyle's *Chartism* was Bonamy Price's essay "Chartism and Church Extension." Price argues that because "we have drawn together immense populations round certain areas, solely for the purposes of wealth, and we have cared for little else," the consequence has been the creation of a rootless society centering on the workplace rather than on the social life that could be offered by the church. He further observes that socialism has the attraction of providing "wholesome amusements" such as music and dancing for the poorer classes, an area of interest neglected by the church. His proposed solution is the construction of more churches and what would now be termed community centers, providing that social focus that Carlyle imagines Gurth had in Cedric's hall.

55. For example, the *Monthly Review*, whose reviewer, like that of the *Monthly Magazine*, was seemingly at a loss to comprehend Carlyle's argument, noted that he was "understood to be a Conservative, a Tory" (151[February 1840]: 246). Carlyle was less than delighted with this summary of his political opinions.

56. See the *Dictionary of National Biography* and Rokewood's obituary in the *Gentleman's Magazine* (172[1842]: 659–661).

57. These ideas are illustrated in Pugin's *Contrasts*, where pictures of a benevolent medieval past are set against a harsh Utilitarian present.

58. Digby, *Broad Stone of Honour* 2:239–240.

59. Living in a world determined by such solemn pronouncements as "All is race; there is no other truth," Disraeli's Tancred makes a discovery compatible with Digby's exalted view of the Crusaders — namely, that at least in terms of divine revelation, the most privileged race is not his own but the "Arabian" (Disraeli's word for Semitic). Unfortunately, this discovery leaves Tancred little else to do in the novel. Daniel Schwarz observes that *Tancred* "ends

inconclusively without establishing its dramatic correlative for its theological message" (*Disraeli's Fiction*, 102).

60. Disraeli, *Sybil*, 21–22; 1:3. Subsequent references to this edition are cited in the text as *Sybil*, by page number and book and chapter numbers.

61. In calling this character Devilsdust, perhaps Disraeli was creating his own version of Carlyle's Teufelsdröckh. In a novel where names are always significant — even to the point of the perversity of the demagogue Bishop Hatton and his Catholic brother Baptist — Devilsdust finally adopts the name of his town, and thus replaces the Egremonts as the "real" Mowbray.

62. Digby, *Broad Stone of Honour* 3:81.

63. That is, freeman. This would seem to be a Norman as opposed to a Saxon name, but Sybil and her father misinterpret both name and person as Saxon.

64. W. R. Greg expressed contempt for Disraeli's contrivance of a noble-born Chartist as early as 1845 (quoted in Stewart, *Disraeli's Novels Reviewed*, 213). More recently, Daniel Schwarz has seen the marriage between Sybil and Egremont as an avoidance of the questions raised and argues that the novel "leaves the polemic of the early chapters behind" (*Disraeli's Fiction*, 123).

65. Brantlinger, *Spirit of Reform*, 104.

66. Although Fredric Jameson states that "it would be a mistake to conclude that the ideologemes of a given period are more directly accessible to us in so-called popular literature of mass culture," he concedes that "a certain derivate literature is a potential storehouse of such materials," and Yonge's writings, with their unambivalent political stance, are surely useful pointers to these "ideologemes" (*Political Unconscious*, 185).

67. A character in *Abbeychurch* remarks: "How much interest Ivanhoe makes us take in Saxons and Normans!" (p. 132).

68. Christabel Coleridge, *Charlotte Mary Yonge*, 1.

69. The final publication of Yonge's long life was "Reasons Why I Am a Catholic and Not a Roman Catholic" (1901). Nevertheless, Yonge was not entirely blind to the pitfalls of High Anglicanism: in *The Pillars of the House* a young High Church priest is deliberately portrayed as an insufferable prig.

70. Christabel Coleridge records that the proceeds of *The Heir of Redclyffe* were used to buy a missionary ship to help convert Australian Aborigines to Anglicanism, and those of a later successful novel, *The Daisy Chain*, to a missionary college at Kolimarama (*Charlotte Mary Yonge*, 210). It was thought inappropriate for a lady to benefit personally from the profits of her writing.

71. The speaker on this topic is Augustus Mills, nephew of the antiquarian needleworker Mrs. Turner (see chap. 2).

72. In Yonge's *Pillars of the House; or Under Wode, Under Rode* the second of the thirteen Underwood children, Edgar, becomes a Pre-Raphaelite painter, leads a rakish life (at least by Yonge's standards), presents a fraudulent check, and is eventually scalped by Indians in California. Of Edgar's portrait of Brynhilda, his siblings feel that "the Pre-Raffaelitism of the hauberk was

too like worsted stockings" (3:145), while his roommate Malone's portraits of Ruth and Rachel are said to be "made coarse and vulgar by being treated with vile reality — looking like Jewish women out of fruit-shops" (3:155).

73. Yonge, *Heir of Redclyffe* 1:6–7; ch. 1.

74. Battiscombe, *Charlotte Mary Yonge*, 20.

75. Yonge, *Cameos from English History*, 21. Subsequent references are cited in the text as *Cameos*, by page number.

76. Since Richard is presented as an example for children, Yonge focuses on his early life and ignores his later reputation for loose living.

77. There seems to be some confused thinking in Yonge's theology: her major criticism of Rome is the lust for "temporal power," yet clearly in the case of England, she believes that church and state should be one — indeed, that the church may be the best property owner. Perhaps the logic is that French and Italians are prone to corruption and that the English clergy are not.

Chapter 4

1. As Freeman pointed out in his 1860 essay, Becket's very name causes problems: he is known variously as St. Thomas of Canterbury, Thomas of London, Thomas Becket, and Thomas à Becket — the last being found no earlier than the Reformation. All the names have interpretative implications, but here I shall principally use Becket, as the form favored by most of the writers discussed.

2. The concept of a "spirit of the age" (*zeitgeist*) is itself, of course, principally a product of nineteenth-century historical thinking. Yet interestingly, in discussing Becket, Hume spoke of "the genius of the age."

3. Edwin Abbott's account of the Becket miracles actually began as an exercise in New Testament scholarship and implies that the Gospel miracles may have taken their present form in a similar manner (see note 6).

4. According to Berington, the story of Rosamund, Eleanor, and the bower or labyrinth is derived from "the fabling Bromton," a compilation from earlier chronicles with additions from popular stories of late date. Berington is incorrect in ascribing to "Bromton" the origin of the Saracen princess story, which is copied from the *Quadrilogus* in the compilation supposedly by John of Brompton; but since Brompton's Chronicle had been printed by Roger Twysden in 1652, this version was probably more readily available to English scholars than the *Quadrilogus* itself.

5. Southey, *Book of the Church* 1:143. This history of the English church, declar-

edly a statement against Roman Catholic emancipation, follows Foxe's English Protestant reading of the conflict.

6. The fullest discussion of the cult of St. Thomas is the remarkable analysis by Edwin A. Abbott, *St. Thomas of Canterbury, His Death and Miracles*. Abbott concludes that many of the "healings" may have been authentic and attributable to psychosomatic reaction, changes in regimen, and possibly induced vomiting.

7. For example, the *Thomas Saga Erkibiskups*, a thirteenth-century Icelandic work edited by Eirikr Magnusson for the Rolls Series; and Latin works written in Italy summarized in Robertson's appendix to Benedict of Peterborough (*Materials* 2:283–298).

8. A good example of early acceptance of the oppositional nature of the Becket story is the portrayal in the Becket Leaves, in the British Museum. Thought to be Matthew Paris's illustrations for his own history and dated at about 1230–1240, they show conflicts between rich and poor, between soldiers and ordinary citizens, and between the king and Becket. Nothing here, however, explicitly opposes Saxons and Normans.

9. Foxe, *Actes and Monuments* 2:196.

10. Hume, *History of England* 1:167.

11. Berington, *Reign of Henry the Second*, xxi. Subsequent references are cited in the text as Berington, by page number.

12. Thierry, *History of the Conquest* 1:xxv.

13. Thierry, *Histoire de la Conquête*, introduction.

14. Turner, *Middle Ages* 1:225.

15. Exceptions include John Foxe, who, as Robertson pointed out, must have had access to the anonymous Life of Thomas in the archbishop's collection at Lambeth and hence states that Thomas's mother was a Norman called Rose; Berington, who pointed out the inconsistencies as early as 1790; and Lingard, who follows the more reliable sources in stating that Becket's parents came from Normandy.

16. *The Pictorial History of England* (1840), which was largely the work of George Craik and Charles Macfarlane, makes the statement clearly, but as Herman Merivale pointed out in the *Edinburgh Review*, this section is actually plagiarized from Thierry: "In many of the most picturesque and animated portions of the story, the writer [Macfarlane] has transferred the Frenchman's narrative bodily into his own work" (*Edinburgh Review* 74[1842]:439).

17. Darley, *Thomas à Becket* 1.1. Subsequent references are cited in the text as *TBDC*, by act and scene.

18. Palgrave's ostensible review of Thierry bears the title "Hume and His Influence on History," presumably because Thierry is scarcely mentioned. The discussion of Thierry appears in the *Quarterly Review* in "Anglo-Saxon History," a review of recent Anglo-Saxon publications (74:286).

19. Thierry was known to be a strong supporter of the July Monarchy, but since he wrote the *History of the Conquest* before such a government was conceived, Palgrave seems to be confounding writings of the young, republican Thierry with the political opinions of the older, liberal Thierry.

20. Palgrave, "Conquest and the Conqueror," 288.

21. Michelet's history, doubtless partly because of its strongly anti-English position, gained only a limited popularity in England. John Stuart Mill reviewed the earlier part in the *Edinburgh Review* in 1844, and subsequently two translations — by W. K. Kelley in 1844–1846 and G. H. Smith in 1844–1847 — were published, but fewer British historians show knowledge of Michelet than of Thierry.

22. Wilson, *To the Finland Station*, 144.

23. Palgrave notes that Becket was born "within the sound of Bow-Bell," the definition of a true Cockney ("Conquest and the Conqueror," 292).

24. Giles's title completely ignores the earlier work done by Hurrell Froude on the Vatican collections (see chap. 4).

25. Robertson, "Recent Publications on Becket," 54.

26. Milman, *History of Latin Christianity* 4:311.

27. Morris, *Life and Martyrdom*, v.

28. Robertson, *Becket, Archbishop of Canterbury*, 87.

29. Kingsley, *Roman and the Teuton*, 223.

30. Hook, *Essays in Ecclesiastical Biography* 2:130–131.

31. Hook, *Archbishops of Canterbury* 2:356.

32. Thomas More is now also a Roman Catholic saint but was not canonized until 1935.

33. Cobbett, *History of the Protestant "Reformation,"* 179.

34. *The History of the Contest* is included in Froude, *Remains* 2:31. The use of the term "high-church" is, of course, anachronistic but points the parallel with contemporary debates.

35. Michelet, *Le Moyen Age*, 299.

36. Eyton, *Itinerary of King Henry II*, iii.

37. Stanley, *Historical Memorials of Canterbury*, 145. Subsequent references to this first U.S. edition are cited in the text as *HMC*, by page number.

38. One wonders how Robertson and Stanley would have reacted had they known that an interest in flagellation survived in England, and that the Liberal party idol Gladstone himself was in all probability a flagellant.

39. Robertson, *Becket, Archbishop of Canterbury*, 87.

40. Stanley's sources include William Fitzstephen and Unknown Biographer I, whom he assumes to be Roger of Pontigny. But here he is drawing on the statements of Benedict of Peterborough and Edward Grim that Becket's torments were "unknown to us," the whole of Christendom, rather than the English, being implied.

41. Abbott, *St. Thomas of Canterbury* 1:41.

42. Fitzstephen. *Vita Sancti Thomae* 3:137.

43. Stanley doubts Fitzstephen's account of his own part during the murder — perhaps justifiably, although elsewhere he treats Fitzstephen's testimony as reliable.

44. Robertson asserts that Grim was a secular clerk on no stronger evidence than the version of Herbert of Bosham, whose loquacious life of St. Thomas Robertson treats elsewhere with extreme caution (*Materials* 2:45; also cited in the text as *Materials*, by volume and page numbers).

45. Hughes, *Tom Brown at Oxford*, 101–102.

46. The cause of the Muscular Christians' preoccupation with "unmanliness" would require a more detailed analysis than is appropriate here — but Thomas Hughes remarks without a hint of irony in his memoir of Stanley that the future dean, who had attended Rugby School a few years before him, "was certainly not bullied, although he came in frills, a cap, and with a pink watch-ribbon; and was nicknamed 'Nancy'. . ." ("Arthur Penrhyn Stanley," 240).

47. Morris, *Life and Martyrdom*, 41.

48. Lingard, *History of England* 2:75. Although the play itself does not support this reading, in the introduction to his *Thomas à Becket: A Historical Play* (1829), Douglas Jerrold had suggested that Becket's mind "was blighted by its own fires."

49. Ironically, those Anglicans whose theology placed most value on a conversion experience were most inclined to deny such a change of heart to Becket.

50. Most assertions concerning how English the Saxon church had been are so vague that they can scarcely be criticized. Lingard made an attempt to argue that the Saxon church had been truly Roman Catholic in his 1806 book, *The Antiquities of the Anglo-Saxon Church*; but there are difficulties with doctrines that the papacy had not articulated at an early date, such as the favorite "proof" cited by the Saxonists, the comments of Ælfric on the Mass that were interpreted as against transubstantiation. Lingard nevertheless set forward an informed argument for seeing continuity since the initial conversion of the Anglo-Saxons, such as in a paper inspired by the Tractarian controversy, "The Ancient Church of England and the Liturgy of the Anglican Church" (1841).

51. That Hamilton's reading of the Becket story was not unique in the United States is indicated by the introduction to the American printing of the Becket episode from Milman's *History of Latin Christianity*. The printer announces: "By an accident of position, he [Becket] questioned with the terrible power of genius the divine right of kings, and the grateful people of England, a hundred thousand at a time, flocked as pilgrims to his tomb." Probably Milman would never have suspected that his Broad Church reading, in which he comments: "The liberties of the church, as they were called, were but the establishment of one tyranny — a milder perhaps, but not less rapacious

tyranny — instead of another" (p. 243), would be interpreted as an attack on the divine right of kings — particularly since the doctrine had not been formulated in Henry II's time.

52. Hollister, *Thomas à Becket: A Tragedy*, 1.1.

53. In the ludicrous death scene, for instance, FitzUrse accidentally slays his beloved, Becket's ward, before Becket is stabbed. The dying Becket reveals that he once loved a Saxon lady, Rosamund, but the king took her from him, and FitzUrse was the result of this union — whereupon FitzUrse commits suicide.

54. Hamilton, *Thomas à Becket*, 6. Subsequent references are cited in the text as Hamilton, by page number. The phrase is almost a direct quotation from Thierry's *Histoire de la Conquête* (3:79).

55. Freeman, *Historical Essays*, 82.

56. Jauss has noted that "in order to become conscious of the otherness of a departed past, a reflective consideration of its surprising aspects is called for" ("The Alterity and Modernity of Medieval Literature," 183), but Freeman does not reveal a commitment to such a perspective.

57. Ironically, one of the few points on which Michelet and Freeman (and also Robertson) might have agreed was that the struggle between the king and the archbishop involved the question of the primacy. Michelet, whose concept of race includes regional geography, believes that the primate of Canterbury (he prefers the spelling Kenterbury) was the patron of the liberties of the men of Kent. Unfortunately, Michelet apparently does not know where Kent is; possibly, he assumes it to be synonymous with Wessex (*Le Moyen Age*, 297).

58. Freeman, *History of the Norman Conquest* 5:666.

59. Robertson, *Materials* 1:xxvi.

60. James Anthony Froude, *Thomas Becket*, 16; 1.

61. Anthony Froude is not being entirely fair. These late stories are collected in the appendix to the second volume of Robertson's *Materials*. Intriguingly, even Becket's harshest critics did not choose to expand on the number of stories that feature his wine drinking. Perhaps excessive alcohol consumption did not seem a particularly alien vice.

62. James Anthony Froude, *Thomas Becket*, 200.

63. Markham Sutherland, the hero of Anthony Froude's 1849 novel, relates: "Just as I was laying off being a boy, we fell under a strong Catholicising influence at home." In the novel, the source of this influence is not clearly stated, but beyond question Markham's experiences are based on Froude's own, and this incident is associated with Hurrell Froude's connection with Newman. Similarly, Markham's statement that "I believe I may date from this point the first disturbance my mind experienced, and however long I went on laying the blame upon myself, I never recovered it" seems indicative

that Froude did blame the Newman circle for his own loss of faith (*Nemesis of Faith*, 121–122).

64. DeVere, *St.Thomas of Canterbury*, 3.
65. Ibid., 257.
66. Irving's production was reviewed favorably in the *Athenaeum* (11 February 1893). He read from it at the Alfred Millenary celebrations (see chap. 6).
67. Alfred Tennyson, *Becket* 1.1. Henry alludes to the contest for power between the German emperor Henry IV and Pope Gregory VII (see chap. 5).
68. Ibid., 5.2.
69. "As for the introduction of Rosamund, that, of course, is a purely dramatic question. But to many it will seem that the scene is one for men alone" (Abbott, *St. Thomas of Canterbury* 1:148).

Chapter 5

1. "In the year 1066 occurred the other memorable date in English History, viz. *William the Conqueror, Ten Sixty-Six*. This is also called *The Battle of Hastings*, and was when William the Conqueror (1066) conquered England at the Battle of Senlac (Ten Sixty-Six)" (Sellar and Yeatman, *1066 and All That*, 24).
2. Freeman, *Norman Conquest* 3:503. Subsequent references are cited in the text as *NC*, by volume and page numbers.
3. Although Edward Bulwer-Lytton is only one of several names used by the man who died Lord Lytton, I retain it as the most familiar.
4. Bourdieu's distinctions between *doxa*, orthodoxy, and heterodoxy obviously cause difficulties when applied to any one specific culture. I can only again revert to the instance of Carroll's Alice and her sense of "orthodoxy" in historical interpretation.
5. Burrow, *Liberal Descent*, 194–195.
6. Bulwer-Lytton, *England and the English* 2:63.
7. *Last of the Barons*, in *The Works of Edward Bulwer Lytton*, vol. 7, preface.
8. Bulwer-Lytton's preface to *The Last of the Barons* was written for the collected edition of his novels.
9. Perhaps for this reason, in searching for an "English" hero, Charles Kingsley chose not Harold but his contemporary Hereward.
10. Foxe sees divine vengeance falling most heavily upon him, however, for the murder of Prince Alfred (Foxe, *Actes and Monuments* 2:92).
11. *Harold* in *Works of Edward Bulwer-Lytton*, vol. 1, 398; 10:2. Subsequent

references are cited in the text as *H/WBL,* by page numbers and book and chapter numbers.

12. Bulwer-Lytton adapts William of Malmesbury's story of the king's saintly mildness expressed in a comment to a recalcitrant peasant, "I would hurt you, if I could," into a statement of impotent malice (*H/WBL,* 241; 1:3).

13. See the Lives edited by Luard for the Rolls Series.

14. Walter Farquhar Hook went so far in his *Lives of the Archbishops of Canterbury* as to claim that Edward was fully aware that he was "incapable of performing the duties of a husband" but went through with the marriage in order to appease Godwin (1:492).

15. Freeman, *Reign of William Rufus,* e.g. 1:157–160.

16. See Ingram, *Saxon Chronicle,* entry for 1066.

17. Alfred Tennyson, *Harold: A Drama* 4.1. Subsequent references are cited in the text as *Harold,* by act and scene.

18. Stephens, *Edward A. Freeman* 1:241.

19. Freeman frequently returns to this story as his favorite example of "comparative mythology"; *Norman Conquest* 1:489–503; 543–550; 779–787.

20. Stephens, *Edward A. Freeman* 2:203.

21. In Orderic's words, "quibusdam signis" (Orderic, *Ecclesiastical History* 2:178).

22. The account of Harold, son of Harold, given by Freeman in *The Reign of William Rufus* is inspired by a scant reference in William of Malmesbury and is entirely the product of the historian's imagination (2:134–135). However, Kingsley claimed that Harold had a daughter (see chap. 6).

23. In the generally pro-Saxon Chronicle of Florence of Worcester, Harold and Leofwine plunder when they land in southwest England, a spot identified by Freeman with Porlock. When they reach the Isle of Wight, however, which was part of Harold's earldom of Wessex, they merely take what their troops need. Since Florence makes a clear distinction between the two actions, Freeman cannot use this evidence to support his theory that at Porlock Harold merely took the supplies he needed (Forrester, *Florence of Worcester,* 150).

24. See Gooch's discussion of Ranke's use of authorities in *History and Historians in the Nineteenth Century,* (p. 97). For a modern appraisal of Ranke, see Hayden White's *Metahistory,* where Ranke's objective of a history very different from Scott's is emphasized (pp. 163–190).

25. The sentence reveals Freeman's relative standards of truthful nations: "The English writers are silent; from the German writers we learn next to nothing; the Scandinavian history of this age is still at least half mythical; the Norman writers never held truth to be of any moment when the relations of England and Normandy were concerned . . ." (*Norman Conquest* 1:471).

26. Orderic, *Ecclesiastical History* 2:138.

27. See Bulwer-Lytton, *H/WBL,* 465; 12:6; Freeman, *Norman Conquest* 3:435–439.

28. Of these, the most famous story is of Edward's prophetic vision that the Seven Sleepers had turned over, which was confirmed by an embassy to Ephesus. The miracle stories bear a strong resemblance to those told by William of Malmesbury and date from approximately seventy years after Edward's death.

29. Luard, *Edward the Confessor*. Subsequent references are cited in the text as *Edward*, by page number.

30. For example, *Norman Conquest* 2:500, where "the Biographer" is a major source.

31. See Stenton's *Bayeux Tapestry*.

32. Freeman, *William the Conqueror*, 3.

33. Forrester, *Florence of Worcester*, entry for 1066.

34. Palgrave, *History of Normandy* 3:296; 3:305–306.

35. Bulwer-Lytton also seems to imply a connection with *Macbeth* when Harold consults the witch Hilda; but writers sympathetic to Harold are usually disinclined to stress his ambition.

36. Tennyson strongly disliked Bulwer-Lytton but nevertheless openly acknowledged a debt to the novelist's *Harold* (Ricks, *Tennyson*, 184–185).

37. James, "Tennyson's *Harold*, " 188.

38. See Bale's *King Johan*, 134. Kingsley made the assertion in a review of Froude's *History of England* in *Macmillan's Magazine* and repeated it in a lengthy correspondence with Newman. Although the *Apologia Pro Vita Sua* showed more sophistication of argument than Kingsley's writing, in a perverse way this demonstrated Kingsley's point: the Romans are better at disputations, because they have less commitment to "simple truth." See appendices to Martin J. Svaglic's edition of Newman's *Apologia*, 356–384.

39. No Victorian writer seems to have doubted that Harold was struck by an arrow in the eye, probably because of the high regard given to the Norman chronicler Wace, but an opinion now widely held is that the story originated with the Bayeux Tapestry itself. Charles Gibbs-Smith comments:

> It is sometimes said that both the figures are Harold, seen first being shot in the eye, and then, having wrenched the arrow out, being hacked down by a Norman. This theory is quite untenable: in no part of the Tapestry, nor in any other comparable work, is the same individual introduced twice within the span of a horse, or for that matter twice within the same section of the story.
>
> (Stenton, *Bayeux Tapestry*, 188)

The theory may indeed be quite untenable, but Wace's source, or since he was a priest at Bayeux very probably Wace himself, seemingly did read the tapestry in this way.

40. The story is included in Michel's *Chroniques Anglo-Normandes.*
41. Burrow, *Liberal Descent,* 195.
42. Freeman, *English Constitution,* 151.
43. Yonge, *Cameos from English History,* 64.
44. But William is elsewhere said to have used mutilation as a punishment — for example, Hereward's followers are said by Florence to have lost their hands or eyes.
45. For example, in Freeman's *William the Conqueror* William is said to have shown a "distinct unwillingness to take human life except in fair fighting on the battlefield" (p. 17).
46. Thus the third edition, a slight strengthening from the first edition, reads: "If there ever was lawful ruler in this world, such of a truth was Harold . . ." (Freeman, *Norman Conquest* 3:47).
47. Early sources make much of this point, for if we assume that victory gives legitimacy to the papal office, Robert was the pope's appointment, while Stigand was virtually appointed by the English and granted his pallium by the antipope. In launching his campaign against Harold, William of Normandy was thus able to appeal to the spurned authority of the pope.
48. Hook, *Archbishops of Canterbury* 1:529.
49. For example, most (Hook being the exception) believe that he opposed the Berengarians, who rejected transubstantiation; that he opposed a married clergy; and that he reasserted the authority of the pope in ecclesiastical appointments.
50. Stephen, "Hildebrand," in *Essays in Ecclesiastical Biography* 1:27–28.
51. The idea that Hildebrand plotted the Norman Conquest seems to be based on one statement from a letter written to William in 1080:

> I am sure that you know how devoted I was to your interests before I was raised to the summits of priestly rule, how useful I showed myself to you and with what zeal I labored to advance you to your royal state. So much so that I had to bear from certain of my brethren the almost infamous charge of having lent my aid to bringing about so great a sacrifice of human life. But God is my witness how conscientiously I acted, trusting as I did in your excellent qualities and believing that the higher you might rise the more useful you would be to God and to Holy Church. (Emerton, *Pope Gregory VII,* 154)

But the pope's claim always to have supported William — made in the hope of securing his continued allegiance — is hardly evidence that the Norman Conquest was a Roman Catholic plot.

52. W.R.W. Stephens, *Hildebrand*, 82–83.

53. Freeman, *Norman Conquest* 3:402. Freeman very probably overstates the permanent nature of the supposed Celtic influx from northern France's Bretons, whom he calls the "Welsh of lesser Britain."

54. Bernal, *Black Athena*, 281–283.

55. Lord Acton, as noted, was Roman Catholic yet still accepted the theory of the Teuton kindred.

56. Here I use the word "culture" in a more anthropological sense than Arnold, who tends to use it in the sense of "high culture," the stock of shared literary, as opposed to social, knowledge.

57. For example, Bulwer-Lytton calls Prussia "that country in which, throughout the whole world, education is most admirably administered" (*England and the English* 1:230).

58. "Schools and Universities on the Continent," in *Complete Prose Works of Matthew Arnold* 4:16. Subsequent references to this collection are cited in the text as *PWMA*, by volume and page number.

59. Walter William Skeat began publishing his edition of *Piers Plowman* in 1867; he began editing Chaucer in the 1870s. For Victorian editing of Chaucer see Ruggiers, *Editing Chaucer: The Great Tradition*.

60. Martin Bernal observes that even in recent years attitudes towards the actual Philistine race "can be explained only in terms of the 19th-and 20th-century view of 'Philistines' as the exact opposite of the Hellenes — as enemies of culture" (*Black Athena*, 450). Yet some of the people that Matthew Arnold would have termed Philistines were self-styled Hellenes, Gladstone himself being the obvious example.

61. Carlyle, *Sartor Resartus*, 87.

62. "Heinrich Heine" in *Complete Prose Works of Matthew Arnold* 3:112.

63. "Culture and Anarchy," ibid. 5:143–146.

64. See "Friendship's Garland," ibid., vol. 5.

65. In fact, older middle-class Dissenters had particular reason to despise the form of culture offered by the universities, since under the Test Acts they had been excluded from it.

66. For examples of artworks using Saxon themes, see chap. 6. Even the revival of beards (these are protrayed as strange and Bohemian in Charles Kingsley's 1848 novel *Yeast*, but manly and English in his 1866 novel *Hereward the Wake*) may perhaps be influenced by Saxon ideals.

67. In fact, although George Augustus Sala frequently refers to both Britons and Americans as "Anglo-Saxons," and seems to have become a spokesman for the class of Anglo-Saxons who shocked Arnold's sensibilities, this entertaining and prolific journalist was not himself of English stock: his father was Italian, his mother a West Indian of mixed race, and he was educated in France.

68. For the textual history of this work, see *Complete Prose Works of Matthew Arnold*, vol 5.

69. Arnold refers to the habit of visiting the battlefields as humane but neutral spectators (ibid., 348, note).

Chapter 6

1. Austin, *Victoria the Wise*, 24.
2. Alf Jones, the narrator of Graham Greene's *Doctor Fischer of Geneva* (1980) observes that he had been given the name Alfred by his Anglo-Saxonist father and "this Christian name, for some inexplicable reason, had become corrupted in the eyes of our middle-class world; it belonged exclusively to the working class and was usually abbreviated to Alf" (p. 18). The reason may not be inexplicable: perhaps the middle class abandoned Alfred simply because it was so middle class. Jones, however, is about 50: Alfred has now also been abandoned by the working class.
3. The biography of the Prince Consort, authorized by Victoria, gives much of the credit for their marriage to the young queen's Anglophile German advisors, especially her Saxon uncle, Leopold of Belgium, and Baron Stockmar (Martin, *Prince Consort* 1:18).
4. Disraeli, *Sybil*, 50; 1:6.
5. Kemble, *Saxons in England*, preface.
6. Burrow, *Liberal Descent*, 162–163.
7. Sala provides a typical instance of the change in attitude towards the Prince Consort. In *Twice Round the Clock* (1859) he had commented on Albert's general unprinceliness: "I should say that his Royal Highness's coat was seedy" (p. 74). Writing in 1894, however, Sala recalls how the Prince Consort's "dignified, decorous, and blameless character became at once a model to all English gentlemen" (*Things I Have Seen* 2:94).
8. Braudy, *Frenzy of Renown*, 275–277, 335–336.
9. One of the most publicized criticisms was that of Liberal Member of Parliament A. S. Ayrton at a constituency meeting in 1866, where the queen was defended by John Bright.
10. See Darby and Smith, *Prince Consort*.
11. The Princess Royal was enthusiastic in her recognition of her father in Tennyson's Arthur. Hallam Tennyson *Alfred Lord Tennyson* 1:481).
12. Swinburne, "Under the Microscope," 403.
13. Ricks, *Poems of Tennyson*, 1467.
14. Besant's speech is quoted by Alfred Bowker in *The Alfred Millenary*, (p. 37).
15. For a photograph of the statue see Besant, *Queen's Reign*, 67.
16. Perhaps following in the Norse tradition of tracing the lineage of all kings back to Odin, Kingsley traces Alexandra's bloodline back to Harold's daugh-

ter Gyva and Waldemar, King of Russia, "from whom derive, by the Mother's side, Waldemar I, King of Denmark" (*Hereward*, 232; 18).

17. Ricks, *Poems of Tennyson*, 1224.

18. Victoria's correspondence, while suggesting that she did not entirely approve of France, nevertheless reveals that she accepted the the family of Napoleon III as royalty and Empress Eugénie as her sister queen (Buckle, *Letters of Queen Victoria* 2:63).

19. See Dwight, *Modern Philology*, chaps. 1 and 2, for a discussion of contemporary perspectives on comparative philology.

20. Cox, "Science of Language," 67. The ideas were not, of course, so new to German scholars.

21. Burrow, *Evolution and Society*, 109.

22. Müller, *Science of Language*, 27. Subsequent references are cited in the text as *SL*, by page number.

23. See, for example, Jones's 1784 "On the Gods of Greece, Italy, and India" (*Works* 1:229–280). This is not to suggest that Jones believed that the different speakers of Indo-European languages were equal in the present, but rather that they shared common origins (Said, *Orientalism*, 75–79).

24. See Martin Bernal's discussion of the Aryan Model in *Black Athena*, (pp. 1–2).

25. The phrase is from Tennyson's sonnet to Kemble, which Hallam Tennyson states to have been written when Kemble "gave up the thought of taking Orders, and devoted himself to Anglo-Saxon history and literature." The sonnet was published in 1830, but perhaps because of its strong anticlerical sentiment was not reprinted (Ricks, *Poems of Tennyson*, 257).

26. Dowling, *Language and Decadence*, xiii.

27. Freeman, *Comparative Politics*, iii. Subsequent references are cited in the text as *CP*, by page number.

28. Freeman seems to have borrowed the phrase "German Ocean," a Teutonic name for the North Sea, from Müller, who uses it in *The Science of Language* (p. 333).

29. Stubbs, *Constitutional History of England* 1:3. Subsequent references are cited in the text as *CHE*, by volume and page number.

30. The label "Anglo-Saxon" continues to cause difficulties. The Oxford English Dictionary describes it as the name for a particular form of Old English applied to the whole. A recent book on language in Britain, W. B. Lockwood's *Languages of the British Isles Past and Present*, innocently states: "Two chief dialect groupings may be traced in Old English: Anglian and West-Saxon, corresponding to the usage of the districts north and south of the Thames respectively, hence the term Anglo-Saxon, often used as a synonym for Old English" (p. 16).

31. The year of Alfred's death was said to be 901 in a number of sources, notably some versions of the Anglo-Saxon Chronicle. A so-called Alfred Committee had also celebrated the millenary of his birth at Wantage in 1849: see the

Alfred Committee's *Whole Works of Alfred the Great,* 3 vols. (Oxford and Cambridge: Alfred Committee, 1852). Modern scholars favor the year 899 as the date of Alfred's death. See, for example, a recent appraisal of Alfred, Allen J. Frantzen's *King Alfred.*

32. The title is based on *The Proverbs of Alfred,* an English poem probably written in the twelfth century. Considering that this is the best evidence that a memory of Alfred survived the Conquest, the nineteenth-century admirers of Alfred drew comparatively little attention to it. Subsequent references are cited in the text as *ED,* by page number.

33. For example, John Rusk wrote in *The Beautiful Life and Illustrious Reign of Queen Victoria,* "Absolute truthfulness and sincerity were the qualities which dominated her character" (p. 448). This analysis of Victoria's character and of Britain during her reign is not as one-sided as the title might suggest.

34. Bowker, *King Alfred Millenary,* 3. Subsequent references are cited in the text as *KAM,* by page number.

35. Bowker, *Alfred the Great,* 4–5. Subsequent references are cited in the text as *AG,* by page number.

36. Besant, *Queen's Reign,* 6.

37. Ibid., 60. Since little is known concerning Anglo-Saxon needlecraft, it would be interesting to know the source of Besant's information. Perhaps he was merely following the tradition that the Bayeux Tapestry was worked by Englishwomen.

38. Bowker, *Alfred the Great,* 7. This somewhat simplistic view of literary history would seem at least to ignore Marie de France and to discount the Norman elements in Chaucer.

39. Bowker, *Alfred Millenary,* 74.

40. This is one of the very few references to the Normans during the Alfred commemoration, and is far removed from the theory of the Norman Yoke: the Conquest merely strengthened English identity; it did not substantially alter it.

41. Freeman and Cox, *Poems Legendary and Historical,* 198.

42. Said notes examples of this sense of an Anglo-Saxon "burden" in the face of other races' irresponsibility even in the years immediately preceding the 1914–1918 war (*Orientalism,* 31–36).

43. Kingsley, "The Strategy of Providence," in *Roman and the Teuton,* 305.

44. See Horsman's *Race and Manifest Destiny.* The term "manifest destiny" is especially a product of American Anglo-Saxonism. Frederick and Lois Bannister Merk, for example, note: "A particularly United States version of the Saxon myth is the duty of the United States to regenerate backward peoples of the continent" (*Manifest Destiny,* 33). Nevertheless, British writers share something of this sense of "destiny."

45. Kingsley, *Roman and the Teuton,* 303.

46. See, for example, David G. Ritchie's 1889 essay *Darwinism and Politics,* where

he argues that Darwin "looks forward to the elimination of the lower races by the highest civilised races throughout the world" (p. 7). Darwin himself seems to have preferred the phrase "struggle for existence" to "survival of the fittest."

47. Bulwer-Lytton, dedicating *England and the English* to Talleyrand in the early 1830s, maintained that this hatred no longer existed, but even his own works hardly bear out the assertion (1:42).

48. The attribution to Macaulay of two articles from the January 1825 edition of the *Edinburgh Review*, "West Indian Slavery" and "Hayti," is not definite. They may have been written by, or in collaboration with, Henry Brougham. In either case, they are a reasonable summary of the Whig — and also the Tory Evangelical — conception of race.

49. One rare exception is L. D. Nelme's *Essay towards the Investigation of the Origin and Elements of English Language and Letters* (1772), where Nelme argues that the "monosyllabic" base of the Anglo-Saxon language proves it to be the closest to the tongue spoken before Babel. Nelme's essay is of interest in connecting a Norman Yoke theory with a philological theory but does not seem to have had much influence.

50. Arnold characterizes the *Daily Telegraph* (now a conservative paper) as the Liberal "voice" (*Friendship's Garland*, 66–67).

51. Tennyson, "Britons Guard Your Own," in Ricks, *Poems of Tennyson*, 997–999. Originally published in the *Examiner* in 1852.

52. For example, in 1859 *Punch* featured a cartoon in which Napoleon III was depicted as a porcupine with bayonets for quills.

53. Hughes, *Life of Alfred the Great*. The second edition (1871) contains these thoughts on Napoleon III in a preface evidently written before the outcome of the Franco-Prussian War was certain.

54. Stephens, *Edward A. Freeman* 2:2.

55. Michelet particularly refers to Waterloo as a battle (against the French) fought by the whole world but a victory claimed by England (*Le Moyen Age*, 220).

56. Quoted by Stephens, *Edward A. Freeman* 2:3.

57. Since Disraeli was under considerable pressure from Victoria to aid the Turks, by Freeman's logic, the queen of England must have been Semitic.

58. Quoted by Stephens, *Edward A. Freeman* 2:212. Freeman was assuming by this date, after the Franco-Prussian War, that the French had already been "got rid of."

59. Ibid. 1:280–282.

60. Correspondence between Gladstone and his wife reveals that both found the idea, which Gladstone saw in a letter in the *Daily News* in November 1862, highly comical (Bassett, *Gladstone to his Wife*, 141–142).

61. For "progressive" attitudes towards Greece, see Bernal, *Black Athena*, 330–336.

62. Greece eventually did have a Teutonic king. Victoria's son Alfred prudently rejected the offer of the crown, which eventually was taken by Prince William George of Schleswig-Holstein-Sunderburg-Glücksburg.

63. "Schemes of thought and perception can produce the objectivity that they do produce only by producing misrecognition of the limits of the cognition that they make possible, thereby founding immediate adherence, in the doxic mode, to the world of tradition experienced as a 'natural world' and taken for granted" (Pierre Bourdieu, *Theory of Practice*, 164).

64. For example, in the late 1850s the *Punch* writers made several jokes on how fat Albert had become, something that his memorials, depicting him as a valiant knight, fail to reflect.

65. Bulwer-Lytton suggests that Nelson was one of the few Englishmen consciously to realize that "the best model of conquering France was seriously to inculcate, as a virtue, the necessity of detesting them" (*England and the English* 1:43).

66. Michelet, *Le Moyen Age*, 19 (my translation).

67. Buckle, *Letters of Queen Victoria* 2:62 (memorandum for September 1870). The Schleswig-Holstein question involved a threat by Palmerston that Britain would use force if necessary to defend the Danish provinces against annexation. When Prussia called his bluff, Palmerston did not receive government support for intervention and was forced to resign.

68. In fact, Albert died before the Schleswig-Holstein question came to a head; Victoria may have been projecting her own policies onto her dead husband.

69. Jameson, *Political Unconscious*, 186.

70. For example, Stephens demonstrates Freeman's fondness for children by quoting letters showing his amusement at a little girl expressing anti-Semitic sentiments (*Edward A. Freeman* 2:235).

71. Hitler, *Mein Kampf*, 666.

72. Zig Layton-Henry observes: "Unemployment is, of course, both a cause and an exacerbating factor as immigrants [to Britain] are a convenient scapegoat and focus for the resentment and frustration of unemployed white youths, and one which racist organisations like the National Front and the British Movement are only too willing to exploit" (*The Politics of Race in Britain*, 115). See also Layton-Henry's analysis of the National Front (Ibid., 87–107).

Works Cited

Abbott, Edwin A. *St. Thomas of Canterbury: His Death and Miracles.* London: Black, 1894.

Ackerman, Robert W. and Gretchen P. *Sir Frederic Madden, A Biographical Sketch and Bibliography.* New York: Garland, 1979.

Acton, Lord [John Emerich Edward Darlberg]. *A Lecture on the Study of History, Delivered at Cambridge June 11 1895.* London: Macmillan, 1895.

Alfred the Great, Deliverer of his Country. London, 1753.

Arnold, Matthew. *Complete Prose Works of Matthew Arnold.* Edited by R. H. Super. 11 vols. Ann Arbor: Michigan University Press, 1960–1977.

Arnold, Thomas. *Introductory Lectures on Modern History.* Oxford: J. H. Parker, 1842.

————. *The Miscellaneous Works of Thomas Arnold, D.D.* 2d U.S. ed. New York: Appleton, 1846.

Asser, John. *Annales Rerum Gestarum Alfredi Magni.* Edited by Francis Wise. Oxford, 1723.

————. *Asserius de Rebus Gestis Ælfredi.* Edited by W. H. Stevenson. Oxford: Clarendon, 1904.

Austin, Alfred. *"England's Darling."* London: Macmillan, 1896.

————. *Victoria the Wise.* London: Eyre and Spottiswood, 1901.

Bale, John. *King Johan.* Edited by Barry B. Adams. San Marino: Huntington Library, 1969.

Bassett, A. Tilney, ed. *Gladstone to His Wife.* London: Methuen, 1936.

Battiscombe, Georgina. *Charlotte Mary Yonge: The Story of an Uneventful Life.* London: Constable, 1943.

Behlman, Rudy, ed. *The Adventures of Robin Hood.* Warner Bros. Screenplay Series. Madison: University of Wisconsin Press, 1979.

Benzie, William. *Dr. F. J. Furnivall, Victorian Scholar Adventurer*. Norman, Okla.: Pilgrim Books, 1983.

Berington, Joseph. *History of the Reign of Henry the Second, and of Richard and John . . . In which the Character of Thomas a Becket is Vindicated from the Attacks of George Lord Lyttelton*. Birmingham, 1790.

Bernal, Martin. *Black Athena*. Vol. 1. New Brunswick: Rutgers University Press, 1987.

Besant, Sir Walter. *The Queen's Reign and Its Commemoration 1837–97*. London: Warner, 1897.

———. *The Story of King Alfred*. 1901. The Library of Useful Stories. New York: Appleton, 1930.

Bicknell, Alexander. *The Life of Alfred the Great, King of the Anglo-Saxons*. London, 1777.

———. *The Patriot King, or Alfred and Elvida*. London, 1788.

Blackmore, Sir Richard. *Alfred, an Epick Poem*. London, 1723.

Blackstone, Sir William. *Commentaries upon the Laws of England*. 1765–69. Edited by Joseph Chitty. 4 vols. London: Water, 1826.

Blake, E.O., ed. *Liber Eliensis*. London: Royal Historical Society, 1962.

Bosworth, Joseph. *The Elements of Anglo-Saxon Grammar*. London: Harding, 1823.

Bourdieu, Pierre. *Outline of a Theory of Practice*. Translated by Richard Nice. Cambridge: Cambridge University Press, 1972.

Bowker, Alfred, ed. *Alfred the Great: Containing Chapters on His Life and Times*. London: Macmillan, 1899.

———. *The Alfred Millenary*. London: Macmillan, 1902.

Brantlinger, Patrick. *The Spirit of Reform: British Literature and Politics, 1832–1867*. Cambridge: Harvard University Press, 1977.

Braudy, Leo. *The Frenzy of Renown*. New York: Oxford University Press, 1986.

Buckle, George Earle, ed. *The Letters of Queen Victoria*. 2d and 3d Series. London: John Murray, 1926–1932.

Bulwer-Lytton, Edward. *England and the English*. 2 vols. New York: Harper, 1833.

———. *The Works of Edward Bulwer Lytton*. 8 vols. New York: Collier, n.d.

Burke, John. "The Rolls of Battle Abbey." *Patrician* 1 (May 1846): 31–44.

Burrow, J. W. *Evolution and Society*. Cambridge: Cambridge University Press, 1966.

———. *A Liberal Descent: Victorian Historians and the English Past*. 1981. Reprint. Cambridge: Cambridge University Press, 1983.

Butterfield, Sir Herbert. *The Whig Interpretation of History*. London: Bell, 1931.

Byron, Lord George Gordon. *The Complete Poetical Works*. Edited by Jerome McGann. 5 vols. Oxford: Clarendon, 1980–1986.

Cameron, Kenneth. *English Place Names*. London: Batsford, 1961.

Carlyle, Thomas. *Chartism*. Corrected Edition. London: Chapman and Hall, 1890.

———. *Past and Present*. London: Chapman and Hall, 1890.

———. *Sartor Resartus*. London: Chapman and Hall, 1890.

Carr, Ernest H. *What Is History?* 1961. New York: Knopf, 1972.

Carroll, Lewis. *The Annotated Alice*. Edited by Martin Gardner. 2d ed. Harmondsworth: Penguin, 1970.

Cartwright, John. *An Appeal on the Subject of the English Constitution*. London, 1797.

————. *The English Constitution Produced and Illustrated*. London: Cleary, 1823.

————. *Take your Choice*. 2d ed. London, 1777.

Chandler, Alice. *A Dream of Order*. University of Nebraska Press, 1970.

Cobbett, William. *A History of the Protestant "Reformation," in England and Ireland, Showing how this event has improverished and degraded the main body of the People in those Countries. In a series of letters addressed to all sensible and just Englishmen*. London: Clement, 1824–1827.

Coleridge, Christabel. *Charlotte Mary Yonge: Her Life and Letters*. London: Macmillan, 1903.

Coleridge, Samuel Taylor. *Collected Letters of Samuel Taylor Coleridge*. Edited by Earl Leslie Griggs. 6 vols. Oxford: Clarendon, 1956–1971.

Coleridge, Samuel T. *Essays on His Times*. Edited by David V. Erdman. 3 vols. Princeton: Bollingen, 1978.

Connolly, L. W. *The Censorship of English Drama, 1737–1824*. San Marino: Huntington Library, 1976.

Conybeare, John J. "Account of the Exeter Ms." *Archaeologia* 17 (1814):180–188.

————. "Observations on the Metre of Anglo-Saxon Poetry." *Archaeologia* 17 (1814): 257–274.

————. *Illustrations of Anglo-Saxon Poetry*. Edited by Daniel Conybeare. London: Harding and Lepard, 1826.

Cordasco, Francisco. *The Bohn Libraries: A History and Checklist*. New York: Burt Franklin, 1951.

Cottle, Amos, trans. *Icelandic Poetry or the Edda of Saemund*. Bristol, 1797.

Cottle, Joseph. *Alfred, an Epic Poem in Twenty-four Books*. 2 vols. 1800. Newburyport, Mass.: W. B. Allen, 1814.

Cox, George W. "Lectures on the Science of Language." *Edinburgh Review* 115 (June 1865): 67–103.

Croker, John Wilson. *"Waverley." Quarterly Review* 11 (1814): 354–377. [Authorship sometimes ascribed to William Gifford.]

Curry, Kenneth, ed. *New Letters of Robert Southey*. 2 vols. New York: Columbia University Press, 1965.

Darby, Elisabeth, and Nicola Smith. *The Cult of the Prince Consort*. New Haven: Yale University Press, 1983.

Darley, George. *Thomas à Becket: A Dramatic Chronicle*. London: Moxon, 1840.

de Certeau, Michel. *Heterologies: Discourse on the Other*. Translated by Brian Massumi. Minneapolis: University of Minnesota Press, 1985.

DeVere, Aubrey Henry. *St. Thomas of Canterbury: A Dramatic Poem*. London: Henry King, 1876.

Dickens, Charles. *A Child's History of England*. Vol. 15 of *The Complete Works of Charles Dickens*. 20 vols. New York: Bigelow and Brown, n.d.

Digby, Kenelm Henry. *The Broad Stone of Honour; or, The True Sense and Practice of Chivalry*. 1826. Rev. ed. 4 vols. London: Lumley, 1844–1846.

Disraeli, Benjamin. *Sybil; or, The Two Nations*. 1845. Reprint. Harmondsworth: Penguin, 1954.

————. *Tancred; or, the New Crusade*. 1847. Reprint. London: John Lane, 1905.

Dorey, T. A., ed. *Tacitus*. London: Routledge and Kegan Paul, 1969.

Dowling, Linda. *Language and Decadence in the Victorian Fin de Siècle*. Princeton: Princeton University Press, 1986.

Duchesne, André, ed. *Historiae Normannorum Scriptores Antiquae*. Paris, 1699.

Dwight, Benjamin W. *Modern Philology: Its Discoveries, History, and Influence*. 1st ser., 3d ed. New York: Scribner, 1864.

Ellis, Sir Henry, ed. *Introduction and Indexes to Domesday*. 2 vols. London: Public Records Office, 1833.

Elstob, Elizabeth. *The Rudiments of Grammar for the English-Saxon Tongue*. London, 1715.

————. , and William Elstob, eds. *An English-Saxon Homily on the Birthday of St. Gregory, anciently used in the English-Saxon Church*. London, 1709.

Emerton, Ephraim, ed. and trans. *The Correspondence of Pope Gregory VII: Selected Letters from the Registrum*. New York: Columbia University Press, 1932.

English Historical Society. "General Introduction to the English Historical Society." In *Bede's Ecclesiastical History*. Edited by Joseph Stevenson. London: English Historical Society, 1841.

Evans, Joan. *A History of the Society of Antiquaries*. Oxford: Oxford University Press, 1956.

Eyton, R. W., ed. *The Court, Household, and Itinerary of King Henry II*. London: Taylor, 1878.

Fairfield, Leslie P. *John Bale, Mythmaker for the English Reformation*. W. Lafeyette, Ind.: Purdue University Press, 1976.

Forrester, Thomas, ed. *The Chronicle of Florence of Worcester, with Continuations*. London: Bohn, 1854.

Foucault, Michel. *The Archaeology of Knowledge*. Translated by A. M. Sheridan Smith. New York: Pantheon, 1972.

————. *The Order of Things, an Archaeology of the Human Sciences*. 1970. Reprint. New York: Vintage Books, 1973.

Foxe, John. *Actes and Monuments [Book of Martyrs]*. 1560. Reprint. Edited by George Townsend. 7 vols. London: Seeley, 1843.

Frantzen, Allen J. *King Alfred*. Boston: Twayne, 1986.

Freeman, Edward A. *Comparative Politics*. London: Macmillan, 1873.

————. *The Growth of the English Constitution from the Earliest Times*. London: Macmillan, 1872.

————. *Historical Essays*. 1st ser. 2d ed. London: Macmillan, 1872.

———. *The History of the Norman Conquest of England, Its Causes and Results*. 3d ed. 6 vols. Oxford: Clarendon, 1877.

———. , and George Cox. *Poems Legendary and Historical*. London: Longmans, 1850.

———. *The Reign of William Rufus*. 2 vols. Oxford: Clarendon, 1882.

———. *William the Conqueror*. Twelve English Statesmen Series. London: Macmillan, 1888.

Froude, James Anthony. *The Life and Times of Thomas Becket*. New York: Scribner's, 1878.

———. *The Nemesis of Faith*. London: John Chapman, 1847.

Froude, Richard Hurrell. *Remains of the Reverend Richard Hurrell Froude*. Edited by John Henry Newman and John Keble. 2 vols. in 4. London and Derby: Rivington, 1838–1839.

Gaimar, Geffrei. *L'Estorie des Engles*. Edited by Thomas Duffus Hardy and Charles Trice Martin. Rolls Series. London: Longmans, 1888–1889.

Garnett, Richard. "Antiquarian Book Clubs." *Quarterly Review* 82 (1848): 309–342.

Geertz, Clifford. *The Interpretation of Cultures: Selected Essays*. New York: Basic Books, 1973.

Giles, John Allen, ed. *The Life and Letters of Thomas à Becket, Now First Gathered from the Contemporary Historians*. 2 vols. London, 1846.

Gooch, George Peabody. *History and Historians in the Nineteenth Century*. 1913. Rev. ed. London: Beacon Press, 1959.

Graves, Charles L., ed. *Mr. Punch's History of Modern England*. 4 vols. London: Cassell, 1921.

Gray, Thomas. *The Complete Poems of Thomas Gray; English, Latin, and Greek*. Edited by H. W. Starr and J. R. Hendrickson. Oxford: Clarendon, 1966.

Green, John Richard. *A Short History of the English People*. London: Macmillan, 1875.

Greene, Graham. *Doctor Fischer of Geneva, or The Bomb Party*. New York: Simon and Schuster, 1980.

Grierson, Sir Herbert, ed. *Letters of Sir Walter Scott*. 12 vols. London: Constable, 1832–1837.

Hallam, Henry. *View of the State of Europe in the Middle Ages*. 1818. New ed. 3 vols. London: John Murray, 1872.

Haller, William. *The Elect Nation: The Meaning and relevance of Foxe's "Book of Martyrs."* New York: Harper and Row, 1963.

———, ed. *The Leveller Tracts*. New York: Columbia University Press, 1944.

Hamilton, Alexander. *Thomas à Becket: A Tragedy in Five Acts*. New York: Dick and Fitzgerald, 1863.

Henry, Robert. *The History of England on a New Plan*. 3 vols. London, 1771–1793.

Hick, William. "The Presentation of the National Petition, and the Movement of Mr. Duncombe." *Northern Star*, June 1841. Reprinted in *An Anthology of Chartist Literature*. Edited by U. V. Kovaleva. Moscow, 1956.

Hickes, George. *Linguarum vett. Septentrionalum Thesaurus Grammatico-Criticus et Ar-chaeologicus.* 2 vols. Oxford, 1705–1712.

Hill, Christopher. "The Norman Yoke." In *Puritanism and Revolution.* London: Secker and Warburg, 1958.

———. *"The World Turned Upside-Down": Radical Ideas during the English Revolution.* London: Maurice Temple Smith, 1972.

Hitler, Adolf. *Mein Kampf.* Translated by Ralph Manheim. Boston: Houghton Mifflin, 1971.

Hodgell, Patricia. *The Nonsense of Ancient Days: Sources of Scott's "Ivanhoe."* Ph. D. diss., University of Minnesota, 1987.

Hollister, Gideon Hiram. *Thomas à Becket: A Tragedy, and Other Poems.* Boston: Spencer, 1866.

Home, John. *Alfred, a Tragedy.* London, 1788.

Honey, John Raymond de Symons. *Tom Brown's Universe.* New York: Quadrangle, 1977.

Hook, Walter Farquhar. *Ecclesiastical Biography.* 8 vols. London: Rivington, 1845–1852.

———. *Lives of the Archbishops of Canterbury.* 12 vols. London: Bentley, 1860–1876.

Horsman, Reginald. *Race and Manifest Destiny: the Origins of American Racial Anglo-Saxonism.* Cambridge: Harvard University Press, 1981.

Hughes, Thomas. "Arthur Penrhyn Stanley." *Quarterly Review* 178 (1894): 235–265.

———. *The Life of Alfred the Great.* 2d ed. London: Macmillan, 1871.

———. *Tom Brown at Oxford.* 1861. Reprint. Chicago: Bedford, n.d.

———. *Tom Brown's School Days.* 1859. Reprint. London: Dent, 1964.

Hume, David. *Enquiry concerning Human Understanding.* 1777. Reprint. Edited by L. A. Selby-Bigge. 3d ed. Oxford: Clarendon, 1972.

———. *History of England.* 1754–1762. 2 vols. Philadelphia: M'carty and Brown, 1840.

Ingram, R., ed. *The Saxon Chronicle.* London: Longman, 1823.

Ingulf, Monk of Croyland [ascribed to]. *History of the Abbey of Croyland.* Translated by Henry T. Riley. London: Bohn, 1854.

"Irving's Production of Tennyson's *Becket.*" *Athenaeum,* 11 February 1893: 193–194.

James, Henry. "Tennyson's *Harold.*" In *Views and Reviews by Henry James, Now First Collected.* Boston: Bell, 1908.

Jameson, Fredric. *The Political Unconscious: Narrative as a Socially Symbolic Act.* Ithaca: Cornell University Press, 1981.

Jauss, Hans Robert. "The Alterity and Modernity of Medieval Literature." Translated by Timothy Bahti. *New Literary History* 10 (Winter 1979): 181–229.

———. *Toward an Aesthetic of Reception.* Translated by Timothy Bahti. Minneapolis: University of Minnesota Press, 1982.

Jefferson, Thomas. *The Writings of Thomas Jefferson.* Edited by Andrew A. Lipscomb and Albert Ellery Bergh. 20 vols. Washington: Thomas Jefferson Memorial Association, 1903–1904.

Jeffrey, Francis. *"Ivanhoe." Edinburgh Review* 33 (1820): 1–59.

Jerrold, Douglas. *Thomas à Becket: A Historical Play.* London: Richardson, 1829.

Jones, Sir William. *The Works of Sir William Jones.* 6 vols. London, 1799.

Kemble, John Mitchell, ed. *Beowulf.* 2d ed. 2 vols. London: Pickering, 1835–1837.

————, ed. *The Poetry of the Codex Vercellensis with English Translation.* 2 vols. London: Ælfric Society, 1843–1855.

————. *The Saxons in England.* 2 vols. London: Longmans, 1849.

Keynes, Sir Geoffrey. *William Pickering, Publisher.* Rev. ed. London: Galahad Press, 1969.

Kiernan, Kevin S. *Beowulf and the Beowulf Manuscript.* New Brunswick: Rutgers University Press, 1981.

Kingsley, Charles. "Froude's *History of England*, vols. VII and VIII." *Macmillan's Magazine* 9 (January 1864): 211–224.

————. *The Roman and the Teuton: Lectures Delivered before the University of Cambridge.* New ed. London: Macmillan, 1889.

————. *The Works of Charles Kingsley.* 20 vols. Hildesheim: Georg Olms, 1968–1969.

Kliger, Samuel. *The Goths in England.* Cambridge: Harvard University Press, 1957.

Knowles, James Sheridan. *Alfred the Great; or, the Patriot King.* London: Ridgeway, 1831.

Laing, David. *List of Members, Rules, and Catalogue of the Bannatyne Club.* Edinburgh: Bannatyne Club, 1867.

Lappenberg, J. *History of England under the Anglo-Saxon Kings.* Translated by Benjamin Thorpe. London: John Murray, 1845.

Layton-Henry, Zig. *The Politics of Race in Britain.* London: Allen and Unwin, 1984.

Levine, Philippa. *The Amateur and the Professional.* Cambridge: Cambridge University Press, 1986.

Liebermann, F., ed. *Die Gesetze der AngelSachsen.* 3 vols. Halle: Max Niemeyer, 1903.

————. *The National Assembly in the Anglo-Saxon Period.* Halle: Max Niemeyer, 1913.

Lingard, John. "The Ancient Church of England and the Liturgy of the Anglican Church." *Dublin Review* 9 (August 1841): 167–196.

————. *The History of England from the First Invasion by the Romans to the Accession of William and Mary.* 6th ed. 10 vols. London: Dolman, 1855.

L'Isle, William. *Divers Monuments in the Saxon Tongue.* London, 1638.

Lockhart, John Gibson. *Memoirs of the Life of Sir Walter Scott.* 1837–1838. 10 vols. Boston: Houghton and Mifflin, 1901.

Lockwood, W. B. *Languages of the British Isles Past and Present.* London: Andre Deutsch, 1975.

Logan, John. *Poems, and Runnamede, a Tragedy.* 1781. Reprint. Edinburgh: Bell, 1812.

Luard, Henry Richards, ed. *Lives of St. Edward the Confessor.* Rolls Series. London: Longmans, 1858.

Lukács, Georg. *The Historical Novel.* 1938. Reprint. Translated by Hannah and Stanley Mitchell. London: Merlin, 1962.

Lyttelton, George, Lord. *The History of the Life of King Henry the Second, and of the Age in which he lived.* 4 vols. London: 1767–1771.

Macaulay, Catherine. *Observations on the Reflections of the Right Hon. Edmund Burke on the Revolution in France.* Boston, 1791.

Macaulay, Lord. *The Works of Lord Macaulay, Complete.* 8 vols. London: Longmans, 1875.

MacDougall, Hugh A. *Racial Myth in English History: Trojans, Teutons, and Anglo-Saxons.* Montreal: Harvest House, 1982.

McGann, Jerome J. *The Romantic Ideology.* Chicago: University Chicago Press, 1983.

Magnusson, Erikr, ed. *Thomas Saga Erkibyskups.* Rolls Series. London: Longmans, 1875.

Martin, Theodore. *The Life of His Royal Highness the Prince Consort.* 4 vols. 2d ed. London: Smith, Elder, 1875.

Merivale, Herman. "The Pictorial History of England." *Edinburgh Review* 74 (1842): 430–473.

Merk, Frederick, and Lois Bannister Merk. *Manifest Destiny and Mission in American History: A Reinterpretation.* New York: Knopf, 1970.

Michel, Francisque, ed. *Bibliothèque Anglo-Saxonne.* Paris: Silvestre; London: Pickering, 1838.

————, ed. *Chroniques Anglo-Normandes.* 3 vols. Rouen, 1836–1840.

Michelet, Jules. *Le Moyen Age* (1833). Reprint. Paris: Robert Laffont, 1981.

Milman, Henry Hart. *History of Latin Christianity.* 8 vols. New York: Sheldon, 1867.

Milton, John. "Outlines for Tragedies." In vol. 18 of *The Works of John Milton.* 18 vols. New York: Columbia University Press, 1938.

Mitchell, Jerome. *The Walter Scott Operas.* Tuscaloosa: University of Alabama Press, 1977.

Monthly Review. Anonymous Review of Carlyle's *Chartism. Monthly Review* 151 (1840):241–245.

Morris, John. *The Life and Martyrdom of St. Thomas Becket, Archbishop of Canterbury, and Legate of the Holy See.* London: Longmans, 1859.

Müller, F. Max. "Comparative Mythology." *Oxford Essays* (1856 ser.): 1–87.

————. *Lectures on the Science of Language.* 1st ser. London: Longmans, 1861.

Nedham, Marchamont. *The Case of the Commonwealth of England Stated.* 1650. Reprint. Edited by Philip Knachel. Charlottesville: University of Virginia Press, 1969.

Nelme, L. D. *Essay towards the Investigation of the Origin and Elements of English Language and Letters.* 1772. Reprint. Menston: Scolar Press, 1972.

Newman, John Henry. *Apologia Pro Vita Sua.* 1864. Reprint. Edited by Martin J. Svaglic. Oxford: Clarendon, 1967.

Nichols, John, ed. *Biographical and Literary Anecdotes of William Bowyer, Printer, and of Many of his Learned Friends.* London, 1782.

Nichols, John G. *Descriptive Catalogue of the Works of the Camden Society.* Westminster: J. B. Nichols, 1862.

Nicol, G. and W. *Catalogue of the Library of the Late John Duke of Roxburghe.* London: Nicol, 1812.

Nicolas, Sir Nicholas Harris. *Observations on the State of Historical Literature, and on the Society of Antiquaries and other Institutions for its Advancement in England.* London: Pickering, 1830.

O'Keeffe, John. *Alfred, or the Magic Banner.* In *The Dramatic Works of John O'Keeffe.* 4 vols. London, 1798.

Orderic [Vitalis]. *Ecclesiastical History.* Edited by Marjorie Chibnall. 6 vols. Oxford: Clarendon, 1968–1980.

Paine, Thomas. *Common Sense addressed to the Inhabitants of America.* Albany, 1791.

————. *Rights of Man.* Albany, 1791.

Palgrave, Sir Francis. "Anglo-Saxon History." *Quarterly Review* 34 (1826): 248–298.

————. "The Conquest and the Conqueror." *Quarterly Review* 74 (1844): 281–325.

————. *A History of the Anglo-Saxons.* 1831. Reprint of 1867. Rev. ed. London: Ward Lock, 1887.

————. *The History of Normandy and of England.* 4 vols. London: John Parker, 1851–1864.

————. "Hume and his Influence on History." *Quarterly Review* 73 (1844): 536–592.

————. *The Rise and Progress of the English Commonwealth — Anglo-Saxon Period.* 2 vols. London: John Murray, 1832.

Pauli, G. Reinhold. *The Life of King Alfred.* Translated by Benjamin Thorpe. London: Bohn, 1853.

Peacock, Thomas Love. *Maid Marian.* 1822. Vol. 5 of *The Novels of Thomas Love Peacock.* Edited by Richard Garnett. 10 vols. London: Dent, 1891–1892.

Pedersen, Holgar. *Linguistic Science in the Nineteenth Century, Methods and Results.* Translated by John Webster Spargo. Cambridge: Harvard University Press, 1931.

Percy, Thomas. *Reliques of Ancient English Poetry.* 3 vols. London, 1765.

Petheram, John. *A Historical Sketch of the Progress and Present State of Anglo-Saxon Literature in England.* London: Lumley, 1840.

Powell, Robert. *The Life of Alfred or Alured.* London, 1634.

Price, Bonamy. "Chartism and Church Extension." *British and Foreign Review* 9 (1840): 1–31.

Pugin, Augustus W. N. *Contrasts; or, a Parallel between the Noble Edifices of the Middle Ages, and the Corresponding Buildings of the Present Day, Shewing the Decay of Taste.* 2d ed. London: Dolman, 1841.

Pye, Henry James. *Alfred; an Epic Poem, in Six Books.* London: J. Wright, 1801.

Rapin-Thoyras, Paul de. *The History of England.* Translated by N. Tindal. 3d ed. 4 vols. 1743–1747.

Ricks, Christopher. *Tennyson.* New York: Macmillan, 1972.

Ritchie, David G. *Darwinism and Politics.* New York: Scribner's, 1889.

Ritson, Joseph. *On the Abstinence from Animal Food as a Moral Duty.* London: Phillips, 1802.

————, ed. *Robin Hood: A Collection of all the Ancient Ballads . . . to which are prefixed Historical Anecdotes of his Life.* London, 1795.

Robertson, James Craigie. *Becket, Archbishop of Canterbury.* London: John Murray, 1859.

————. "Recent publications on Becket." *English Review* (September 1846): 37–62.

————, ed. *Materials for the History of Archbishop Thomas Becket.* Rolls Series. 7 vols. London: Longmans, 1875–1785.

Rokewood, John Gage, ed. *Chronica Jocelini de Brakelonde de Rebus Gestis Sampsonis Abbatis Monasterii Sancti Edmundi.* London: Camden Society, 1840.

Roxburghe Club. *List of Members, Catalogue of Books, and Rules of the Roxburghe Club.* London: Roxburghe Club, 1892.

Ruggiers, Paul G., ed. *Editing Chaucer: The Great Tradition.* Norman, Okla.: Pilgrim Books, 1984.

Rusk, John. *The Beautiful Life and Illustrious Reign of Queen Victoria.* Probably U.S., c. 1902.

Said, Edward W. *Orientalism.* 1978. Reprint. New York: Vintage Books, 1979.

Sala, George A. *Things I Have Seen and People I Have Known.* 2 vols. London: Cassell, 1894.

————. Twice Round the Clock, or the Hours of the Day and Night in London. 1859. Reprint. New York: Humanities Press, 1971.

Schwarz, Daniel R. *Disraeli's Fiction.* New York: Barnes and Noble, 1979.

Scott, Sir Walter. *Tales of the Crusaders.* Abbotsford ed. Philadelphia: Lippincott, 1868.

————. *Ivanhoe.* Edited by A. N. Wilson. Harmondsworth: Penguin, 1984.

————. *The Minstrelsy of the Scottish Border.* Edited by T. F. Henderson. 4 vols. Edinburgh: Oliver and Boyd, 1932.

Sellar, W. C., and R. J. Yeatman. *1066 and All That.* 1930. Reprint. London: Magnum Books, 1980.

Senior, Nassau. "Novels by the Author of *Waverley.*" *Quarterly Review* 26 (1822): 109–148.

Shelton, Maurice, trans. *William Wotton's Short View of George Hickes's Grammatico-Critical and Archaeological Treasury of the Ancient Northern Language.* 2d ed. London, 1737.

Six Odes presented to that justly-celebrated historian Mrs. Catherine Macaulay . . . at Alfredhouse. Bath: R. Cruttwell, 1777.

Smiles, Samuel. *Memoir and Correspondence of the Late John Murray.* 2 vols. London: John Murray, 1891.

Somner, William. *Dictionarium Saxonico-Latino-Anglicum.* Oxford, 1659.

Southey, Robert. *The Book of the Church.* 2 vols. London: John Murray, 1824.

Spelman, Sir John. *Ælfredi Magni Anglorum Regis Invictissimi Vita.* Edited by Obadiah Walker [?]. Oxford, 1678.

————. *The Life of Ælfred the Great.* Edited by Thomas Hearne. Oxford, 1709.

Spenser, Edmund. *The Faerie Queene.* Edited by J. C. Smith and E. de Selincourt. 1912. Reprint. London: Oxford University Press, 1975.

Stanley, Arthur Penrhyn. *Historical Memorials of Canterbury.* 1855. 1st U.S. ed. from 11th British ed. New York: Randolph, 1888.

————. , ed. *Life and Correspondence of Thomas Arnold.* 7th ed. London: Fellowes, 1852.

Stanley, Eric Gerald, ed. *Continuations and Beginnings: Studies in Old English Literature.* London: Nelson, 1966.

Stenton, Sir Frank, and Simone Bertrand, George Wingfield Digby, Charles H. Gibbs-Smith, Sir James Mann, John L. Nevinson and Francis Wormald. *The Bayeux Tapestry: A Comprehensive Survey.* 2d ed. London: Phaidon, 1965.

Stephen, James. "Hildebrand." In *Essays in Ecclesiastical Biography,* vol. 1. London: Longmans, 1853. Originally published in *Edinburgh Review* (1845).

Stephens, W.R.W. *Hildebrand.* London: Macmillan, 1888.

————. *The Life and Letters of Edward A. Freeman.* 2 vols. London: Macmillan, 1895.

Stewart, Robert Wilson, ed. *Disraeli's Novels Reviewed, 1826–1968.* Metuchen, N.J.: Scarecrow Press, 1975.

Strachey, Lytton. *Eminent Victorians.* New York: Putnam, 1918.

Strutt, Joseph. *A Complete View of the Dress and Habits of the People of England from the Establishment of the Saxons in Britain to the Present Time.* 2 vols. London, 1796–1799.

————. *Queenhoo-Hall, a Romance.* 4 vols. Edinburgh: Constable, 1808.

Stubbs, William. *The Constitutional History of England, in Its Origin and Development.* 5th ed. 3 vols. Oxford: Clarendon, 1891.

Swift, Jonathan. *A Proposal for the Correcting, Improving, and Ascertaining the English Tongue.* London, 1712.

Swinburne, Algernon. "Under the Microscope." In vol. 16 of *The Complete Works of Algernon Charles Swinburne.* Edited by Edmund Gosse and Thomas J. Wise. 20 vols. London: Heinemann, 1926.

Tacitus, P. Cornelius. *Agricola and Germania.* Tranlated by H. Mattingley. Harmondsworth: Penguin, 1948.

Taylor, Edgar, ed. and trans. *Master Wace, His Chronicle of the Norman Conquest from the Roman de Rou.* London: Pickering, 1837.

Tennyson, Alfred, Lord. *Becket.* London: Macmillan, 1884.

————. *Becket: A Tragedy in Four Acts, As Arranged for the Stage by H. Irving*. New York: Macmillan, 1893.

————. *Harold: A Drama*. Boston: Osgood, 1877.

————. *The Poems*. Edited by Christopher Ricks. London: Longmans, 1972.

————. *A Variorum Edition of Tennyson's Idylls of the King*. Edited by John Pfordresher. New York: Columbia University Press, 1973.

Tennyson, Hallam. *Alfred, Lord Tennyson, a Memoir*. 2 vols. London: Macmillan, 1897.

Thackeray, William M. "Proposals for a Continuation of *Ivanhoe*." *Fraser's Magazine* 34 (1846): 237–245; 359–367.

————. *Rebecca and Rowena*. London: Chapman and Hall, 1850.

Thierry, Augustin. *Histoire de la Conquête de l'Angleterre par les Normandes*. 10th ed. 4 vols. Paris: Furne, 1860.

————. *History of the Conquest of England by the Normans*. Translated by William Hazlitt [the Younger]. 2 vols. London: Bohn, 1856.

Thompson, A. Hamilton. *The Surtees Society 1834–1934*. Durham: Surtees Society, 1939.

Thompson, E. P. *The Making of the English Working Class*. 1963. Reprint. New York: Vintage Books, 1966.

[Thomson, James, and David Mallet]. *Alfred, a Masque*. London, 1740.

Toynbee, Arnold. *A Study of History*. Abridged by D. C. Somerville. 2 vols. London: Oxford University Press, 1947.

Turner, Sharon. *History of the Manners, Landed Property, Government, Laws, Poetry, Literature, Religion, and Language of the Anglo-Saxons*. 3 vols. London: Longmans, 1799–1805.

————. *The History of the Anglo-Saxons, with a Vindication of the Genuineness of the Ancient British Poems*. 6th ed. 3 vols. London: Longmans, 1836.

————. *The History of England during the Middle Ages*. 1814–1823. 2d ed. 5 vols. London: Longman, 1825.

Verstegen, Richard. *A Restitution of Decayed Intelligence in Antiquities*. London, 1628.

Walpole, Horace. *The Yale Edition of Horace Walpole's Correspondence*. Edited by W. S. Lewis. 48 vols. New Haven: Yale University Press, 1937–1983.

Whitaker, Thomas D., ed. *Visio Willi de Petro Plouhman, ascribed to Robert Langland*. London: John Murray, 1813.

White, Hayden V. *The Content of the Form: Narrative Discourse and Historical Representation*. Baltimore: Johns Hopkins Press, 1987.

————. *Metahistory: The Historical Imagination in Nineteenth-Century Europe*. Baltimore: Johns Hopkins Press, 1973.

————. *Tropics of Discourse: Essays in Cultural Criticism*. 1978. Reprint. Baltimore: Johns Hopkins Press, 1985.

Wiley, Raymond, ed. and trans. *John Mitchell Kemble and Jakob Grimm, a Correspondence 1832–1852*. Leiden: Brill, 1971.

William of Malmesbury, *Chronicle of the Kings of England.* Translated by John Sharpe; revised by J. A. Giles. London: Bohn, 1848.

Wilson, Edmund. *To the Finland Station.* New York: Harcourt, Brace, 1940.

Winstanley, Gerrard. *The Law of Freedom and Other Writings.* Edited by Christopher Hill. Harmondsworth: Penguin, 1973.

Wright, C. E., and Ruth C. *The Diary of Humfrey Wanley.* 2 vols. London: London Bibliographical Society, 1966.

Wright, Thomas. *Essays on Subjects Connected with the Literature, Popular Superstitions, and History of England in the Middle Ages.* 2 vols. London: John Russell Smith, 1846.

Yonge, Charlotte M. *Abbeychurch; or, Self Control and Self Conceit.* London: Mozley, 1848.

———. *Cameos from English History.* London: Macmillan, 1868.

———. *The Heir of Redclyffe.* 2 vols. Leipzig: Tauschnitz, 1855.

———. *The Pillars of the House; or, Under Wode, Under Rode* 4 vols. London: Macmillan, 1873.

Index